THE *New* ELSON'S POCKET MUSIC DICTIONARY

by **Louis C. Elson**
Professor of Music
New England Conservatory

Edited by
Matthew Herman, D.M.A.

PREFACE TO THE 1909 EDITION

In this book will be found all the important terms used in music with their pronunciation and concise definition. Where clear explanation could not be given in a few words, necessary space has been taken.

The Italian terminology is given preference to a large extent, for it has most general use. In this connection it may be stated that some Italian words are quite similar to their English equivalents and can be easily translated: for instance, *abbandono*, "with abandon," *affabile*, "affable," *carezzando*, "caressingly," etc. There are many terminal variants in Italian words, such as *dolore, dolente, dolorosamente, dolentemente*, etc. In a condensed work, such as this, only the root-forms are given, but as many as possible of these.

Where compound terms are not given, look up the words separately.

For practical and immediate use in the classroom, I believe that the little volume will be found sufficient to the needs of the teacher.

LOUIS C. ELSON

PREFACE TO THE 2009 *"NEW* ELSON'S"

In this new century of nearly limitless electronic communication and information sharing, it is hard to imagine that there would be a need for a tiny pocket dictionary for music. Nevertheless, musicians everywhere have continued to use *Elson's Pocket Music Dictionary* as a trusted resource in their classrooms, rehearsals, and individual practice. There will always be something special about the tactile joys of flipping through a book to seek information.

With the continued popularity of Elson's dictionary, it became necessary to update the book for a new century. The scope of musical change and evolution over the past 100 years has been vast, and much of the original information in Elson's had remained unchanged since its 1909 printing. This new edition, beyond the necessary updates to original entries, incorporates the new technologies and theories of 20th- and 21st- century music. Instruments and styles of music from around the world have also been added, including jazz and popular music. The list of composers has been edited and updated to reflect those individuals who have made the most significant contributions to music from antiquity to the present day.

Despite the updates and additions, this book remains a pocket reference dictionary. For the purposes of space, the definitions are terse, providing only the most basic and necessary information about each item. Readers who desire or require detailed information on a specific subject are encouraged to refer to a full-sized music dictionary or encyclopedia.

I am deeply indebted to Daniel Dorff, who was the original driving force behind this revision. He is responsible for much of the initial organization required for a project of this magnitude, as well as collaborative editing throughout the dictionary.

I would also like to thank Jennifer Adam, Susan Galeone, Kyle Herman, Judith Ilika, Brendan McGeehan, Len Oranzi, Elizabeth Scott, Todd Shilhanek, Kim Trolier, and George Tsontakis for generously contributing ideas and input in their various areas of expertise.

MATTHEW HERMAN, D.M.A.
June 2009

THE ELEMENTS OF NOTATION

The STAFF consists of five lines and four intervening spaces. CLEFS indicate how specific notes are mapped on to the staff. In the example below, the position of middle C is shown in those clefs that are most widely used at present.

bass (F) clef   treble (G) clef   alto (C) clef   tenor (C) clef

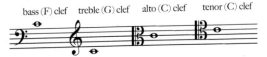

The following clefs incorporate the octave symbol to represent octave transposition up or down.

sopranino clef   tenor clef (modern)   subbass clef

The final set of clefs are of historical importance, but are now rarely used.

soprano clef   mezzo-sop. clef   baritone clefs

NOTES are placed on the STAFF to represent both the PITCH (name of the note) by their position on the STAFF, and the time-value or duration of the note according to their shape.

RESTS indicate periods of timed silence. The terms in parentheses indicate British usage.

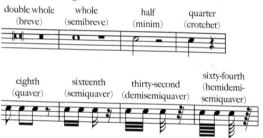

double whole (breve)	whole (semibreve)	half (minim)	quarter (crotchet)

eighth (quaver)	sixteenth (semiquaver)	thirty-second (demisemiquaver)	sixty-fourth (hemidemi- semiquaver)

The TIME SIGNATURE, or METER, is a guide to counting the musical pulse. The lower numeral shows the rhythmic unit that defines the beat, or counting unit; the upper numeral shows how many of those beats fit into a measure.

simple duple   simple triple   simple quadruple

1 & 2 &   1 & 2 & 3 &   1 & 2 & 3 & 4 &

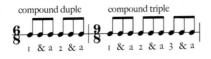

SCALES are consecutive successions of adjacent notes. The most common scale patterns follow below, with whole steps signified by brackets and half steps by angled lines. Although the examples below all begin on C, a scale may start on any note, the starting point defining the KEY of that scale. The sharps and/or flats that result from maintaining these patterns are placed at the beginning of the staff as a KEY SIGNATURE.

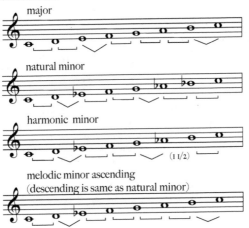

The CHROMATIC SCALE is composed exclusively of HALF-STEPS. In the ascending scale, the half-step succession is spelled with sharps to raise certain notes; in the descending scale, flats are used to lower certain notes.

chromatic scale
(ascending and descending)

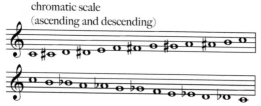

For further scales, see *Church modes*, *Octatonic scale*, *Pentatonic scale*, and *Whole-tone scale* in the main dictionary.

In addition to letter names, there are several interrelated ways to label pitches by syllables; this system is sometimes referred to as SOLFÈGE.

Diatonic solfège

| Do | Re | Mi | Fa | Sol | La | Ti | Do |

Chromatic solfège

| Di | Ra | Ri | Me | Fi | Se | Si | Le | Te |

An INTERVAL is the distance between two notes, counted by steps of a scale. Therefore, from C to D is the interval of a second, because D is the 2nd note in an C scale. Apart from their numerical name, INTERVALS are in addition classified as Major, Minor, Perfect, Augmented, and Diminished, according to their notation and content. The following table of intervals, in this case based on C, establishes a measurement for corresponding intervals in any other key. The letter "P" stands for perfect, "M" for major, "m" for minor, "+" for augmented, and "°" for diminished.

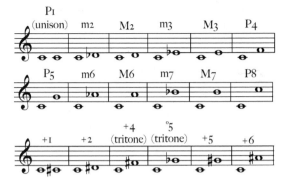

CHORDS are a combination of three or more notes sounded simultaneously. The basic chord unit is a combination of three notes separated by thirds, called a TRIAD. The MAJOR TRIAD uses the 1st, 3rd, and 5th note of a MAJOR SCALE, and the MINOR TRIAD uses the 1st, 3rd, and 5th note of a MINOR SCALE. The DIMINISHED TRIAD is constructed entirely with minor thirds, and the AUGMENTED TRIAD is constructed entirely with major thirds.

CHORDS constructed with four notes often form SEVENTH CHORDS, each of which has a different character based on the intervals and tensions between its notes.

Each of the above CHORDS may be built upward from any pitch.

INVERSIONS of the order of notes from top to bottom are still considered the same chord. When the lowest note is the fundemental note of the chord, it is said to be in ROOT POSITION.

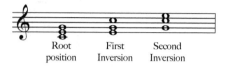

| Root position | First Inversion | Second Inversion |

CHORD FUNCTIONS can be described in several different ways. In a given key, the major triad built from the 1st note in the scale is called the Tonic chord. It is often labeled with a Roman numeral I, indicating a chord built from the 1st note of the scale. The example below shows these diatonic triads, in both major and minor, and their Roman numeral labels. Upper-case numerals indicate major chords, and lower-case indicates minor or diminished chords.

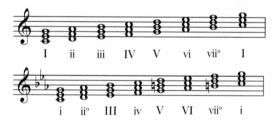

I   ii   iii   IV   V   vi   vii°   I

i   ii°   III   iv   V   VI   vii°   i

FUNDAMENTAL TEMPO MARKS
FROM THE SLOWEST TO THE FASTEST

These terms are merely the most familiar descriptive terms. They do not convey a specific tempo, but rather a mood; for specific tempo instructions, it is necessary to indicate a metronome marking specifying how many beats per minute, for example, ♩ = 100, meaning 100 beats per minute.

Larghissimo – Extremely slow

Largo – Very slow and stately

Largamente – Quite slow

Larghetto – Somewhat faster than *Largo*

Grave – Seriously, solemnly

Lento – Slowly

Adagio – Slowly, with great expression

Adagietto – Slightly faster than *Adagio*

Andantino – Faster or lighter than *Andante*

Andante – In tranquil or quiet time, but moving (literally "going")

Moderato – Moderately

Allegretto – With some animation, but less than *Allegro*

Allegro – Lively, animated in movement

Vivace – Vivaciously, with more rapid movement than *Allegro*

Presto – With great rapidity

Prestissimo – With extreme rapidity

SPEEDING UP

Accelerando – With gradual, though definite, increase in speed

Doppio movimento – Double movement, twice as fast

Più mosso, Più moto – With more motion or speed

Stretto - With growing excitement or tension

Stringendo - Accelerating with excitement

SLOWING DOWN

Allargando – Slowing down and broadening, gradually or suddenly

Meno mosso, Meno moto – With less speed or motion

Molto meno mosso – Much slower than the previous movement.

Morendo – Dying away, gradually slower and softer

Rallentando – Slowing; *synonymous with ritardando*

Ritardando – Slowing; *synonymous with rallentando*

Ritenuto – Slowing more suddenly and dramatically than a ritardando

COMMON MODIFIERS

Assai - very

Meno – less

Moltissimo – extremely; intensified form of Molto

Molto – very

Più – more

Pochissimo – very slightly; intensified form of Poco

Poco – a little bit

STANDARD DYNAMIC MARKINGS

_ff_ = fortissimo (very loud)

_f_ = forte (loud)

_mf_ = mezzo-forte (medium loud)

_mp_ = mezzo-piano (medium quiet)

_p_ = piano (quiet)

_pp_ = pianissimo (very quiet)

n, niente = nothing (silent)

$<$ _crescendo_ = increasing in loudness

$>$ _decrescendo_ or _diminuendo_ = decreasing in loudness

COMMON MUSIC SYMBOLS

♯ = sharp

✕ = double sharp

♭ = flat

♭♭ = double flat

♮ = natural

> = accented

≥ = accented and sustained

∧ = _marcato,_ short and accented

· = _staccato,_ separated from surrounding notes, usually meaning short

_ = _legato,_ sustained and connected

⁔ = _détaché,_ sustained, but detached

⌒ = _fermata,_ hold

// = _luftpause,_ a break in the music

' = breath mark (slight break)

𝄋 = _segno,_ the sign used for _Dal segno_

$\oplus$ = *coda* sign

$\boxed{\exists}$: = repeat sign

$\mathcal{X}$. = repeat previous measure

$\mathcal{W}$. = repeat previous two measures

$\mathbf{\text{w}}$ = mordent

$\mathbf{\text{w}}$ = inverted mordent

∞ = turn

$\mathbf{tr}\sim$ = trill

8/8va/8ba/8vb = play one octave up/one octave down

15/15ma/15ba = play two octaves up/two octaves down

$\flat$ = grace note

$\mathbf{Ped.}$ = depress the damper pedal (piano symbol)

$\ast$ = lift the damper pedal (piano symbol)

V = upbow

$\sqcap$ = downbow

∘ = natural harmonic

◇ = artificial harmonic

"LOAN WORDS" FROM ITALIAN

Many words in the English-speaking musician's vocabulary are of Italian origin and have become "loan words," meaning the foreign word has become absorbed into English. As a result, "correct" pronunciations and plurals depend on whether one is intending these words as Italian or English.

The Italian plurals of the familiar words *concerto* and *solo* are *concerti* and *soli*. However it is equally correct to consider these loan words into English and pluralize them as *concertos* and *solos*. The same is true for hundreds of other Italian terms.

The correct pronunciations of Italian words such as *adagio* and *capriccio* are in 3 syllables, the letter *i* only indicating the soft pronunciation of the preceding consonant. However, it has become customary among English-speaking musicians to give the *i* its own extra syllable. Therefore the dictionary shows both pronunciations (such as *ah-DAH-jo*, *ah-DAH-ji-o*). In all cases the first and shorter pronunciation is correct Italian, and the second pronunciation is the accepted English-language style.

PRONUNCIATION GUIDE

For ease of reading, and to accommodate the many languages incorporated into this dictionary, phonetic pronunciation guides are given. Each language has subtle inflections of vowels and consonants, and the following guide is a fast way to approximate certain sounds.

CAPITAL letters indicate the accented syllable.

VOWELS

a = cat
ah = father
ai = air
ay = play
e = egg
ee = beet
er = her
e[r] = the vowel of her, without the following r sound
i = bit
igh = sigh
o = oboe
oo = boot
ow = cow
oy = toy
u = put
uh = luck
ü = German and French sound like oo with lips rounded

CONSONANTS

ch = cheese
g = always indicates hard g, as in get
kh = German sound as in Bach
n = like American n in most languages, but in French words very nasal and with the tongue not reaching the teeth
r = in Italian words the tongue is more forward than in English; in French soft and from the back of the mouth; in German more gutteral and from the top of the mouth
sh = in German, the final ch and g are similar to English sh but from the back of the throat
zh = French sound like a voiced sh

LANGUAGES

Following is a guide to abbreviations for the languages of words defined in the dictionary:

Chin. = Mandarin
Cz. = Czech
Eng. = English
Fr. = French
Ger. = German
Gr. = Greek
Heb. = Hebrew
Hin. = Hindu
It. = Italian
Jap. = Japanese
Lat. = Latin
Port. = Portuguese
Rus. = Russian
Sp. = Spanish
Yid. = Yiddish

THE *New* ELSON'S POCKET MUSIC DICTIONARY

I   Roman numeral indicating the tonic chord, based on the first degree of a scale.

2   Figured bass symbol indicating that the root of the chord is a 2nd above the bass note.

II   Roman numeral indicating the supertonic chord, based on the second degree of a scale.

III   Roman numeral indicating the mediant chord, based on the third degree of a scale.

4   Figured bass symbol indicating that the root of the chord is a 4th above the bass note.

IV   Roman numeral indicating the subdominant chord, based on the fourth degree of a scale.

V   Roman numeral indicating the dominant chord, based on the fifth degree of a scale.

6   Figured bass symbol indicating a first-inversion triad.

6/4   Figured bass symbol indicting a second-inversion triad.

VI   Roman numeral indicating the submediant chord, based on the sixth degree of a scale.

7   Figured bass symbol indicating that the bass is the root of a triad including the 7th degree of the scale.

VII   Roman numeral indicating the leading tone chord, based on the seventh degree of a scale.

A   1. The sixth tone of the diatonic major scale of C, also called *La*. 2. The major scale with three sharps in its signature. 3. A 440 (A above middle C), the standard tuning note, whose sound wave vibrates at 440 cycles per second. While A 440 is "standard," it is by no means a universal value, some ensembles or specific instruments choosing a slightly higher or lower number of cycles per second for the tuning reference. 4. Abbreviation for alto.

A (It., ah)   By, for, to, at, in, etc.

a2, a3 (It., ah DOO-e, ah tre)   Indicates that both, or all three, musicians should play, in contrast to the marking *solo*. Note there is no accent in the Italian *a2* or *a3*, although in French *à2* and *à3* are correct.

AABA   A common musical form, often called "song form," in which the A Theme is heard twice, followed by a contrasting middle section, or "B Theme," and then a return to the first theme.

ABA   A musical form, often called Ternary Form, in which an initial main theme is followed by a contrasting theme, and then the first theme is repeated.

A&R Artist & Repertoire, the department of a recording company coordinating performers with suitable songs.

Ab (Ger., ahb) Off. Used in organ music.

A balata (It., ah bah-LAH-tah) In the style of a ballad.

Abandon (Fr., ah-bahn-don) Without restraint.

A battuta (It., ah bah-TOO-tah) As beaten; strictly in time.

Abbandonatamente (It., ah-bahn-do-nah-tah-MEN-te) Vehemently; violently.

Abbandono (It., ah-bahn-DO-no) With passionate expression.

Abbellire (It., ah-be-LEE-re) To embellish with ornaments.

Abellimento (It., ah-be-lee-MEN-to) A decoration, ornament, or embellishment.

Abendmusik (Ger., ah-bend-moo-ZEEK) Evening or night music; serenade.

Abgestossen (Ger., AHB-ge-shtos-n) Detached, struck off, staccato.

Abkürzung (Ger., AHB-kür-tsoong) Abridgment, abbreviation.

Abnehmend (Ger., AHB-nay-mend) Diminishing.

Abrégé (Fr., ah-bray-zhay) Abridgment; also the trackers in an organ.

Absolute Music "Pure" music with no extramusical associations, the opposite of program music.

Absolute Pitch Often called pitch memory or perfect pitch, the ability to name any pitch heard with no reference other than memory.

Abstossen (Ger., AHB-shtos-n) Staccato.

Abwechselnd (Ger., AHB-vex-lnd) Alternating, changing. In organ playing, alternately; in choir singing, antiphonally; in dance music, change of movements.

A cappella (It., ah kah-PE-lah) In the chapel style, referring to unaccompanied vocal music.

A capriccio (It., ah kah-PREE-cho) In a capricious style; according to the taste of the performer.

Accarezzevole (It., ah-kah-re-TZE-vo-le) Cajoling; in a persuasive and caressing manner.

Accelerando (It., ah-che-le-RAHN-do) Accelerating.

Accelerato (It., ah-che-le-RAH-to) Accelerated.

Accent A stress or emphasis on a certain note.

Accento (It., ah-CHEN-to) Accent.

Accentuare (It., ah-chen-too-AH-re) To accentuate.

Accessory notes Notes situated one degree above or below the principal note of a turn. The upper note of a trill is also called the accessory or auxiliary note.

Acciaccato (It., ah-chah-KAH-to)   Brusquely, forcibly.

Acciaccatura (It., ah-chah-kah-TOO-rah)   A very short grace note before the principal note; it is distinguished from the appoggiatura by a slash through the note's flag.

Accidentals   Sharp, flat, natural, double-sharp, and double-flat symbols introduced apart from the key signature. In more recent music, quarter-tone symbols may also be called accidentals.

Accompaniment   Secondary parts or voices that support the leading melody.

Accopiato (It., ah-ko-pee-AH-to)   Bound, tied, joined together.

Accord (Fr., ah-kor)   A chord; a concord; consonance.

Accordamento (It., ah-kor-dah-MEN-to)   Consonance, unison, harmony of parts.

Accordatura (It., ah-kor-dah-TOO-rah)   Concord, harmony. Also, the set of notes to which the open strings of an instrument are tuned.

Accordion   An instrument consisting of two oblong sound boxes enclosing metal reeds, the flexible connection between the two boxes forming a bellows. The keyboard for the right hand provides a chromatic scale, and buttons for the left provide fundamental bass notes and chords.

Acid rock   A form of rock music, popular in the late 1960's and early 1970's, characterized by improvisation, long instrumental solos, and drug-influenced lyrics and light shows.

Accrescendo (It., ah-kre-SHEN-do)   Increasing in loudness.

Acoustic   Literally meaning natural sound, a non-amplified or non-electric instrument, such as an acoustic guitar.

Acoustics   1. The science of sound.   2. The sound qualities of a performance hall or environment.

Action   1. The mechanism attached to the keys of a piano or organ   2. The mechanism attached to the pedals of a harp, which changes the pitch of the strings by shortening them.   3. The distance between the strings and the neck of a guitar.

Acuta (Lat., ah-KOOT-ah)   A mixture stop in the organ.

Acute   High, in reference to pitch.

Adagietto (It., ah-dah-JE-to, ad-dah-ji-E-to)   1. A short adagio.   2. A movement somewhat less slow than adagio.

Adagio (It., ad-DAH-jo, ah-DAH-ji-o)   Slow, but quicker than largo and slower than andante.

Adagissimo (It., ah-dah-JEE-see-mo)   Extremely slow.

Added Sixth   A triad plus the sixth note above the tonic, such as C-E-G-A.

Additive synthesis   The electronic creation of complex sound waves by combining numerous simpler waveforms.

Addolorato (It., ah-do-lo-RAH-to)   Sorrowful.

A demi jeu (Fr., ah d-mee zhü)   With half the power of the instrument.

A demi voix (Fr., ah d-mee vwah)   At half voice; whispered.

A deux (Fr., ah DÜH)   For two instruments or voices.

A deux mains (Fr., ah-düh man)   For two hands.

Adiratamente (It., ah-di-rah-tah-MEN-te)   Angrily, sternly.

Adirato (It., ah-di-RAH-to)   Angry, stern.

Adjunct notes   Unaccented auxiliary notes.

Ad libitum (Lat., ahd LIB-i-tum)   1. At will; at pleasure; changing the rhythm of a particular passage at the discretion of the performer. 2. A part that may be omitted if desired. 3. In jazz, the term "ad lib." generally refers to an improvised solo over an accompaniment.

ADSR   Attack, decay, sustain, and release. In electronic music synthesis, this describes the envelope, or loudness pattern, of a given note. For example, one of the timbral differences between a xylophone and a violin is the very different sustain they have during any single note.

A due (It., ah DOO-e)   See a2.

A dur (Ger., ah door)   The key of A major.

Aeolian (ay-O-lee-in)   A modal scale corresponding to A to A on the white keys of the piano. It is the same as the natural minor scale. Also see *Mode* and *Minor scale*.

Aeolian harp   An instrument consisting of a soundbox and strings so constructed that a current of air sets the strings in vibration.

Aerophone   A musical instrument that uses a vibrating body of air to produce sound, such as a flute, trumpet, or organ.

Affabile (It., ah-FAH-bee-le)   In a pleasing manner.

Affannato (It., ah-fah-NAH-to)   Sad, distressed.

Affannoso (It., ah-fah-NO-zo)   With anxious expression.

Affettivo (It., ah-fe-TEE-vo)   Affecting; pathetic.

Affetto (It., ah-FE-to)   Feeling; tenderness; pathos.

Affettuosamente (It., ah-fet-too-o-zah-MEN-te)   With tenderness and feeling.

Affettuoso (It., ah-fet-too-O-zo)   With tender and passionate expression.

Afflitto (It., ah-FLEE-to)   Afflicted, mournfully

Afflizione (It., ah-flee-tsee-O-ne)   Sorrow, distress.

Affrettando (It., ah-fret-TAN-do)   Hurrying; quickening.

Affrettate (It., ahf-fret-TA-te)   To hurry, quicken.

After-note   A brief ornamental note occurring on an unaccented part of the measure, and taking its time from the note preceding it.

Aftertouch   The ability of a keyboard to monitor pressure on a key after being struck, and to allow the volume (or other parameters) to continuously vary based on this pressure, unlike traditional keyboard instruments.

Agevole (It., ah-JEH-vo-le)   Lightly; easily; with agility.

Agilità (It., ah-JEE-lee-tah)   Lightness, agility.

Agilmente (It., ah-jeel-MEN-tay)   Lightly.

Agitamento (It., ah-jee-tah-MEN-to)   Agitation, restlessness.

Agitato (It., ah-jee-TAH-to)   Agitated, restless.

Agité (Fr.) (ah-zhee-tay)   Agitated.

Agnus Dei (Lat., ahn-yoos DE-ee)   Lamb of God; one of the movements in a Mass.

Agogic accent   A note that receives extra emphasis, due to being longer than the surrounding notes.

Agraffe   A metallic support of the string in a piano, between the pin and bridge, serving to check vibration at that part.

Agréments (Fr., a-gray-mahn)   Embellishments applied in harpsichord music, particularly referring to the French Baroque.

Aigrement (Fr., aygr-mahn)   Sharply, harshly.

Aigu (Fr., ay-gü)   Acute, high, sharp, shrill.

Air   A short song or melody, with or without words.

Air à boire (Fr., ayr ah bwahr)   A drinking song.

Air de cour (Fr., ayr du coor)   A secular song from France, during the late Renaissance.

Air varié (Fr.) (ayr vah-ri-ay)   Aria with variations.

Ais (Ger., ah-IS)   The note A sharp.

Aisément (Fr., ay-zay-mahn)   Easily, freely.

Ajoutez (Fr., ah-zhoo-tay)   Add. Used in organ music.

À la Russe (Fr., ah lah rüs)   In Russian style.

Alberti Bass   A left-hand piano accompaniment characterized by arpeggios, named for composer Domenico Alberti.

Albumblatt (Ger., AHL-boom-blaht)   Album leaf; a short piece, most typically grouped in collections of piano music of modest difficulty.

Al coda (It., ahl KOH-dah)   To the coda.

Alcuna licenza (It., ahl-KOO-nah lee-CHEN-zah)   Rhythmic license to use rubato.

Aleatoric music   Music whose elements include chance or randomness.

Al fine (It., ahl FEE-ne)   To the end.

Al (It., ahl) **All** (It., ahl) **Alla** (It., ah-lah) **Alle** (It., ah-le) **Agli** (It., ahl-yee) **Allo** (It., ah-lo)   To the; in the style or manner of.

Alla breve (It., ah-lah BRE-ve)   Originally 4/2 rhythm, so called from the fact that one *breve*, or double-whole-note, filled each measure. Today the term is more generally applied to 2/2 rhythm.

Alla caccia (It., ah-lah KAH-cha) In the style of hunting music.

Alla camera (It., ah-lah KAH-me-rah) In the style of chamber music.

Alla cappella (It., ah-lah kah-PE-lah) 1. In the church or sacred style, derived from Alla Breve style, the measure being sub-divided. 2. Unaccompanied vocal music.

Allargando (It., ah-lahr-GAHN-do) Growing slower.

Alle (Ger., ahl-le) All the instruments or singers; tutti.

Allegramente (It., ah-le-grah-MEN-te) Gaily, joyfully, quickly.

Allegretto (It., ah-le-GRE-to) Rather light and cheerful but not as quick as allegro.

Allegrissimo (It., ah-le-GREE-see-mo) Extremely quick and lively; the superlative of Allegro.

Allegro (It., ah-LE-gro) Quick, lively; a rapid, vivacious movement.

Alleluia (Lat., al-le-LOO-yah) Praise the Lord; Hallelujah.

Allemande (Fr., all-mahnd) Traditionally, a moderate dance or melody in 2/4 or 4/4; after the late 18th century, the term for a dance in triple meter.

Alle saiten (Ger., ah-le ZIGH-ten) All the strings. Release the soft pedal.

All' Espagnuola (It., ahl es-pahn-yoo-O-lah) In Spanish style.

All' Inglese (It., ahl een-GLAY-ze) In English style.

All' Italiana (It., ahl ee-tah-lee-AH-nah) In Italian style.

Allmählich (Ger., ahl-ME-leesh) Little by little.

All' Ongarese (It., ahl on-gah-RAY-ze) In Hungarian style.

Allonger (Fr., al-lon-zhay) To lengthen, prolong, delay.

Allonger l'archet (Fr., al-lon-zhay lahr-shay) To lengthen or prolong the stroke of the bow in violin music.

Allontandosi (It., ahl-on-tan-DO-see) Gradually disappearing in the distance; further and further away.

All'ottava (It., ahl o-TAH-vah) At the octave; play the passage one octave higher (or lower) than written.

Al niente (It., ahl nee-EN-te) Diminuendo to silence.

Alphorn A large, fairly straight, wooden keyless horn from the Alps.

Al rigore di tempo (It., ahl ri-GO-re di TEM-po) In very vigorous and strict time.

Al Segno (It., ahl SEN-yo) Go to the 𝄋 sign, indicating a jump back to an earlier measure.

Alt (It., ahlt) High. This term is sometimes applied to the notes above the treble staff.

Al Tedesco (It., ahl te-DES-ko) In German style.

Alteration Changing a pitch out of the key signature through a chromatically changed note.

Altered chord A chord in which one note (or more) is chromatically changed from the natural diatonic scale tones.

Altgeige (Ger., AHLT-gigh-ge)   The viola.

Altieramente (It., ahl-tee-er-ah-MEN-te)   With grandeur; haughtily.

Altisono (It., ahl-TEE-so-no)   Sonorous.

Altissimo (It., ahl-TEE-see-mo)   The highest; extremely high in pitch, generally referring to extended high ranges of instruments beyond the traditional high register.

Alto (It., AHL-to)   The term means "high" and has several applications. 1. In vocal terminology the word applies to the lowest female voice or the similar vocal range in an unchanged boy's voice. 2. The French term for *Viola*. 3. Alto flute, Alto clarinet, Alto saxophone, and the less familiar Alto horn, are medium-high members of these instrumental families.

Alto clef   The C clef on the third line of the staff, as illustrated on page 3.

Alto clarinet   A secondary instrument of the clarinet family, the alto clarinet is primarily seen in band music and has been only an optional part in recent years. The alto clarinet is pitched a 5th below B♭ Clarinet. It is properly called E♭ Alto Clarinet, sounding down a minor 6th – therefore written middle C on alto clarinet sounds as the E♭ below it in concert pitch.

Alto flute   A secondary instrument of the flute family, often used for special dark effects in orchestral music throughout the 20th century; more recently the alto flute has become a staple in flute choirs, which often have several altos. The alto flute sounds a 4th below the standard C Flute, and a 4th below where it is notated.

Alto saxophone   One of the primary instruments of the saxophone family, traditionally the most common saxophone for recital and concerto repertoire. The alto is also a standard jazz instrument. The alto saxophone is pitched in E♭, sounding down a minor 6th – therefore written middle C on alto saxophone sounds as the E♭ below it in concert pitch.

Altra (It. fem., AHL-trah)   **Altro** (It. masc., AHL-tro)   Other, another.

Altri (It., ahl-tree)   Others; often used for an orchestral string part to distinguish the section players from a soloist within that part.

Altra volta (It., AHL-trah VOL-tah)   Another time.

Alzamento (It., ahl-tsah-MEN-to)   An elevating of the voice; lifting up.

Alzando (It., ahl-TSAN-do)   Raising; lifting up.

AM   See *amplitude modulation*.

Amabile (It., ah-MAH-bee-le)   Amiable, gentle, graceful.

Amabilmente (It., ah-mah-beel-MEN-te)   Amiably, gently.

Amaro (It., ah-MAH-ro)   Grief, bitterness, affliction.

Ambrosian Chant   Sacred melodies collected and introduced into the church by St. Ambrose. See *Chant*.

Amen (Heb., ah-men)   So be it. A word used as a termination to prayers, and therefore as the last section of much sacred music.

A moll (Ger., ah moll)   The key of A minor.

Amore (It., ah-MO-re)   Tenderness, affection, love.

A moresco (It., ah mo-RES-ko)   In Moorish style.

Amorevole (It., ah-mo-RE-vo-le)   Tenderly, gently, lovingly.

Amorevolmente (It., ah-mo-re-vol-MEN-te)   With tenderness.

Amorosamente (It., ah-mo-ro-zah-MEN-te)   Tenderly.

Amoroso (It., ah-mo-RO-zo)   Tenderly.

Amphibrach (Gr., AHM-fi-brakh)   A rhythmic foot comprising one short, one long and one short note or syllable. See *Foot.*

Amplifier   An audio processor used to control the loudness (or otherwise color the sound) of an instrument or other sound source.

Amplitude   1. The loudness or volume of a sound.   2. The height of a sound wave, which in turn determines its volume.

Amplitude modulation   To vary the amplitude of an electronic signal; used in electronic communication and music synthesis.

An (Ger., ahn)   On; to; in organ music, draw, or add.

Anacrusis (Gr., ah-nah-KROO-sis)   Upbeat or pickup.

Analog   Information, such as an audio signal, that is conveyed, stored, or synthesized by continuous waves; the opposite of digital.

Anapest (Gr., AHN-ah-pest)   A rhythmic foot containing two short notes or syllables, and a long one. See *Foot.*

Anche (Fr., ahnsh)   1. The reed of the oboe, bassoon, clarinet, etc. 2. The various reed stops in an organ.

Ancora (It., ahn-KO-rah)   Still; *ancora più mosso* means still a little faster.

Andacht (Ger., ahn-dakht)   Devotion.

Andante (It., ahn-DAHN-te)   A movement in moderate time but flowing easily, gracefully; literally, "going."

Andantino (It., ahn-dahn-TEE-no)   The diminutive of Andante, it is generally used *quicker* than Andante.

Andare (It., ahn-DAH-re)   To go; go on.

Anfang (Ger., AHN-fahng)   The beginning.

Angemessen (Ger., AHN-ge-MES-n)   Comfortable, suitable.

Angenehm (Ger., AHN-ge-naym)   Agreeable, pleasing, sweet.

Anglaise (Fr., ahn-glayz)   In English style; a tune adapted for an English air or country dance, resembling a hornpipe.

Anglico (It., AHN-glee-ko)   See *Anglaise.*

Angoscia (It., ahn-GO-shah)   Anguish.

Angosciamente (It., ahn-go-shah-MEN-te)   Anguishedly.

Ängstlich (Ger., ENGST-leesh)   Uneasy, anxious.

Anhang (Ger., AHN-hahng)   Coda; appendix; postscript.

Anima (It., AH-nee-mah)   Liveliness, animation.

Animato (It., ahn-ee-MAH-to)   Animated; with life and spirit.

Animé (Fr., ahn-ee-may)   Animated, lively, spirited.

Animoso (It., ahn-ee-MO-zo)   In an animated manner; lively, energetic.

Anlage (Ger., AHN-lah-ge)   The plan or outline of a composition.

Anlaufen (Ger., AHN-louf-n)   To increase in sound; to swell.

Anleitung (Ger., AHN-ligh-toong)   Introduction, instruction.

Anmuthig (Ger., AHN-moo-teesh)   Agreeable, sweet, pleasant.

Ansatz (Ger., AHN-sahts)   1.The embouchure of a wind instrument; the setting of the mouth of a wind player. 2.The attack of a vocal phrase.

Anschlag (Ger., AHN-shlahg)   1. A stroke or attack; the touch in piano playing. 2. A double grace note.

Anstimmen (Ger., AHN-stim-en)   To begin to sing; to tune up.

Anstimmung (Ger., AHN-stim-oong)   Intonation, tuning.

Answer   1. The response to the subject of a fugue, given by the second voice, either above or below. Also see *Tonal answer* and *Real answer*. 2. The second phrase of a parallel period.

Antecedent   1. The subject of a fugue or canon. 2. The first phrase of a parallel period.

Anthem   A short, sacred choral composition, the words of which are often selected from the Bible.

Antibacchius (AHN-ti-BAH-ki-us)   A rhythmic foot of three syllables, the first two long or accented and the last short. See *Foot*.

Anticipation   One or more harmonic voices or parts moving to their particular position in a new chord, in advance of the other parts or in advance of the next strong beat.

Antico (It., ahn-TEE-ko)   Ancient.

Antiphon   1. The response made by one part of the choir to another, or by the congregation to the priest in the Roman Catholic service. 2. A sacred composition based on this alternation.

Antiphony   Music in which two or more separated ensembles of singers and/or instrumentalists alternate, or overlap, in ways that exploit their contrasting locations to add an extra element of musical interest.

Antique Cymbals   See *Crotales*.

Antithesis   In fugues, the *subject* is sometimes called a *thesis*, in which case the *answer* is called an *antithesis*.

Antwort (Ger., AHNT-vort)   Answer.

Anwachsend (Ger., AHN-vahkh-send)   Swelling, increasing.

Aperto (It., ah-PAIR-to) 1. Open, clear, distinct. 2. In piano music, it signifies that the damper pedal is pressed down. 3. In organ music, it refers to an open pipe.

A piacere (It., ah pee-ah-CHER-e) At pleasure, generally meaning the soloist may take liberties with rhythm in a given passage.

Aplomb (Fr., ah-plom) Firm, in exact time; steadiness, coolness.

Apollo In mythology, the god of music, said to be the inventor of the lyre.

Appassionatamente (It., ah-pah-see-o-nah-tah-MEN-to) Passionately.

Appassionato (It., ah-pah-see-o-NAH-to) Passionate.

Appenato (It., ah-pe-NAH-to) Grieved, distressed.

Appoggiato (It., ah-po-JAH-to) Leaning on, drawn out.

Appoggiatura (It., ah-po-jah-TOO-rah, ah-po-jee-ah-TOO-rah) An embellishment, generally notated like a grace note with no slash, sometimes called a long grace note, even though it is played on the beat. The appoggiatura is by nature a non-chord tone on a strong beat, whose expressive quality comes in its delayed resolution. The notation as a grace note disguises the fact that it is a dissonance on a strong beat, because the proper chord tone appears to be on the beat but is heard later. Being an ornament used in many musical traditions, there is extensive literature and some disagreement about the correct duration and interpretation of appoggiatura notation.

Apprestare (It., ah-pres-TAH-re) To prepare, or put in a condition to be played.

Âpre (Fr., AH-pruh) Harsh.

A punta d'arco (It., a poon-tah DAHR-ko) With the point of the bow.

À quatre mains (Fr., ah kahtr-man) For four hands.

Arabesque A phrase, melody, or composition with ornate embellishments, named after highly-ornamented Moorish architecture.

Arbitrio, al (It., ahr-BEE-tree-o) At the will or pleasure of the performer.

Arcato (It., ahr-KAH-to) Bowed; played with the bow.

Archet (Fr., ahr-shay) see *Arco*.

Archlute A plucked-string continuo instrument of the 17th century; combining the body of a tenor lute with the neck extension of the theorbo.

Arch-top guitar A steel-stringed acoustic guitar with an arched top or "belly"; popular in jazz and blues music.

Arco (It., AHR-ko) 1. The bow for a string instrument. 2. An instruction to play with the bow (rather than pizzicato).

Ardente (It., ahr-DEN-te) With fire; glowing, vehement.

Ardentemente (It., ahr-den-te-MEN-te) Ardently, vehemently.

Ardito (It., ahr-DEE-to) Bold; with energy.

Ardore (It., ahr-DO-reh) With ardor and warmth.

Aria (It.) (AH-ree-ah) **Arie** (It. pl.) (AH-ree-e) **Arien** (Ger. pl., AH-ri-en) **Arietta** (It.) (ah-ree-ET-tah) **Ariette** (Fr., ah-ree-et) **Ariettina** (It., ah-ree-et-TE-nah)   An air (song) sung by a single voice generally with accompaniment.

Aria buffa (It., ah-ree-ah BOO-fah)   A comic or humorous air.

Aria cantabile (It., ah-ree-ah kahn-TAH-bee-le)   An air in a graceful and melodious style.

Aria concertata (It., ah-ree-ah kon-cher-TAH-tah)   An air with orchestral accompaniment in a concertante style.

Aria di bravura (It., ah-ree-ah dee brah-VOO-rah)   A florid air in bold, marked style and permitting great freedom of execution.

Aria parlante (It., ah-ree-ah pahr-LAHN-te)   An air in declamatory style, like a recitative in tempo.

A rigore del tempo (It., ah ree-GO-re del TEM-po)   In strict time.

Arioso (It., ah-ree-O-zo)   Melodious, graceful; a short piece in the style of an aria, often describing an instrumental composition.

Armonica (It., ahr-MO-nee-kah)   See *Glass harmonica*.

Armoniosamente (It., ahr-MO-nee-o-zah-MEN-te)   Harmoniously.

Armonioso (It., ahr-mo-nee-O-zo)   Concordant, harmonious.

Arpa (It., AHR-pah)   The harp.

Arpa doppia (It., AHR-pah DO-pee-ah)   1. The double action harp; 2. a harp with two strings for each note.

Arpeggiando (It., ahr-pe-jee-AHN-do)   Played in a harp-like broken-chord style.

Arpeggiato (It., ahr-pe-jee-AH-to)   Played in a harp-like broken-chord style.

Arpeggiator   A feature of some synthesizers that automatically plays in arpeggio-style using whatever pitches are held down on the keyboard.

Arpeggio (It., ahr-PE-jee-o)   1. Playing the notes of a chord one at a time, rather than simultaneously. 2. A rapid arpeggio is notated as a chord preceded by an arpeggio sign. The symbol means to play from the bottom upward, but the addition of a downward arrow indicates the opposite.

Arpeggione (It., ahr-pe-JOH-ne)   An instrument fretted and tuned like a guitar that is played with a bow.

Arraché (Fr., ah-rah-shay)   Very strong pizzicato.

Arrangement   The adaptation of a composition to instruments or voices for which it was not originally designed. This may involve a literal transfer of the composition to a different scoring, or a freer creative reworking.

Ars antiqua (Lat., ahrs ahn-TEE-kwah)   Literally, "old art," the term generally indicates music of the 12th and 13th centuries, especially that

24

by early polyphonists Leonin and Perotin. This repertoire is considered the beginning of free composition and counterpoint.

Arsis (Gr., AHR-sis)   An upbeat.

Ars nova (Lat., ahrs NO-vah)   Literally, "new art," the term generally indicates music of the 14th century, especially that by Machaut and Landini, representing a new flowering of complex music in layers of counterpoint.

Articolato (It., ahr-tee-ko-LAH-to)   Articulated; distinctly enunciated.

Articulation   The details of how notes are performed, such as slurred, tongued, staccato, legato, and other similar nuances.

Artifical harmonics   Those harmonics on string instruments using fingered pitches (rather than open strings) to produce the fundamentals over which harmonics are produced.

Art song   A song, generally for voice and piano, in the concert-music tradition (as distinct from folk or popular music).

As (Ger., ahs)   The note A flat.

Ases (Ger., ahs-ayz)   The note A double-flat.

ASCAP   American Society of Composers, Authors, and Publishers.

As dur (Ger., ahs doer)   The key of A flat major.

As moll (Ger., ahs moll)   The key of A flat minor.

Asperges me (Lat., ahs-PER-ges may)   The opening of the Mass in the Catholic service. Not a movement of the musical Mass itself, but sung during the purification of the altar at the beginning of the service.

Asprezza (It., ah-SPRE-tsah)   Roughness, dryness, harshness.

Assai (It., ah-SAH-ee)   Very, extremely.

Assai più (It., ah-SAH-ee pee-oo)   Much more.

Assez (Fr., ah-say)   Enough, sufficiently.

Assoluto (It., ah-so-LOO-to)   Absolute, free, alone, one voice.

Assonanz (Ger., ah-so-NAHNTS) **Assonanza** (It., ah-so-NAHN-tsah)   Similarity, or consonance of tone.

Atem (Ger., AH-tem)   Breath.

A tempo (It., ah TEM-po)   Returning to the established tempo, after some deviation.

Atemlos (Ger., AH-tem-los)   Breathlessly.

Atonal   1. Literally, music which does not have a tonal center. 2. Often used to describe music of harsh dissonance, regardless of any tonal organization. 3. Some theorists only use this term to define music organized by twelve-tone rows, although this is not the standard definition. 4. The term has also been used incorrectly to describe music with no key signature (which is not necessarily devoid of tonal centers).

Attacca (It., ah-TAH-kah)   Continue immediately to the next section or movement.

Attacca subito (It., ah-TAH-kah SOO-bee-to) An emphatic clarification to take no time at all in continuing to the next section.

Attack The intensity of the beginning of a note.

Attendant keys Those scales having most sounds in common with the scale of any given key; the relative keys. In C major the attendant keys are: its relative minor A, the dominant G, and its relative minor E, the subdominant F, and its relative minor D.

Attenuator In electronic music, a control that adjusts the amplitude of a signal, generally to decrease or increase volume, but potentially to alter any other parameter.

Atto (It., AH-to) An act of an opera or play.

Aubade (Fr., o-bahd) Morning music; a morning concert in the open air.

Audace (It., ow-DAH-che) Bold, spirited, audacious.

Audio A general term for sound, in music it usually refers to the output of a music playback system.

Augenmusik (Ger., OW-gen-moo-zeek) Music written so that features of the notation illustrate the meaning of the music or words.

Auf (Ger., owf) On, upon, in, at, etc.

Auf dem Oberwerk (Ger., owf dem O-ber-vayrk) On the upper-work or highest row of keys in organ playing.

Aufführung (Ger., OWF-für-roong) Performance.

Aufgeregt (Ger., OWF-ge-regt) With agitation; excitedly.

Aufgeweckt (Ger., OWF-ge-vekt) Sprightly, cheerful, wide awake.

Aufhalten (Ger., OWF-hahlt-n) To stop; to slow; to keep back.

Auflösungszeichen (Ger., owf-LE[R]-zoongz-tsigh-shen) See *Natural*.

Aufschwung (Ger., OWF-shvoong) Upswing.

Aufstrich (Ger., OWF-streesh) Upbow.

Auftakt (Ger., OWF-tahkt) Arsis, upbeat.

Augmentation Changing the rhythmic values of a theme into notes of longer duration than the original presentation.

Augmented A chromatically raised note.

Augmented chord A triad consisting of the root note, a major third above it, and a chromatically raised (augmented) fifth, such as C-E-G#.

Augmented intervals Major or perfect intervals raised by a half step. These may occur either within a key signature or by alteration.

Augmented sixth chord Any chord featuring an augmented sixth that resolves outward to an octave. See *French sixth, German sixth,* and *Italian sixth* for examples.

Augmented triad See *Augmented chord*.

Aulos (Gr., OW-los) An ancient Greek double-reed wind instrument.

Aus (Ger., ows) From; out of.

Ausdruck (Ger., OWS-drook) Expression.

Ausdrucksvoll (Ger., OWS-drooks-fol) Expressive.

Ausgabe (Ger., OWS-gah-be) Edition.

Ausgehalten (Ger., OWS-ge-hahlt-n) Sustained.

Ausgelassen (Ger., OWS-ge-LAHS-n) Wild, with abandon.

Ausgewählte (Ger., ows-ge-VEL-te) Selected.

Aushalten (Ger., OWS-hahl-t'n) To hold on; to sustain a note.

Auskomponierung In Schenkerian analysis, a musical elaboration from the deep structure of a piece to its surface; literally, "composing out."

Authentic cadence A final cadence; the progression of the dominant to the tonic. A perfect authentic (or complete) cadence involves root-position dominant and tonic chords, and ends with the tonic in the top voice. An imperfect authentic (or incomplete) cadence is weakened either by inverted chords or the lack of the tonic in the top voice.

Authentic mode A church mode or scale in which the tonic pitch was the lowest tone of the scale, as illustrated in the definition for *Church mode*.

Autoharp A type of strummed zither with buttons that are pre-set to produce certain standard chords.

Auxiliary notes Notes (generally graces) immediately above or below a principal or harmonic note.

Avant garde A subjective term used in the 20th century to describe music (or other arts) that were very progressive, experimental, or "before their time."

Avec (Fr., ah-VEK) With.

Ave Maria (Lat., AH-ve mah-REE-ah) "Hail, Mary." A hymn or prayer to the Virgin Mary.

Ave Maris Stella (AH-ve MAH-ris STE-lah) A hymn of the Catholic Church, the words meaning "Hail, Star of the Sea."

Ave Regina (Lat., AH-ve re-JEE-nah) Vesper hymn to the Virgin Mary.

À volonté (Fr., ah vo-lon-tay) At will; at pleasure.

Axe Slang for any musical instrument.

B 1. The seventh note in the scale of C; it is called *Si* in much of the world, but *H* in Germany, and *ti* in American solfège tradition. 2. The major scale with five sharps in its signature. 3. In Germany, B indicates the pitch known elsewhere as B♭.

Baßbrechung, Bassbrechung (Ger., BAHS-brekh-oong) Literally, bass arpeggiation; in Schenkerian analysis, the underlying I-V-I progression that supports the *urlinie*.

Babillage (Fr., bah-bee-yahzh) Playful chatter.

Baby grand The smallest-size grand piano.

Back beat In 4/4 pop music, emphasis on beats 2 and 4.

Backing tracks   In recording, separate layers of music providing the supporting instruments.

Backup group   Typically a small group of singers that accompanies a lead vocalist.

Badinage (Fr., bah-di-nahzh)   Playfulness, sportiveness.

Badinerie (Fr., bah-di-ne-ree)   Playfulness, sportiveness.

Bagatelle (Fr., bag-ah-tel)   Literally a trifle or toy, a short easy piece of music, often for solo piano.

Bagpipe   An instrument with one or more reed pipes attached to a wind bag or bellows. The most elaborate are Irish and Scottish, the latter having three or four drone or single-note pipes and a "chanter," or fingered pipe, for the melody.

Baguala (Sp., bah-GWAH-lah)   A genre of music from Northwest Argentina, consisting of both indigenous and Spanish elements.

Balalaika (Rus., bah-lah-LIGH-kah)   A plucked string instrument in traditional Russian music, consisting of a triangular body and three strings (sometimes doubled).

Baldamente (It., bahl-dah-MEN-te)   Boldly.

Ballabile (It., bah-LAH-bee-le)   In the style of a dance.

Ballad   1. In folk music traditions, a strophic song used to tell a story, often tragic or heroic in character. 2. A light style of music used both in singing and dancing.

Ballade (Fr., bah-LAHD)   One of the French *formes fixes* of the late Middle Ages and early Renaissance, featuring rigid rules for the repetition of verse, refrain, and music. Also see *Formes fixes*, *Rondeau*, and *Virelai*.

Ballerina (It., bahl-le-REE-nah)   A female dancer.

Ballerino (It., bahl-le-REE-no)   A male dancer.

Ballet (Fr., bal-lay)   **Balleto** (It., bahl-LET-to)   Representation of a story, or abstract movement, by means of dance or pantomime accompanied by music.

Ballo (It., BAHL-lo)   A dance or dance tune.

Band   1. A large ensemble of woodwind, brass, and percussion players, sometimes described more specifically as Concert Band, Symphonic Band, Marching Band, Military Band, Wind Ensemble, Wind Symphony, or Wind Orchestra, depending on the function, instrumentation, and personnel distribution of the ensemble. 2. A smaller instrumental group in popular music such as a rock band, jazz band, or dance band.

Bandmaster   The conductor of a band; this term is generally used only for military bands.

Bandola (Sp., bahn-DO-lah)   An instrument resembling a lute.

Bandoneon (Sp., bahn-DO-nee-on) A small accordion of German origin, characterized by buttons on both sides that play different notes when the bellows are pushed or pulled. It has recently entered concert music as the favored instrument of Argentinian composer Astor Piazzolla.

Bandora, Bandurria (Sp., bahn-DO-rah, bahn-doo-REE-ah) A species of Spanish guitar.

Banjo A 5-string picked instrument consisting of an guitar-like neck with fretted fingerboard attached to a circular, parchment-covered body, over which the strings vibrate; the shortest string is a drone. The banjo was used in traditional African-American and Dixieland music, and later became a staple of bluegrass and country music.

Bar 1. Synonymous with measure. 2. A line drawn perpendicularly across the staff to divide it into measures. See *Double bar.*

Barbershop quartet A male vocal quartet specializing in 4-part harmony (characterized by many chromatic chords and dominant sevenths on secondary degrees) popular in America in the early 20th century.

Barcarola (It., bahr-kah-RO-lah) **Barcarolle** (Fr., bahr-kah-rol) A work song of Venetian gondoliers (boatmen), generally in 6/8.

Bariolage (Fr., bar-ee-o-lahzh) A flashy passage, usually for violin, in which open strings are especially used to facilitate fast passagework across several strings;

Baritone (Eng.), **Bariton** (Fr., bah-ri-TON) **Baritono** (It., bah-ree-TO-no) 1. A male voice between bass and tenor. 2. The baritone horn. See *Euphonium.* 3. See *Baryton.*

Baritone clef The F clef on the third line of the staff, as illustrated on page 3.

Baritone saxophone The lowest member of the saxophone family to be in common use, the baritone is a common member of concert band, jazz ensembles, saxophone quartets, and is not uncommon as a solo instrument in jazz and R&B music. Sounding an octave below the alto saxophone, the E♭ Baritone Saxophone transposes by an octave plus a major 6th, meaning written middle C played by the "bari" sounds as E♭ an octave plus a major 6th below.

Bar line See *Bar.*

Barocco (It., bah-ROK-ko) See *Baroque.*

Baroque (Fr., bah-ROK) The historical period of music from roughly 1600 through 1750, whose composers include Purcell, Vivaldi, Handel, and Bach. This period began the flowering of traditional harmony, melody with accompaniment, and formally composed instrumental music. The term Baroque refers to the complicated ornamentation and surprising harmonies typical of music in this period.

Barré (Fr., bar-ray) In guitar playing, a temporary nut (bar) formed by placing the forefinger of the left hand across some of the strings. The term grand barré is used when all 6 strings are covered.

Barrel organ A small, portable organ whose tones are produced by the revolution of a cylinder covered with metal pins and staples carefully positioned to play one or more tunes.

Bartók pizzicato   In contrast to a traditional pizzicato or pluck of the string on instruments of the violin family, this technique involves pulling the string up high from the fingerboard so its release causes a dramatic snapping sound. The technique, popularized through the music of Bela Bartók, is also called "snap pizzicato."

Baryton (Fr., bah-ri-ton)   An instrument of the viol family, consisting of six to seven gut strings on a fretted fingerboard (played with a bow) and 9 to 24 sympathetic wire strings on the back of the fingerboard (plucked with the thumb of the left hand).

Bass   1. The lowest male voice. 2. The lowest part in a musical composition. 3. The lowest pitch in a musical texture or chord. 4. The term alone is often used to describe the string contrabass, defined under the latter term. 5. The lowest member of certain instrumental families, as defined separately below.

Bassa (It., BAH-sah)   Low, often used in the term 8va bassa, meaning to play an octave lower than indicated.

Bass bar   A strip of wood fixed inside the belly of a bowed string instrument, running under and supporting the left foot of the bridge.

Bass clarinet   The lowest commonly-used member of the clarinet family, the bass clarinet is a standard instrument in bands and frequently used in orchestras. The Bb Bass Clarinet sounds an octave lower than a Bb Clarinet and often has extra low notes, extending the bottom range. The notated middle C on this instrument sounds as Bb a major ninth lower than written. Some European music of the late 19th and early-to-middle 20th century also score for Bass Clarinet in A, an instrument which is no longer commonly found.

Bass clef   The F clef, placed upon the fourth line, as illustrated on page 3.

Bass, double   See *contrabass*.

Bass drum   A very large and low drum of indefinite pitch.

Basset horn (It. *Corno di Bassetto*)   An rarely-used instrument of the clarinet family similar in shape, tonal quality and compass to the modern alto clarinet. This instrument flourished during Mozart's era.

Bass flute   The lowest member of the flute family to be in relatively common use, it is almost never found in orchestra or band writing. Bass flutes are often used in large flute ensembles, and can be heard on jazz recordings. The instrument is rather quiet and is often used when miking is available. The bass flute is built with a big curve at the headjoint and sounds an octave lower than the C Flute, and an octave lower than notated.

Basse fundamentale (Fr., bahs foon-da-men-tahl)   Fundamental bass; a bass line that shows only the roots of each chord.

Bass, ground   See *ground bass*.

Bass guitar   An instrument one octave lower than the guitar, it is generally a solid-body electric, usually fretted, and usually with 4 strings tuned to E-A-D-G, matching the strings of the acoustic Contrabass and the bottom 4 strings of the guitar. On rare occasion, bass guitars may have an extra B-string below the E, or C-string above the G.

Basso   (It., BAH-so)   1. See *Bass*. 2. An 8-foot organ stop.

Bass oboe   An uncommon double-reed instrument one octave below the oboe.

Basso buffo   (It., BAH-so BOO-fo)   A humorous operatic bass singer.

Basso cantante   (It., BAH-so kahn-TAHN-te)   A bass voice of baritone quality; a lyric bass.

Basso concertante   (It., BAH-so kon-cher-TAHN-te)   The principal bass; also, the lighter and more delicate parts performed by the violoncello or bassoon.

Basso continuo   (It., BAH-so kon-TEE-noo-o)   In baroque music, this describes the harmonic framework showing a bass part and numeric symbols, often called figured bass, instructing a keyboard player in what chords to play, giving the keyboardist great latitude in improvising the accompaniment. Note that basso continuo is not an instrument, but rather a technique of writing for several instruments. See *Figured bass*.

Bassoon   (Ger. *Fagott*, It. *Fagotto*)   1. A double-reed woodwind instrument of deep pitch, with a compass of over three octaves. The bassoon ordinarily forms the bass of woodwind family, and is capable of expressive and light solo work in all registers. The only other modern instrument in the bassoon family is the contrabassoon (or double bassoon) which sounds an octave lower. 2. A reed stop in the organ which imitates the tones of the bassoon.

Basso ostinato   (It., BAH-so os-tee-NAH-to)   A brief bass figure constantly repeated.

Basso profundo   (It., BAH-soh proh-FOON-doh)   A bass voice that extends below the common bass range.

Bass saxophone   A very low member of the saxophone family occasionally found in concert band or saxophone ensembles. Sounding an octave below the tenor sax, the B♭ Bass Saxophone transposes at 2 octaves plus a major 2nd, meaning its written middle C sounds as the B♭ 2 octaves plus a second below.

Bass trombone   A wide-bore trombone featuring extended tubing, usually activated by two valves, to chromatically extend the low range of the instrument. The contrabass trombone, a rarer instrument, sounds a fourth lower than the bass trombone.

Bass tuba   A brass instrument, available in several sizes and valve configurations, forming the bass of the brass family for all concert band music, and frequently used in music for large orchestra. See *Tuba*.

Bass viol   See *Contrabass*.

Baton   A conductor's stick.

Battement (Fr., bah-te-MAHN)   Banging, or beating.

Batterie (Fr., bah-te-ree)   1. The roll of the drum. 2. The percussion instruments of an orchestra collectively.

Battery   The percussion instruments of an orchestra collectively.

Battre (Fr., bah-truh)   To beat, either for a conductor to show beats, or to strike percussion instruments. "Battre à4" means for a conductor to beat in 4.

Battuta (It., bah-TOO-tah)   1. A beat, pulse, or measure. 2. Struck, as in the instruction *col legno battuta*, meaning to strike the strings with the wood side of the bow (rather than bowing the strings).

Bazouki (Gr., bah-ZOO-kee)   A pear-shaped, plucked string instrument with either three or four doubled strings and a long neck; used in traditional Greek music and, more recently, Celtic music.

B dur (Ger., bay door)   The key of B♭ major.

Be (Ger., bay)   Flat, B♭.

Beam   The horizontal or diagonal line that connects groups of eighth notes, sixteenth notes, thirty-second notes, etc., in place of separate flags.

Bearbeitet (Ger., be-AHR-bigh-tet)   Arranged; adapted.

Beat   1. The musical pulse. 2. The rise or fall of the conductor's hand or baton marking the pulse. 3. To conduct and show the pulse. 4. An acoustical throbbing heard when two unison tones are slightly out of tune with each other.

Beater   General term for any percussion mallet or stick.

Bebop   A progressive style of jazz that originated in the 1940s, characterized by exploratory harmonies, free improvisation, complex rhythms, fast tempos, and a general approach to be exploratory music rather than functional dance music or recognizable songs.

Bebung (Ger., BE-boong)   A shaking or vibration; a German organ stop.

Bec (Fr., bek)   The mouthpiece of a wind instrument.

Becarré (Fr., beh-KAHR)   See *Natural*.

Becken (Ger., BEK-n)   Cymbals.

Begleiten (Ger., be-GLIGHT-n)   To accompany.

Beguine (beh-GEEN)   A lively, syncopated Latin-American dance in 4/4 time.

Bel   A unit of acoustical measure, see *Decibel*.

Bel canto (It., bel KAHN-to)   Literally, "beautiful song." While it could be applied to all good singing, it specifically describes a tender, pure, and sympathetic legato, the opposite of bravura singing.

Belieben (Ger., be-LEEB-n)   Pleasure; at pleasure.

Bell 1. Any hollow metal instrument, set in vibration by a clapper inside or a hammer outside. 2. Any solid metal instrument of specific pitch, such as the glockenspiel. 3. The flared end of wind and brass instruments (so called due to its bell-like shape, rather than sound or function).

Bellezza (It., be-LE-tsah)   Beauty of tone and expression.

Bell gamba A gamba stop in an organ; the top of each pipe spreading out like a bell.

Bellicosamente (It., be-lee-ko-zah-MEN-te) See *Bellicoso*.

Bellicoso (It., bel-lee-KO-zo)   In a martial and warlike style.

Bell lyre A portable glockenspiel, convenient for marching bands.

Bellows A pneumatic appendage for supplying organ pipes with air.

Belly The soundboard of a string instrument, over which the strings are extended.

Bémol (Fr., bay-mol) **Bemolle** (It., bay-mo-le)   The flat symbol ♭.

Ben (It., ben) **Bene** (It., BAY-ne)   Well, good.

Bend A short, smooth change in pitch similar to a portamento or glissando; used on guitar, harmonica and synthesizer, among other instruments.

Benedictus (Lat., be-ne-DIK-tus)   One of the movements in a Mass.

Bene placito (It., BE-ne PLAH-chee-to)   At will; at pleasure.

Ben marcato (It., ben mahr-KAH-to) **Bene marcato** (be-ne mahr-KAH-to)   Well marked in a distinct and strongly accented manner.

Bequadro (It., bay-QUAH-dro)   See *natural*.

Berceuse (Fr., bair-soos)   A cradle song; a lullaby.

Bergamasca (It., ber-gah-MAHS-kah) **Bergamasques** (Fr. ber-gah-mahsk)   A kind of rustic dance.

Bes (Ger., bes)   The note B double-flat.

Beschleunigen (Ger., be-SHLOYN-i-gen)   To accelerate.

Bestimmt (Ger., be-SHTEEMT)   With decision. Distinct.

Betonend (Ger., be-TO-nend) **Betont** (Ger., be-TONT)   Accented.

Betonung(en) (Ger., be-TO-noong [-en])   Accent(s).

Betrübt (Ger., be-TRÜBT)   Afflicted, grieved.

Bewegt (Ger., be-VEGT)   Animated.

Bewegung (Ger., be-VE-goong)   Motion, movement.

Big band A jazz ensemble usually made up of 5 saxophones, 3-4 trumpets, 3-4 trombones, piano, bass, drums, and guitar, and occasionally further instruments, generally playing dance music, and often featuring vocalists.

Binary form A two-part musical structure where one section is followed by a contrasting section, often represented as "AB." Also see *Rounded binary form*.

Binary measure Two beats to a measure.

Bis (Lat., bis) 1. Twice; indicating that the passage marked is to be repeated. 2. A subdivision of some section or number of a musical work, as 1 *bis*, 2 *bis*, etc. 3. A slang term yelled to request an encore.

Bisbigliando (It., bees-beel-YAHN-do) Literally "whispering," the term describes a soft tremolo on the harp.

Biscroma (It., bees-KRO-mah) Thirty-second note.

Bitonal A musical passage featuring two simultaneous key centers.

Biwa (Jap., BEE-wah) A Japanese lute.

Bizzarramente (It., bee-tsah-rah-MEN-te) Oddly.

Bizzarria (It., bee-tsah-REE-ah) Written in a capricious, fantastic style; sudden, unexpected modulations.

Bizzaro (It., bee-TSAH-ro) Whimsical, odd, fantastical.

Blasen (Ger., BLAHZ-n) 1. To blow. 2. Wind instruments.

Blasinstrumente (Ger., BLAHZ-een-stroo-men-te) Wind instruments.

Blasmusik (Ger., BLAHZ-moo-ZEEK) Music for wind instruments.

Blechinstrumente (Ger., BLEKH-een-stroo-men-te) Brass instruments.

Blockflöte (Ger., BLOK-flö-te) 1. Recorder. 2. An organ stop composed of large scale-pipes, the tone of which is full and broad.

Bluegrass A folk style from the American south featuring quick tempos, busy textures, and elaborate vocals. It usually features fiddle, banjo, mandolin, guitar, and bass, and is traditionally without percussion.

Blue notes Chromatically lowered third, fifth, and seventh degrees of a major scale that create the characteristic sound of the blues, particularly when in simultaneous conflict with those diatonic notes in other instruments. Most typically these pitches involve bending and are not meant to be perfectly in tune.

Blues A kind of American music whose musical style derived from spirituals and work songs, and whose lyrics generally bemoan a challenging life or lost love, with melody characterized by blue notes, often using a 12-bar harmonic framework. See *Twelve-bar blues.*

Blues harp Slang for a diatonic harmonica. To get blue notes, one bends the pitch and/or uses harmonicas in keys different from the song itself. For example, a C diatonic blues harp has all "natural" notes, so playing a C harp for a song in G major provides the lowered 7th (F natural) automatically.

Bluette (Fr., blü-et) A short, brilliant piece. The word means spark or flash.

BMI Broadcast Music, Inc.

B-moll (Ger., bay-mol) The key of B-flat minor.

Board fade In sound engineering, to fade out a musical passage from the engineering console or software.

Bocal (Fr., BO-kuhl) The small tubular part of a bassoon (or other

34

instrument) that connects the reed to the main body.

Bocca (It., BO-kah)   The mouthpiece of a horn, trumpet, trombone, and similar instruments.

Bocca chiusa (It., BO-kah kee-OO-zah)   With closed mouth; humming.

Bodhran (Gaelic, BOW-rahn)   An Irish frame drum with a goatskin head, played by striking the head with a double-ended wooden rod, or tipper.

Body   1. The resonance box of a string instrument. 2. That primary part of a wind instrument other than mouthpiece, crooks, and bell. 3. The tube of an organ-pipe above its mouth.

Boehm Flute (Ger. , be[r]m)   A modern flute with well-tuned sound holes, either closed by pads or with open rings to be covered by fingertips, with a key mechanism that greatly facilitates execution; invented in the early 19th century by Theobald Boehm.

Bogen (Ger., BOG-n)   1. The bow of a violin and other string instruments. 2. A slur or tie.

Bois (Fr., bwah)   Woodwind.

Boléro (Sp., bo-LAY-ro)   A lively Spanish dance, in 3/4 time, much like the Andalusian cachucha. It is typically accompanied by castanets, and sometimes with singing. Note that Ravel's famous work is *not* a typical boléro rhythm.

Bombarde (Fr., bon-bahrd) **Bombardo** (It., bom-BAHR-do)   1. A powerful reed stop in an organ of 16-foot scale. 2. An old wind instrument of the oboe species.

Bombardon (Fr., Bom-bahr-don)   1. A bass or contrabass tuba. 2. A 16- or 32-foot reed stop on an organ.

Bongos   An Afro-Cuban percussion instrument consisting of two small hand drums: a larger drum, or *hembra* and a smaller drum, or *macho*.

Boogaloo   A Caribbean-inspired rock genre of the 1960s.

Boogie woogie   A jazz piano style popular in the United States during the 1920s and 1930s, characterized by a steady rhythmic ostinato bass in the left hand, and an ornate right-hand part with *swung* rhythm.

Boot   The foot of a reed pipe.

Bop   See *Bebop.*

Bordone (It., bor-DO-ne)   See *Bourdon.*

Bore   The windstream, or diameter, of a woodwind or brass instrument.

Borrowed chord   A chord placed as a substitute for an expected chord, which "borrows" one or more pitches from a different key.

Bossa nova (Port., BO-sah NO-vah)   A Brazilian dance rhythm popular in the late 1950s and 1960s, characterized by a set of syncopations teasing the expectation of where typical Latin syncopation would be heard.

Bottleneck   A glass or metal tube placed over a finger of a guitarist's left hand, to create pitch slides by gliding over the frets.

Bouchée (Fr., boo-shay) 1. In wind instruments, this means muted. 2. For organ pipes, it means stopped.

Bouche fermée (Fr., boosh fair-may) With closed mouth; humming.

Bouffe (Fr., boof) Comic, as in operatic roles and style.

Bourdon (Fr., boor-don) 1. An organ stop, the pipes of which are stopped or covered, and produce the 16-foot, and sometimes the 32-foot tone. 2. A drone bass. 3. A large bell with a deep pitch.

Bourrée (Fr., boo-ray) An old French dance said to have come from Auvergne, but others claim it to be a Spanish dance coming from Biscay, where it is still in use. It is very rapid and hearty, generally in 2/4 or in 2/2 time. (Note the correct spelling.)

Bouts The curved sides of stringed instruments which form a waist.

Bouzouki (Gr. boo-ZOO-kee) A plucked string instrument of Greek origin, consisting of a pear-shaped body, three to four pairs of strings, and an elongated neck. Recently, it has become popular in Celtic music.

Bow An instrument of wood and horsehair, employed to set the strings of an instrument in vibration. The bow, originally curved, as its name implies, has been subject to many changes of shape from time to time, from a large curve to an almost flat form.

Bow hand The right hand; the hand that holds the bow.

Bowing 1. The art of using the bow; playing with the bow. 2. The marks used to guide the player, specifically ⊓ for downbow and ∨ for an upbow.

Bpm Beats per minute, referring to metronome markings.

Brace 1. In music notation, a character at the left of a score, curved or straight, used to connect several staves. It is common to describe the curved symbol as a brace and the squared symbol as a bracket, although the terms may be considered interchangeable. 2. The leather slide that tightens or loosens the cords of a drum.

Bracket See *Brace*.

Brake drum The drum from an automotive brake, usually suspended or mounted and struck with hammers or drumsticks; the sound is similar to an anvil.

Bransle, Branle (Fr., brahnl) 1. A lively old dance in 4/4 time. 2. A dance species of "follow the leader" in which all motions of the leading couple are imitated.

Brass band An ensemble of brass players, often with a percussion section, commonly found in the United Kingdom.

Brass instruments The family of instruments with funnel-shaped mouthpieces, including trumpet, cornet, bugle, flügelhorn, horn, trombone, baritone, euphonium and tuba.

Brass quintet   1. An ensemble consisting of two trumpets, horn, trombone and tuba (or bass trombone). 2. A composition for that ensemble.

Brass trio   1. An ensemble consisting of a trumpet, horn, and trombone. 2. A composition for that ensemble.

Bratsche (Ger., BRAH-chuh)   Viola.

Brautlied (Ger., BROWT-leet)   A bridal hymn; a wedding song.

Bravissima (It. fem., brah-VEE-see-mah)   Intensified form of brava.

Bravissimo (It. masc., brah-VEE-see-mo)   Intensified form of bravo.

Brava (It. fem., BRAH-vah)   Feminine form of bravo.

Bravo (It. masc., BRAH-vo)   An exclamation of enthusiastic approval often used following performances.

Bravura (It., brah-VOO-rah)   Spirit; skill; requiring great dexterity and skill in execution.

Brawl   See *Bransle*.

Break   1. The point of change in the quality of tenor, soprano, and alto voices. A genuine bass voice has no break. The lower range is called *voce di petto*, or chest voice; the upper, *voce di testa*, or head voice; and the place of junction is called the break. A properly cultivated voice should have the break so under control, that the change of the quality should be practically imperceptible. 2. On clarinet, the break in tone where the lower register meets the upper.

Breit (Ger., bright)   Broad.

Breve (It., BRAY-ve)   1. Brief, short; in ancient times the Breve was the shortest note. The notes then used were the Large, the Long, and the Breve. The Breve is now the longest note, equal to two *semibreves* or whole notes. 2. A double whole note, as shown on page 4.

Bridge   1. The part of a stringed instrument, near the tail, that supports the strings. 2. A transitional passage between two thematic sections of a composition.

Brillante (It., bree-LAHN-te) **Brillante** (Fr., bree-yahnt)   Bright, sparkling, brilliant.

Brill Building   The office building at 1619 Broadway in New York City, which served as a songwriting and publishing nexus during the 1930s and 1940s.

Brindisi (It., breen-DEE-zee)   A drinking song.

Brio (It., BREE-o)   Vigor, animation, spirit.

Brioso (It., bree-O-zo)   Lively, vigorous, with spirit.

Brisé (Fr., bree-zay)   Split; broken into an arpeggio.

Broadway   Named after a street in New York City, the term has come to mean the mainstream musical theater genre whose major theaters are located there.

Broken chords   Chords whose notes are not played simultaneously, but successively. See *Arpeggio*.

Broken octaves   Octaves in which the notes are played separately, such as a slight arpeggio in piano playing.

Bruit (Fr., brü-ee)   Noise, rattle, clatter.

Brummen (Gr., BROO-men)   To hum; to growl.

Bruscamente (It., broo-skah-MEN-te)   Abruptly, coarsely.

Brushes   Soft wire mallets with fine tines bunched together, used in place of drumsticks to strike percussion instruments gently; often used in jazz.

Brustwerk   Literally, "breast-work"; the choir organ, with softer, more delicate stops.

Bubblegum music   A genre of rock music of the 1960s aimed at younger listeners.

Bucket mute   A mute lined with a soft substance, like cotton, that muffles the sound of brass instruments by absorbing high frequencies.

Buffa (It., BOO-fah) **Buffo** (It., BOO-fo)   Comic, humorous, in the comic style, also a singer who takes comic parts in the opera.

Buffonescamente (It., boo-fo-ne-skah-MEN-te)   In a burlesque and comical manner.

Bugle   1. A hunting horn. 2. An instrument of copper or brass, similar to the cornet, but higher and more piercing in pitch. Formerly equipped with keys or valves, it now exists only in natural form and is used in military field music.

Burden   1. A regular return of a theme or phrase in a song, at the close of each verse. 2. The drone of a bagpipe.

Burgundian school   The group of northern European composers of the early 15th century pioneering the next generation of harmony and polyphony, including Guillaume Dufay.

Burla (It., BOOR-lah) **Burlando** (It., boor-LAHN-do) **Burlesco** (It., boor-LES-ko)   Facetious, droll, comical; in a playful manner.

Burlesque   Musical comedy, satire, or farce; often a show consisting of many unrelated scenes, songs, and skits, sometimes of a racy nature.

Burletta (It., boor-LET-ta)   A comic operetta; a light musical and dramatic piece, somewhat in the nature of the English farce.

BWV   Bach Werke Verzeichnis; the numerically organized catalogue of J.S. Bach's music.

Byzantine chant   Christian monophonic chants from the Byzantine Empire (330-1453 A.D.)

C   1. The first note of the natural scale, called Ut in France and Do in most other countries. 2. The major scale with no flats or sharps in its signature. 3. A symbol indicating 4/4 or Common Time; the C symbol is not an abbreviation of the word Common, but rather an evolution of a circular rhythmic symbol from the middle ages. A slashed C is similarly used to indicate 2/2, or Cut Time.

c., ca.   Abbreviation for circa, meaning approximately.

Cabaletta (It., kah-bah-LE-tah)   A simple melody of a pleasing and attractive character; an operatic air like the rondo in form; also called cavaletta.

Cabasa (Sp., kah-BAH-sah) A Latin-American percussion instrument using chains of beads to act as a scraper against either a gourd or a ribbed metal surface.

Caccia (It., KAH-chah)   1. Music for chase or hunt. 2. A canon where the voices "chase" each other. 3. See *Catch*.

Cachucha (Spa., kah-CHOO-chah)   A popular Spanish dance in triple time, similar to the bolero.

Cacophony   Disorganized sound or dissonance, often describing a busy texture of conflicting patterns.

Cadence   1. Any division or close of a phrase in melody or harmony, creating a partial punctuation of the phrase, or a final termination. 2. An ornamental passage decorating such a junction. See entries below and also *Cadenza*.

Cadence, authentic   See *Authentic cadence*.

Cadence, church   See *Plagal cadence*.

Cadence, complete   See *Authentic cadence*.

Cadence, deceptive   See *Deceptive cadence*.

Cadence, half   See *Half cadence*.

Cadence, imperfect   See *Half cadence*.

Cadence, incomplete   See *Authentic cadence*.

Cadence, perfect   See *Authentic cadence*.

Cadence, plagal   See *Plagal cadence*.

Cadenza (It., kah-DEN-zah)   An ornamental passage often near the close of a song or solo, either provided by the composer or improvised by the performer. Cadenzas originated as a brief elaboration and texture break, and over the centuries evolved to include significantly long passages for concerto soloists.

Caesura (It., che-ZOO-rah)   1. A brief pause in the music. 2. Sometimes used to describe the abrupt break of a luftpause, notated as //.

Caisse (Fr., kes)   Drum.

Caisse grosse (Fr., kes gros)   Bass drum.

Caisse roulante (Fr., kes roo-lahnt)   Side (snare) drum.

Cakewalk   A syncopated American dance popular in the 1890s, rhythmically related to ragtime.

Calando (It., kah-LAHN-do)   Gradually diminishing the tone and slowing the time; becoming softer and slower by degrees.

Calcando (It., kahl-KAHN-do)   Pressing forward, hurrying.

Calcant (Ger., KAHL-kahnt)   The bellows treader, in old German organs.

Call and response   A type of simple antiphony, typical of both work songs and sacred music, where a leader sings a phrase and the ensemble replies, either by repeating the leader's phrase, or with an answering response.

Calliope (kah-LIGH-o-pee)   A pipe organ of limited compass, the loud and coarse tone being produced by steam.

Calma (It., KAHL-mah) **Calmate** (It., kahl-MAH-te) **Calmato** (It., kahl-MAH-to)   Calmness, tranquility, repose.

Calore (It., kah-LO-re) **Caloroso** (It., kahl-o-RO-zo)   Warmth, animation.

Calypso   A syncopated ballad style from Trinidad popular in the United States during the late 1950s and early 1960s.

Cambiata (It., kahm-bee-AH-tah)   1. A non-chord tone approached by a leap and resolved by a step in the opposite direction. 2. In species counterpoint, a dissonance approached by a descending step and followed by a descending skip of a third. 3. The voice part of an adolescent male whose vocal range is in the middle of changing, generally similar to a baritone.

Camera (It., KAH-me-rah)   Chamber; a term applied to music composed for private performance or small concerts.

Camerata (It., kah-meh-RAH-tah)   A small school of writers and musicians, typically during the Renaissance.

Caminando (It., kah-mee-NAHN-do)   Flowing; with easy and gentle progression.

Campana (It., kahm-PAH-nah)   A bell.

Campanella (It., kahm-pah-NE-lah)   A little bell.

Canaries   An old dance, in lively 4/4 or 6/8, and sometimes 12/8 time, of two strains. It derives its name from the Canary Islands, from where it is supposed to have originated.

Can-can (Fr., kahn-kahn)   A French dance in fast 2/4 time, popular in the 19th century.

Cancellation   A natural sign (♮), used to remove the effect of a previous accidental.

Cancion (Sp., kahn-see-ON)   Song.

Cancrizans (It., kahn-KREE-tsahns) **Cancrizante** (It., kahn-kree-TSAHN-te)   Retrograde movement; going backward; the name comes from crab-like motion.

C&W   Country & Western music.

Canon   Literally meaning "rule," the strictest form of contrapuntal composition, in which each voice exactly imitates the melody sung or played by the first voice. The imitation may be exact repetition, or an exact transformation by a rule, such as "twice the rhythmic value" or "a perfect fifth higher."

Cantabile (It., kahn-TAH-bi-le)   Singing or playing in a melodious and graceful style, full of expression.

Cantando (It., kahn-TAHN-do)   In a singing style, cantabile.

Cantare (It., kahn-TAH-re)   To sing; to celebrate; to praise.

Cantata (It., kahn-TAH-tah) **Cantate** (Fr., kahn-taht) **Cantate** (Ger.) (kahn-TAH-te)   A vocal composition typically in several movements, and traditionally comprising airs, recitatives, and choruses.

Cantica (It., kahn-TEE-kah)   Canticle; laude, or sacred song of the Roman Catholic Church.

Canticle   A sacred hymn or song. One of the non-metrical hymns of praise and jubilation in the Bible.

Cantillation   Hebrew prayers embellished by rising and falling pitch; this tradition of heightened speech evolved into the earliest forms of chant, and later into the original Christian plainchant.

Cantillation marks   Ornamental signs placed over Hebrew texts, indicating pitch direction for chanting, and therefore a forerunner of modern notation showing contour without a staff or fixed pitch reference.

Cantilena (It., kahn-ti-LAY-nah)   1. Any light and simple song, or in instrumental music, a piece of songlike character. 2. The melody or principal part in any composition; generally the highest vocal part.

Canto (It., KAHN-to)   1. Song, melody. 2. The highest vocal part in choral music. 3. A part or division of a poem.

Canto fermo (It., KAHN-to FAIR-mo)   See *Cantus firmus*.

Cantor (It., kahn-TOR)   A liturgical singer; a chanter.

Cantoris (Lat., kan-TO-ris)   In cathedral music, the passages intended for singers on the side of the choir where the cantor or precentor sits. This is usually on the left-hand side on entering the choir from the nave. See *Decani*.

Cantus (Lat., KAN-tus)   A song; a melody; also, the treble or soprano part.

Cantus firmus (Lat., KAN-tus FIR-mus)   The subject or "fixed song" against which other melodic figures are set, "point against point," in contrapuntal writing.

Canzona (It., kahn-TSO-nah)   1. Song; ballad. 2. A graceful and somewhat elaborate air in two or three strains or divisions. 3. An air in two or three parts with passages of fugue and imitation, somewhat similar to the madrigal.

Canzonet   A short song in one, two, or three parts.

Canzonetta (It., kahn-tso-NET-tah)   A short canzone. A little song.

Capellmeister   see *Kapellmeister*.

Capo (It., KAH-po)   The head, beginning, top; generally refers to the beginning of a composition.

Capo (Eng., KAY-po) See *Capotasto.*

Capotasto (It., kah-po-TAH-sto) 1. Originally a piece of wood or ivory with a clamp, and more recently a steel bar covered with clear semi-soft plastic, used by guitar players to form a temporary nut across the fingerboard; this is applied to raise the pitch of all the strings simultaneously, to create a transposition to a higher key. This term is called "capo" for short and sometimes incorrectly referred to as *capo d'astro.* 2. The nut or upper part of the fingerboard of a string instrument.

Capped reed See *Reed, double.*

Cappella (It., kah-PE-lah) 1. A chapel or church. 2. A group of musicians who sing or play in a church. 3. An orchestra.

Cappriccietto (It., kah-pree-CHE-to) A short capriccio.

Capriccio (It., kah-PREE-cho, kah-PREE-chee-o) A fanciful and irregular species of composition; in a capricious and free style.

Capricciosamente (It., kah-pree-cho-zah-MEN-te Capriciously.

Capriccioso (It., kah-pree-CHO-zo, kah-pree-chee-O-zo) In a fanciful and capricious style.

Caprice (Fr., ka-prees) See *Capriccio.*

Capstan The rotating roller on a cassette or open-reel tape player that propels the tape forward across the play, record, and erase heads.

Carattere (It., kah-RAH-te-re) Character.

Caressant (Fr., kah-re-sahn) Caressingly, tenderly.

Carezzando (It., kah-re-TSAHN-do) **Carezzovole** (It., kah-re-tso-VO-le) In a caressing and tender manner.

Caricatura (It., kah-ree-kah-TOO-rah) A caricature; an exaggerated representation.

Carillon 1. A set of chimes, typically built above a church or other steeple, played by a large mechanism initiated by a keyboard (or more recently by computer). 2. Music composed for this instrument. 3. A mixture stop in an organ, to imitate a peal of bells.

Carità (It., kah-REE-tah) Tenderness, feeling.

Carnatic music The traditional music of South India.

Carol A song of joy, exultation, or devotion, most typically celebrating the Nativity.

Cassa (It., KAH-sah) A large drum.

Cassa grande (It., KAH-sah GRAHN-de) The bass drum.

Castanets A pair of clappers used to accompany dancing, formed of small concave shells of ivory or hard wood. Traditionally castanets are used by dancers in Spain and other southern countries to mark the rhythm of the bolero, cachucha, etc., held in their hands as they dance. As symphonic composers began including complex rhythms in castanet writing, instruments also evolved as two mounted shells to sit on a stand or table, facilitating fast or complex non-traditional rhythms.

Castrato (It., kahs-TRAH-to)   A male singer surgically altered before puberty to prevent the voice from changing, with the goal of remaining a male soprano through adulthood; such singers were not necessarily true eunuchs.

Catch   A humorous composition for three or four voices, of English tradition. The parts are so contrived that individual vocal parts enter introducing simple and innocent texts, generally with ample rests between phrases. Then when they repeat as overlapping parts, the newly juxtaposed syllables conjoin resulting in a new composite text, often bawdy.

Catgut   A string material for violins and other instruments of a similar kind, made of the intestines of sheep, lambs, or goats.

Cautionary   An extra accidental not required by the key signature, but rather as a reminder to the performer that either an accidental in a previous bar is no longer in affect, or that an accidental earlier in the bar is still in effect. This is sometimes also called a courtesy accidental.

Cavaquinho (Port., kah-vah-KEEN-o)   A small, four-stringed guitar originating in Portugal.

Cavatina (It., kah-vah-TEE-nah)   An air, traditionally of one strain only; generally of simple and expressive character.

C clef   Any of several clefs resembling the letter K whose placement on the staff indicates the location of middle C, as detailed on pages 3 and 4.

CD   Compact Disc. The term CD tends to refer to audio-format discs, in contrast to CDR or CD-Rom which means data-format discs.

C dur (Ger., tsay door)   The key of G major.

Cebell   The name of an old air in common time, characterized by a quick and sudden alternation of high and low notes.

Cédez (Fr., say-day)   Hold back.

Celere (It., CHE-le-re)   Quick; rapid; with velocity.

Celerità (It., che-le-REE-tah) **Célérité** (Fr., say-lay-ree-tay)   Velocity, rapidity.

Celesta (Fr., se-le-sta, It., che-LE-sta)   An instrument invented by Mustel in Paris in 1886. It consists of steel tuning forks set in sound boxes struck with mallets through a keyboard.

Céleste (Fr., say-lest)   Celestial, heavenly; see *Voix celeste*.

Celestina (It., che-les-TEE-nah)   An organ stop of 4-foot scale, producing a very delicate and subdued tone.

Cello (It., CHE-lo)   A shortened form of violoncello, sometimes spelled with the apostrophe: 'cello. The proper abbreviation for Cello is Vcl. because it refers to the violoncello.

Cembalo (It., CHEM-bah-lo)   Harpsichord.

Cent   Literally "hundreth," a cent equals one hundredth of a half-step; for example, there are 100 cents between A and B♭, allowing musicians to discuss intonation in fine detail.

Ces (Ger., tses)   The note C flat.

Ces dur (tses doer)   The key of C flat major.

Cesura (It., che-ZOO-rah)   See *Caesura*.

Cha-cha   A Latin-American dance in 4/4, less syncopated than most Latin dances, and most notable for its characteristic cha-cha-cha rhythms where the melody and harmony play 3 staccato eighth notes in succession, generally on repeating pitches.

Chaconne (Fr., shah-kon)   1. A traditional form of composition consisting of variations on a brief and recurring chord progression. When a repeating bass line supports the recurring chords, that line is called a Ground Bass. (Pachelbel's familiar *Kanon in D* is a typical example because it is a series of elaborations over a repeating series of 8 chords, supported by a repeating series of 8 bass notes, the roots of each chord). Although they are similar, the chaconne should not be confused with *Passacaglia* in which a melodic line recurs with elaborations. 2. A graceful, slow Spanish movement in 3/4, using the above technique.

Chalumeau (Fr., shahl-u-mo)   1. The lowest register of the clarinet.

Chamade (Fr., shah-mahd)   A drum beat declaring surrender.

Chamber ensemble   A small group of musicians.

Chamber music   The term originated as *any* music suited to a room or small hall, as distinct from music for a large auditorium, church, theater, or symphonic hall. The term refers now to instrumental music for relatively small ensembles, generally without doubling parts. There is no specific definition or maximum number of players.

Chamber orchestra   A general term for an orchestra with a fairly small number of players. There is no specific definition by number of musicians.

Chance music   See *Aleatoric music*.

Change ringing   The art of ringing church bells, most often by hand, employing various mathematical patterns to organize the sequence.

Changes   Jazz term for a progression of chords (short for chord changes) over which soloists improvise.

Changko (CHANG-ko)   An hourglass-shaped drum with two heads of differing pitch and timbre, widely used in traditional Korean music. Also spelled "janggu."

Changing notes   Passing notes or non-chord tones that occur on the accented parts of a measure.

Channel   An individual layer of music or sound, often an isolated instrument, as part of a composite audio mix, particularly used in MIDI sequencing.

Chanson (Fr., shahn-son) Song.

Chant 1. Sacred monophonic vocal music, typically notated only in pitches, allowing the rhythm to follow the natural prosody of the liturgical words. Typically called plainchant, this includes the specific repertoires known as Gregorian, Ambrosian, and Byzantine Chant. 2. To recite musically; to sing.

Chant (Fr., shahn) The voice part; a song or melody; singing.

Chantant, chantante (Fr., shahn-tahn, shahn-tahnt) Adapted to singing; in a melodious and singing style.

Chant, double A chant extending through two verses of a psalm. It should have four reciting-notes and four cadences.

Chanter The melody pipe in a bagpipe.

Chanterelle (Fr., shahn-tuh-rel) Treble string; the E string of the violin. The highest string of any instrument of the violin or lute family.

Chantey, chanty, shanty Sailors' song.

Chapman stick An electronic instrument devised in the 1970's; similar to a wide guitar fingerboard in appearance, it is designed specifically for the technique of finger-tapping on the frets.

Character piece A short instrumental composition with a given mood or character, most often for solo piano.

Charango (Sp., chah-RAHN-go) A small, plucked string instrument with five doubled strings, used in South American music. The body is traditionally crafted from the shell of an armadillo.

Charivari (Fr., shah-ree-vah-ree) Noisy music made with tin dishes, horns, bells, etc.; clatter; a mock serenade.

Charleston An American dance originating in the 1920s, characterized by a syncopated accent on the offbeat of beat 2 in 4/4.

Chart In jazz and other popular music, a written arrangement.

Chasse (Fr., shahs) Hunting; in the hunting style.

Che (It., ke) Then, that, which.

Chef (Fr., shef) Leader, chief.

Chef-d'œuvre (Fr., she doovr) A masterpiece; the principal or most important composition of an author.

Chef-d'orchestre (Fr., she dor-kestr) The conductor of an orchestra.

Chest voice The lowest register of the voice.

Chest, wind See *Wind chest*.

Chiamare (It., kee-ah-MAH-re) To chime.

Chiaramente (It., kee-ah-rah-MEN-te) Clearly, brightly, purely.

Chiarezza (It., kee-ah-RET-sah) Clearness, neatness, purity.

Chiesa (It., kee-E-zah) Church. See *Sonata di chiesa, Trio sonata*.

Chimes 1. A set of tuned bells large enough to be suspended from a rack, also called Tubular Bells or Tubular Chimes. 2. Also see *Wind chimes*.

Chitarra (It., kee-TAH-rah)   Guitar.

Chitarrone (It., kee-ta-RO-neh)   An Italian bass lute of the Renaissance, similar to the theorbo.

Chiuso (It., kee-OO-zo)   Closed; hidden; see *Bocca chiuso*.

Choeur (Fr., kühr)   See *Choir*.

Choir   1. An ensemble of singers. 2. An ensemble of instruments blended as uniformly as singers, such as handbell choir or flute choir. 3. That part of a cathedral or church set apart for the singers.

Choir, grand   In organ playing, the union of all reed stops.

Choir organ   In a large organ, the lowest keyboard is generally the choir organ, which contains some of the softer and more delicate stops, and is used for accompanying solos, duets, etc.

Choke   To quickly stop a ringing percussion instrument such as a cymbal. The choking effect itself adds a percussive sound.

Chops   Slang for a musician's technique, originally referring to the strength of a player's mouth, but now meaning any type of skill.

Choral (Eng.)   Referring to music for choir.

Choral (Ger., ko-RAHL) **Chorale** (Eng.)   A hymn that is typically harmonized in 4 parts in block-chord style with brief cadences at the end of each text line, to be sung several times through with successive stanzas of text. The tradition evolved from the early German Protestant church and continues to the present in church music. The proliferation of chorales has also inspired a large body of sacred art music elaborating on these harmonized tunes.

Chorale prelude   Music for organ (or other instruments) based on a chorale tune, in which newly-composed music begins as the primary theme, and the familiar hymn is later introduced in counterpoint with the new theme.

Chord   The union of several simultaneous pitches; many types of chords are detailed in the prefatory pages of this book.

Chord, dominant   A chord built from the 5th note of a diatonic scale; see page 8.

Chord, inverted   A chord in which the root pitch does not appear as the lowest note.

Chordophone   A musical instrument that produces sound through the vibration of strings, such as a violin, harp, or guitar.

Chorister   A choral singer.

Chorus   1. A group of singers. 2. A composition intended to be sung by a number of voices. 3. A refrain within a vocal or choral work.

Christe eleison (Gr., KREE-ste e-LE-i-son)   "Christ, have mercy"; the middle part of the Kyrie, which is the first movement in a Mass.

Chromatic   1. Proceeding by half-steps.   2. Any music or chord containing notes outside the diatonic scale.

Chromaticism   The use of chromatic (non-diatonic) pitches to add interest or intensity to a musical passage or composition.

Chromatic scale   A scale including all twelve pitches in ascending and/or descending order, illustrated on page 6.

Church cadence   See *Plagal cadence.*

Church modes   Originating in Medieval plainchant, these are the 4 scale patterns (authentic modes) and 4 further variants (plagal modes). The mood and color of each mode is determined by its pattern of half steps and whole steps, as well as the emphasis on its psalm tone and recitation tone. Similar "modal" scales are also utilized in folk and concert music. Examples of these more contemporary modes are shown under the entry for *Mode.*

Ciaccona (It., chah-KO-nah)   See *Chacone.*

Cimbalom (Hung., CHEEM-bah-lom)   A large hammered dulcimer of Hungarian origin.

Cinelli (It., chee-NE-lee)   Cymbals.

Ciphering   The sounding of organ pipes when keys are not touched.

Circle of fifths   A method of chord progression or modulation, using each chord successively as the new dominant of a V-I sequence, thereby traveling through all 12 notes and back to the first chord.

Circular breathing   A technique in which air is simultaneously inhaled through the nose and exhaled through the mouth. This allows sound to be sustained indefinitely.

Cis (Ger., tsis)   The note C sharp.

Cisis (Ger., tsis-is)   The note C double sharp.

Cis dur (Ger., tsiss door)   The key of C-sharp major.

Cis moll (Ger., tsiss mol)   The key of C-sharp minor.

Cither, cithern, cittern (SITH-er, SITH-ern, SIT-tern)   A plucked-string instrument of the Renaissance, smaller than a lute and with a flat back.

Clam   Slang for a wrong note, as in "playing a clam."

Clap   To smack one's hands together creating a percussive sound.

Clapper   The beater inside a bell, on those bells which sound by being shaken, rather than being struck from the outside.

Clarabella (Lat., klah-rha-BE-la)   An organ stop of 8-foot scale, with a soft flutelike tone; the pipes are wood and not stopped.

Clarinet   A rich full-toned woodwind instrument with a single reed mouthpiece and a range well-beyond three octaves. This staple of orchestras and bands consists of a cylindrical tube with open holes to be covered by fingertips, as well as auxiliary keys, terminating in a bell, and with a beak-like mouthpiece. The primary member of the family is the B♭ Clarinet, so called because its middle C sounds as the B♭ immediately below. The A Clarinet is roughly the same size and timbre, and is occasionally substitute for the B♭ Clarinet when pragmatic to play in a sharp key or to reach an extra low note. The main members of the extended family of clarinets includes the smaller E♭ Clarinet (occasionally called Piccolo Clarinet), and the B♭ Bass Clarinet an octave lower. There are many other sizes in less-common or historical usage.

Clarinet, bass See *Bass clarinet*.

Clarinette (Fr., klah-ree-net) **Clarionet** An organ reed stop of 8-foot scale and soft quality of tone.

Clarino (It., klah-REE-no) **Clarion** 1. A small military ancestor of the trumpet, sounding higher and more shrill than the modern instrument. 2. A 4-foot organ reed stop tuned an octave above the trumpet stop.

Classical 1. The musical period from roughly 1750 through 1825 in which form, elegance, and structure were stressed rather than drama and personal expression. Composers of this period include Haydn, Mozart, and Beethoven. 2. The generic term for all "serious" or "art" music evolving from the Classical tradition.

Classical guitar 1. A hollow-bodied acoustic guitar with six nylon strings (the lowest being wound with metal thread); also known as Spanish guitar. 2. The technique of guitar playing in which individual fingers pluck the strings.

Clausula (Lat., KLOW-soo-yah) 1. A cadence. 2. A composition of the 12th or 13th century based on plainchant.

Clavecin (Fr., klah-ve-san) Harpsichord.

Claves A percussion instrument consisting of a pair of thick dowels struck together, originating in Afro-Cuban music.

Clavichord A small keyboard instrument, among the first to be touch-sensitive and therefore a forerunner of the modern piano. Its mechanism pushed a sharp-edged tangent, like the point of a chisel, against a pitched wire; the tone was rather quiet and meant for private use rather than performance.

Clavier See *Klavier*.

Clavierauszug See *Klavierauszug*.

Clavinet An electric keyboard popular among rock bands in the 1970s, the tone of which was raspy and almost harpsichord-like.

Clawhammer A highly-rhythmic fingerpicking style used by banjo players.

Clef A notation symbol used at the beginning of each staff to determine the pitch of notes on that staff. A comprehensive table of clefs is provided on page 3.

Climax The high point of a composition, or one of several high points, generally a dramatic arrival point in thematic resolution, harmony, and volume.

Cloche (Fr., klosh)   Bell.

Close position   Voicing of a chord in which the notes or parts are kept as close together as possible, also called close harmony. The opposite, with spread-out voicing, is called open position.

Cluster   A group of notes a 2nd apart that are played simultaneously; clusters may be diatonic or chromatic, and the term generally describes the dramatic denseness of such a sound more than a precise relationship between notes. On a keyboard instrument, clusters are usually played by a fist, open palm, or forearm; the term also applies when instrumentalists or singers produce pitches resulting together as a cluster. The term is also called a tone cluster.

C moll (Ger., tsay mol)   The key of C minor.

Co (It., ko) **Coi** (It., KO-ee)   With, with the.

Coda (It., KO-dah)   1. Literally a tail or end, the most common use of this term describes a few measures at the end of a composition to make a conclusive ending. Beginning with the later works of Beethoven in the earlier 19th century, the coda often became much longer than a few measures. 2. The final episode of a fugue.

Codetta (It., ko-DET-tah)   1. A short coda or a closing section of a longer work. 2. A connecting passage in a fugue.

Cogli (It. Plur., KOL-yee)   With the, as in "with the others."

Col (It., kol)   With.

Coll', colla (It., kol, KO-lah)   With the.

Colla parte (It., KO-lah PAHR-te)   With the part; indicates a passage where the tempo follows a soloist who is given flexibility.

Coll' arco (It., kol-AHR-ko)   With the bow; the notes are played with the bow, and not pizzicato.

Colla voce (It., KO-lah VO-che)   With the voice; indicates a passage where the tempo follows a singer who is given flexibility.

Col legno (It., kol LEN-yo)   With the wood; indicates a passage for string instruments where the wood side of the bow is used to tap on the strings, rather than bowing with the hair.

Coll'ottava (It., kol o-TAH-vah)   With the octave; indicates a passage in which one plays in the register shown, and also in the next octave above or below, depending on whether this is written above or below the staff.

Coll'ottava bassa (It., kol o-TAH-vah BAH-sah)   Like coll'ottava, but specifically adding the octave below.

Colophon (Fr., kol-o-fon)   Resin.

Color   1. The timbre of an instrument or ensemble. 2. In medieval isorhythms, the repeating pitch pattern, not necessarily synchronized with the repeating rhythmic pattern (talea). See *Isorhythm.*

Coloratura (It., ko-lo-rah-TOO-rah)   A high soprano with the vocal dexterity to perform striking ornamental passages, roulades, and embellishments.

Combination pedals See *Composition Pedals.*

Combination tone An acoustic phenomenon when two notes of almost identical frequency (such as two instruments slightly out of tune), create a resulting third audible sound wave, often of a much lower frequency.

Combo A small group of jazz musicians.

Come (It., KO-me) As, like, the same as.

Come prima (It., ko-me PREE-mah) As at first.

Come sopra (It., ko-me SO-prah) As above; as before.

Come sta (It., ko-me STAH) As it stands; exactly as written.

Comma 1. An extremely small differentiation in pitch barely recognizable by the ear, existing theoretically between enharmonic notes like D# and Eb. 2. In acoustics, a whole step is divided into nine commas. 3. The sign of a comma (,) is often used as a breathing mark in vocal and instrumental music, analogous to a slight break in a spoken phrase.

Common chord See *Pivot chord.*

Common hallelujah meter A stanza of six lines of iambic measure, the syllables of each being in number of order as follows: 8, 6, 8, 6, 8, 8.

Common meter A verse or stanza of four lines in iambic measure, the syllables of each being in number and order, thus: 8, 6, 8, 6.

Common time A time signature of 4/4, often notated with the symbol **C**.

Common tone A note common to two consecutive chords.

Comodamente (It., ko-mo-dah-MEN-te) Easily, smoothily.

Comodo (It., KO-mo-do) Easy, smooth.

Comp In jazz, short for "accompany," as in comping for a soloist.

Compact disc See *CD.*

Compass The range of notes or sounds of which any voice or instrument is capable.

Compiacevole (It., kom-pee-ah-CHE-vo-le) Agreeable, pleasing.

Compiacevolmente (It., kom-pee-ah-che-vol-MEN-te) Agreeably, pleasingly.

Complementary part Extra music added to the subject and countersubject of a fugue.

Complete cadence See *Cadence, authentic.*

Complin (Lat., KOM-plin) The latest evening service of the Catholic church.

Composer A person who writes music. This term may be used for any musical style.

Composition 1. Any musical work. 2. The art of inventing or composing music.

Composition pedals   Pedals connected with a system or mechanism for arranging the stops of an organ.

Composso (It., kom-PO-so)   Composed; set to music.

Composto (It., kom-POS-to)   Composed; set to music.

Compound intervals   Those exceeding an octave.

Compound meter   Any time signature in which each pulse is divisible by three, such as 6/8, 9/4 or 12/8.

Compound stops   Where three or more organ stops are arranged so that by pressing down on key a note from each stop is sounded.

Compound time   See *Compound meter*.

Compression   In audio engineering, to reduce or flatten out the degree of extreme louds and softs.

Con (It., kon)   With.

Concento (It., kon-CHEN-to)   Concord; agreement; harmony of voices and instruments.

Concert   A performance of music.

Concertant (Fr., kon-sair-tahn)   A performer or musician.

Concertante (It., kon-cher-TAHN-te)   Concerto-like; the term can be used in many ways, such as a symphony or solo piece with concerto-like features such as highlighting a solo player.

Concertato (It., kon-cher-TAH-to)   See *Concertante*.

Concert band   An ensemble of woodwind, brass, and percussion instruments, most typically with multiple players on most parts.

Concert grand   The longest size grand piano.

Concertina (It., kon-cher-TEE-nah)   A small instrument, similar to the accordion, the sound boxes being hexagonal in shape instead of oblong. The English concertina has a complete chromatic scale of four octaves.

Concertino (It., kon-cher-TEE-no)   1. A short concerto usually in one movement.   2. The group of soloists in a concerto grosso.

Concertmaster   The principal violinist of an orchestra. While the term is linguistically masculine, it can also be used to describe a female violinist, who may also be called Concert Mistress, or Concert Maestra.

Concerto (It., kon-CHAIR-to)   1. From the Italian word for contrast, a composition for solo instrument and orchestra (or other ensemble such as concert band or chamber ensemble).   2. Works for two or more soloists with ensemble maybe be called simply "Concerto" or "Double Concerto," "Triple Concerto," or "Concerto Grosso."   3. Since the underlying meaning of the term is about contrasting musical texture, some composers have used the term for solo or chamber music in the same spirit, such as J.S. Bach's *Italian Concerto* for solo harpsichord which exploits contrasts between full and spare keyboard registration, much like a traditional concerto would contrast soloist with orchestra.

Concerto for orchestra   A genre evolved in the 20th century, using the concept of soloists and texture contrast, for a composition featuring the orchestra as its own sound palette, without a separate soloist.

Concerto grosso (It., kon-CHAIR-to GRO-so)   1. A concerto of any musical era featuring an ensemble of soloists. 2. A baroque-era concerto using a full orchestra (*ripieno*) and a group of soloists (*concertino*) who may also be principal players within the orchestra, sitting in their conventional locations in performance.

Concert overture   A self-contained work, titled as an overture, that is not the opening of an opera or other theatrical work.

Concert pitch   1. The actual sounding pitch of any instrument. For "non-transposing" instruments, this is synonymous with the pitch they are playing. For transposing instruments, such as clarinet or saxophone, the term describes the resulting pitch in real sound, which is different from the pitch name they are reading and fingering. For example, middle C on an E♭ Alto Saxophone is actually E♭ in concert pitch. 2. This term is occasionally used to describe a tuning standard, such as A440 or A442.

Concertstück   See *Konzertstück*.

Concert tuning   A common technique for contrabass solo playing, where all 4 strings are tuned a whole step higher, to increase brilliance. The bassist then reads and fingers as normal, sounding a whole step higher than the notated pitch names. See *Contrabass*.

Concord   A harmonious combination of sounds; the opposite of discord.

Concords, perfect   The intervals of a perfect fourth, fifth, and octave.

Conduct   To direct a group of instrumentalists and/or singers.

Conductor   A director of a group of instrumentalists and/or singers.

Conductus   Sacred, non-liturgical music of the Ars Antiqua.

Conduttore (It., kon-doo-TO-re)   A conductor.

Conga   An moderate-tempo dance in 2/4 of African origin, in which dancers form a continuously moving chain or line.

Congas   An Afro-Cuban percussion instrument consisting of two to four tall, narrow single-headed drums played with bare hands.

Conical bore   The shape of the main body of wind instruments that are slightly cone-shaped, progressing from a thin diameter at the mouthpiece to a wider diameter at the end of the instrument. The term bore refers to the diameter or inside windstream. Also see *Cylindrical bore*.

Conjunct   Consecutive, adjacent.

Conjunct Succession   Motion to adjacent notes.

Connecting note   See *Common tone*.

Consecutive fifths; consecutive octaves   See *Parallel motion*.

Consequent   1. In a two-phrase melody, this refers to the second, answering phrase. 2. The answer in a fugue, or of a point of imitation.

Conservatoire (Fr., kon-ser-vah-twahr) A French music conservatory.

Conservatory A school or academy of music.

Consolante (It., kon-so-LAHN-te) In a cheering and consoling manner.

Consolatamente (It., kon-so-lah-tah-MEN-te) Quietly, cheerfully.

Console The keyboard, pedals, stops, of an organ, sometimes apart from the sounding portion and connected by cable.

Consonance An accord of sounds agreeable and satisfactory to the ear; the opposite of discord or dissonance.

Consonant Accordant, harmonious.

Consonare (It., kon-so-NAH-re) To tune in unison.

Consoniren (Ger., kon-so-NEER-n) To harmonize; to agree in sound.

Con sordino (It. Sing., kon sor-DEE-no) **Con sordini** (It. Pl., kon sor-DEE-nee) In string and brass instruments, playing with mutes; often abbreviated "con sord." for both singular and plural.

Consort A Renaissance term for a small group of instruments and/or singers.

Contano (It., kon-TAH-no) To count or rest; a term applied to certain parts having rests for the time being, while the other parts continue.

Contemporary music 1. Literally music of the present time, this term has been used for so many types of serious and popular music that it carries no real meaning other than being new. 2. In serious music, it often implies styles that are conspicuously new or challenging.

Continuo (It., kon-TEE-noo-o) See *Basso continuo*.

Continuous controllers In electronic music, methods of sliding pitch, volume, or other parameters through levers, pedals, sliders, wheels, or other physical devices.

Contra (It., KON-trah) Low, under.

Contrabass The double bass or string bass; the deepest instrument of the modern violin family. The strings are tuned a fourth apart, to E, A, D, and G. The contrabass sounds an octave lower than notated; it is typical for some bassists in an orchestra to have C extensions, allowing an extra third lower.

Contrabass clarinet The lowest member of the clarinet family, this instrument is pitched 2 octaves below the B♭ Clarinet, and one octave below the B♭ Bass Clarinet.

Contrabass flute See *Bass flute*.

Contrabassoon The contrabassoon (formerly called double bassoon) is the deepest instrument of the bassoon family. It sounds an octave lower than notated. The contrabassoon is used frequently in orchestras for extra power and depth in the woodwinds, in music as early as Haydn and Beethoven.

Contrabass trombone   See *Bass trombone.*

Contraction   The compression of a theme or fugue subject by removing notes from its center.

Contractor   A musician, or non-playing coordinator, who hires musicians for a performance or ensemble.

Contradance   See *Country dance.*

Contrafagotto (It., KON-trah-fah-GO-to)   1. Contrabassoon. 2. The name of an organ stop of 16- or 32-foot scale.

Contralto (It., kon-TRAHL-to)   The deepest female voice.

Contralto clarinet   A rarely-used low member of the clarinet family, the E♭ Contralto Clarinet sounds one octave below the E♭ Alto Clarinet, placing it between the bass and contrabass members of this family. Middle C on the contralto sounds as the E♭ one octave plus a major sixth below.

Contraposaune (Ger., KON-trah-po-ZOW-ne)   A 16- or 32-foot reed-stop in an organ.

Contrappunto (It., kon-trah-POON-to)   Counterpoint.

Contrappunto doppio (It., kon-trah-POON-to DO-pee-o)   Double counterpoint.

Contrapuntal   Using counterpoint.

Contrary motion   Music in which two parts move in the opposite direction to each other; that is, one rises while the other falls. Also see *Oblique motion* and *Parallel motion.*

Contredance (Fr., kon-truh-dahns)   See *Country Dance.*

Cool jazz   A style of jazz, popular in the 1950's and 1960's, known for moderate tempos, smooth melodic lines and intricate arrangement of the harmony and form; also known as progressive jazz or West Coast jazz.

Coperto (It., ko-PAIR-to)   Covered, muffled; often seen on timpani or other drum parts.

Coppelflöte (Ger., KO-pl-FLE[R]-te)   Coupling flute, an organ stop of the clarabella, or stopped diapason species, intended to be used in combination with some other stop.

Copula (It., KO-poo-lah) **Copule** (Fr., ko-PÜL)   1. On the organ, a coupler by which two rows of keys can be connected together, or the keys connected with the pedals. 2. Codetta. 3. Connecting phrase in a fugue.

Cor (Fr., kor)   A horn; commonly called the French horn.

Corale (It., ko-RAH-le)   Chorale.

Cor Anglais (Fr., kor ahn-glay)   1. English horn; a lower member of the oboe family sounding a 5th lower. Middle C on the English horn sounds as the F below. The instrument is of French origin, not English, and the name is most likely a corruption of "cor anglé," describing the original angled shape of the instrument. 2. An organ reed stop.

Corante (It., ko-RAHN-te) **Coranto** (It., ko-RAHN-to)   See *Courante*.

Corda (It., KOR-dah)   String; see *Una corda*.

Cordatura (It., kor-dah-TOO-rah)   The scale or series of notes to which the strings of any instrument are tuned.

Cor de chasse (Fr., kor de SHAHS)   Hunting horn.

Cornet   1. Formerly called "cornet à pistons," a close relative of the B♭ Trumpet, with the same fingering and range, but with a mellow-sounding conical bore, in contrast to the trumpet's brighter-sounding cylindrical bore. 2. Echo Cornet and Dulciana Cornet are stops on the organ. 3. The Cornet of Shakespearean times was a small member of the Serpent family of brass instruments.

Cornet stop   An organ stop, consisting of from three to five pipes to each note.

Cornett, Cornetto   A medieval instrument made of wood or ivory, with fingering holes like a woodwind and a cup-shaped mouthpiece like a brass instrument.

Corno (It., KOR-no)   French horn.

Corno di bassetto (It., KOR-no dee bah-SE-to)   1. Basset horn. 2. A delicate-toned organ stop (reed) of 8-foot scale.

Corno Inglese (It., KOR-no in-GLAY-ze)   See *Cor Anglais*.

Cornopean   1. An organ reed-stop of 8-foot scale. 2. A crude cornet.

Coro (It., KO-ro)   1. A choir. 2. A piece for many voices.

Corona (It., ko-RO-nah)   A pause or hold.

Corps (Fr., kor)   1. The body of a musical instrument. 2. A group of musicians.

Corps de ballet (Fr., kor duh ba-lay)   The performers in a ballet.

Corrente (It., ko-REN-te)   See *Courante*.

Cortège (Fr., kor-tezh)   A funeral procession.

Cosaque (Fr., ko-sak)   A Cossack dance.

Cotillon (Fr., ko-tee-yon)   A lively dance, a quadrille.

Coulé (Fr., koo-LAY)   A group of two notes, connected by a slur.

Count   Beat, pulse, tempo.

Counterpoint   Literally "point against point," the art of adding one or more parts against a given theme. Counterpoint is the support of one melody by another melody. While there is no precise definition of when multi-part writing becomes considered counterpoint, the concept is to feature simultaneous lines of independent interest, rather than homophony or melody with secondary accompaniment.

Counterpoint, double   Invertible counterpoint in two parts.

Counterpoint, invertible   Counterpoint that is equally successful when when the parts are inverted, meaning the top and bottom parts switch places through octave change.

Counterpoint, quadruple   Counterpoint in four parts, all of which can be inverted.

Counterpoint, triple   Counterpoint in three parts, all of which can be inverted.

Countersubject   The second motive in a fugue, heard against the answer in the second voice.

Countertenor   The highest male voice, it is generally a falsetto, or adult male with an unchanged voice.

Counter theme   See *Countersubject*.

Country   An American popular music genre characterized by pure (non-processed) guitar sounds, a folk-like feel, and true-to-life lyrics often sung with a Southern dialect or twang.

Country and Western   See *Country*.

Country Dance   Also called *Contradance*; *Contredanse* (Fr.); *Contradanza* (It.)   A rustic and sprightly dance of English origin, usually in 2/4 time, in which two lines of dancers faced each other. Contradances inspired Classical composers including Mozart and Beethoven, and in fact the final movement of Beethoven's *"Eroica" Symphony* is made of variations on a contradance he had previously composed.

Coup d'archet   (Fr., koo dahr-shay)   A stroke of the bow.

Coupler   See *Copula*.

Courante   (Fr., koo-rahnt)   From the word for running, an old dance in rapid 3/4 time.

Course   A pair of strings tuned to a unison or octave and played as one; a single string on an instrument with additional multiple-string courses.

Courtesy accidental   See *Cautionary*.

Cover   1. In traditional counterpoint, a covered fifth or covered octave is a parallel fifth or octave that is subtly hidden by other voices. 2. In popular music, a "cover version" is a subsequent performer's interpretation of a previously known song.

Cowbell   A metal bell, similar to that actually hung around a cow's neck, but struck by a beater, rather than an internally shaken clapper.

Crab canon   See *Cancrizans*.

Cracovienne   (Fr., krah-ko-vee-en)   A Polish dance in 2/4 time.

Crash cymbals   A pair of large cymbals (held with handles) that are struck against each other. This term is only used for the held pair of cymbals, and not single mounted cymbals.

Credo   (Lat., KRE-do)   "I believe," one of the principal movements of the Mass; also called The Creed.

Cremona   (It., kre-MO-nah)   1. The name of a superior make of violins. 2. An organ stop.

Crescendo   (It., kre-SHEN-do)   Gradually increasing in loudness;

the term specifically refers to the process of becoming louder, and not the climactic peak itself. It is often abbreviated "cresc." or notated by the symbol $\prec$ indicating the beginning and ending points.

Crescendozug (Ger., kre-SHEN-do-TSOOG)   The swell-box of the organ.

Crescent   A Turkish instrument made of small bells hung on an inverted crescent.

Croche (Fr., krosh)   Eighth note.

Cromhorn (Ger., KROM-horn)   1. A reed-stop in an organ. 2. See *Krumhorn*.

Cromorna-stop, Cromorne (Fr., kro-morn)   A reed-stop in an organ.

Crooks   Small curved tubes added to natural horns, trumpets, and similar unkeyed brass instruments, to change their pitch and adapt them to the key of the piece.

Crossover   A vague term used for music straddling elements of concert and popular music.

Cross relation   The contrast when a note occurs in one chord, and then is chromatically altered in the following chord, or vice versa. For example, when an A Major chord immediately follows or precedes a C Major chord, there is a cross relation between C and C#. Also called a false relation.

Cross rhythm   The mixture of two (or more) rhythmic patterns to create an alluring conflict of attention or expectation. This can occur simultaneously in different instruments, or in alternation of meters in consecutive bars. A very common cross rhythm is the alternation or overlap of 3/4 and 6/8, typical of Spanish and South American dances.

Crotales (kro-TAH-lez)   Small tuned cymbals mounted somewhat like a large glockenspiel, previously called Antique Cymbals. First introduced into the concert repertoire by Debussy, they are more typical of music from the later 20th century.

Crotchet   British term for a quarter note.

Crucifixus (Lat., kroo-chee-FEE-ksoos)   Part of the *Credo* in a Mass.

Crumhorn   See *Krummhorn*.

Crwth (Welsh, *Kruth*) (En. *Crowd.*, *Crowth*)   An old 6-string Welsh instrument resembling the violin; possibly the progenitor of the violin.

Csárdás (Hung., CHAR-dahsh)   A 19th-century Hungarian dance in two parts. The first part is a slow introduction (lassù) and the second is in a quick duple time (friss).

Cue   1. In notation, small unplayed notes shown in a resting part, giving a prominent phrase of the music as a guide to the next entrance of that player or singer. 2. In notation, small notes that may be played to support another instrument if needed to help the balance or in the absence of that other instrument. 3. A conductor's gesture to one or more performers to signal their entrance.

Cuica (Port., KWEE-kah) A Brazilian drum made of a round metal body covered with a skin head, and with a bamboo stick inside that is attached to the center of the head. Played by rubbing on the stick with a wet cloth, the cuica produces a friction-generated sustained tone whose pitch can be raised or lowered by thumb pressure on the skin.

Cup mute A hollow, cone-shaped mute for trumpet or trombone with a large flared lip that forms a cup around the bell. This mute removes low and high frequencies, creating a rounded, muffled tone.

Cupo (It., KOO-po) Dark, obscure.

Cut time Music counted by half notes as the pulse, generally referring to 2/2, and sometimes indicated by the ¢ symbol.

Cycle See *Song cycle*.

Cyclical form A musical structure that includes a recurring theme in various successive movements.

Cycle of fifths See *Circle of fifths*.

Cylindrical bore The shape of the main body of wind instruments that are cylinder-shaped, maintaining a constant diameter from the mouthpiece to the end of the instrument. The term bore refers to the diameter or inside windstream. Also see *Conical bore*.

Cymbale (Fr., sahm-bahl) **Cymbel** (Ger., TSIMB-l) A mixture organ stop with very acute quality of tone.

Cymbals Circular brass plates used for percussion in band or orchestra. They originally came from Turkey. A pair of cymbals struck against each other is called Crash Cymbals. A single mounted cymbal to be played by a beater is called a Suspended Cymbal; also see *Splash Cymbal*, *Sizzle Cymbal*, *Ride Cymbal*, and *Hi-hat*.

Czardas See *Csárdás*.

D 1. The second note in the C scale; foreign and solfège systems call this note *re*. 2. The major scale with two sharps in its signature. 3. Abbreviation for "Da" or "Dal," as *D.S.* – "Dal Segno"; *D.C.* – "Da Capo." 4. Abbreviation for "Deutsch," the cataloguer of Schubert's works; D numbers are to number Schubert's compositions rather than opus numbers.

Da (It., dah) By, from, for, through, etc.

Da capo (It., dah KAH-po) From the beginning; an instruction at the end of the notation for a movement, instructing the performer to return to the beginning, and typically continuing only until a designated final bar in the middle of the notation. In menuets and other dance movements with many internal repeats, these repeats are generally not taken on the second time through.

Da capo al coda (It., dah KAH-po ahl KO-dah) Usually abbreviated

D.C. al Coda, an instruction as defined above, followed by a further instruction to play the second time through only until a designated junction point, and to then jump to the Coda, or ending. The target-like Coda symbol $\oplus$ is often used to indicate both the jumping-off point, and the beginning of the separate coda.

Da capo al fine (It., dah KAH-po ahl FEE-ne) Usually abbreviated D.C. al Fine, an instruction as defined above, followed by a further instruction to play the second time through only until a solid double-bar in the middle of the notation, which is marked Fine, or ending.

Da capo aria (It., dah KAH-po AH-ree-ah) An aria with Da Capo form, thereby resulting in an exact A-B-A structure.

Dal (It., dahl) **Dall'** (It., dahl') **Dalla** (It., DAH-lah) **Dalle** (It., DAH-le) **Dallo** (It., DAH-lo) From the; by the, of the; etc.

Dal segno (It., dal SEN-yo) Often abbreviated D.S., an instruction to jump from the bar marked D.S. back in the music to the junction point marked with the sign $\%$

Dal segno al coda (It., dahl SEN-yo ahl KO-dah) Go back to the $\%$ symbol, and play until the "to coda" indication, then jump to the Coda.

Dal segno al fine (It., dahl SAY-nyo ahl-FEE-neh) Go back to the $\%$ symbol, and play to the end.

Damp 1. To stop a sound from ringing, such as using the dampers on a piano, or muffling a vibrating percussion instrument. 2. A damp sound or acoustic has a ringing or reverberant quality, the opposite of a dry sound.

Damper pedal The pedal on a piano which raises the dampers from the strings, allowing them to vibrate freely. Its use is indicated by the stylized abbreviation $\mathcal{Ped.}$ and cancelled by the $*$ sign indicating to release the pedal. Brackets below the lower staff may also be used to indicate the pedaling.

Dampers A portion of the movable mechanism of the piano, these small felt-covered blocks rest on the strings to prevent undue vibration after the note is released, unless the damper pedal is engaged to disengage the dampers allow the note to continue ringing.

Dämpfen (Ger., DEM-pfen) To muffle, or deaden the tone of an instrument.

Dampfer (Ger., DAHM-pfer) Mute.

Dance 1. Motion to music; in popular music and traditional art music, dance is generally coordinated with the rhythm. In modern dance, interpretive or expressive motion may be inspired by the music's mood without relation to its pulse. 2. A composition used to accompany those who are dancing.

Danse (Fr., dahns) A dance tune.

Danseuse (Fr., dahn-süz) A female dancer.

Danza (It., DAHN-zah) **Danza** (Sp., DAHN-zah) Dance.

DAT Digital Audio Tape; a recording medium popular in the late 20th century, using digital sampling to preserve high audio quality on a cassette-like tape. DAT quickly fell out of favor when computer-based recording became available.

Dauer (Ger., DOW-er) The length or duration of tones.

Daum (Ger., dowm) The thumb.

D.C. Da Capo.

D dur (Ger., day-doer) D Major; the key of D major.

Debile (It., DE-bee-le) **Debole** (It., DE-bo-le) Weak, feeble.

Début (Fr., day-bü) First appearance or public performance. The term is generally used in reference to a performer or ensemble, whereas the introduction of a new composition is called a premiere.

Débutant (Fr. Masc., day-bü-tahn) **Débutante** (Fr. Fem., day-bü-taht) A singer or performer appearing for the first time before the public.

Decani (Lat. Pl., de-KAH-nee) In cathedral music, the passages thus marked must be taken by the singers on the side of the choir where the deacon usually sits.

Decay The fading out of a sound, referring either to overall reverb in a hall, or to the loudness envelope of a given note.

Deceptive cadence A surprise deflection of an expected resolution, when the dominant chord diverts into another harmony (often the submediant) instead of the expected tonic.

Decibel An objective acoustical measurement of the loudness or intensity of a sound, generally written as an abbreviation such as 25dB.

Decima (Lat., DES-i-mah) A *tenth*; an interval of ten degrees in the scale; also the name of an organ stop sounding the tenth.

Decimole Obscure term for a group of ten notes played in the time of eight.

Decisivo (It., de-chee-ZEE-vo) **Deciso** (It., day-CHEE-zo) In a bold and decided manner.

Decke (Ger., DEK-e) 1. The soundboard of a violin or other string instrument. 2. The cover or top in those organ stops which are covered or stopped.

Declamando (It., de-klah-MAHN-do) With declamatory expression.

Decrescendo (It., de-kre-SHEN-do) Gradually diminishing in volume; synonymous with diminuendo. It is most often abbreviated "dim." although "decresc." is also seen. The symbol ➤ is also used to indicate beginning and ending points.

Degli (It., DEL-yee) Of the.

Degree The number of steps up from the first note of a scale.

Dehnen (Ger., DAY-nen) To extend, or prolong.

Dehors, en (Fr., du-or)   1. An instruction to bring out a prominent voice. 2. An instruction to bow on the fingerboard.

Del (It., del)   Of the.

Delay   In audio technology, a device that produces effects such as echo, reverberation, or repeated attacks.

Deliberatamente (It., de-lee-be-rah-tah-MEN-te)   Deliberately.

Delicatamente (It., del-ee-kah-tah-MEN-te)   Delicately.

Delicato (del-ee-KAH-to)   Delicate.

Delirio (It., de-LEE-ree-o)   Frenzy, excitement.

Dell' (It., del) **Della** (It., DE-lah) **Delle** (It., DE-le) **Dello** (It., DE-lo) Of the, by the, etc.

Dem (Ger., dem)   To the.

Demi (Fr., du-mee)   Half.

Demi-cadence (Fr., de-mee kah-dahns)   See *Half cadence*.

Demisemiquaver   British term for 32nd note.

Demo   Short for "demonstration," a recording that demonstrates a performer's or composer's work.

De profundis (Lat., de pro-FUN-dis)   One of the seven penitential psalms.

Des (Ger., des)   The note D flat.

Descant   1. The addition of one or more parts to a melody. The forerunner of modern counterpoint and harmony, this art grew out of the earlier counterpoint called organum. In organum, the parts ran in parallel motion, generally in consecutive fifths or fourths, but in descant, oblique and contrary motion began to appear as early as the 11th or 12th century. The technique is still popular in church and folk music today. 2. In early music, the term also indicates treble or soprano voices.

Des dur (Gr., des door)   D flat major.

Desk   A music stand shared by two string players reading the same part.

Des moll (Ger., des moll)   The key of D flat minor.

Desterità (It., des-ter-ee-TAH)   Dexterity.

Desto (It., DES-to)   Brisk, sprightly.

Destra (It., DES-trah)   Right, as in "mano destra," the right hand.

Détaché (Fr., day-tah-shay)   In bowed string music: detached, staccato.

Determinato (It., de-ter-mee-NAH-to)   Determined, resolute.

Detto (It., DET-to)   The same.

Detune   In electronic music, to alter the system of intonation away from standard tuning.

Deutlich (Ger., DOYT-leesh)   Clear.

Deux (Fr., dü)   Two.

Development   The elaboration of a theme by making new combinations of its figures and phrases. This forms a crucial part in building symphonic and sonata movements.

Devoto (It., de-VO-to) Devout, religious.

Devozione (It., de-vo-tsee-O-ne) Devotion, religious feeling.

Dextra (Lat., DEX-trah) Right, right hand.

Di (It., dee) Of, with, for, from, to.

Dia (Gr., DI-ah) Through, throughout.

Diapase (Gr., dee-a-PAH-se) Diapason.

Diapason (Lat., dee-a-PAH-son, Eng., digh-a-PAY-sun) 1. A whole octave. 2. Among instrument makers, a rule or scale by which they adjust pipes of organs, holes of flutes, etc., to give the proper proportions for intonation. 3. The two foundation stops in an organ (sometimes called Principal) are the open diapason and the stopped diapason. 4. Fixed pitch, or "normal diapason," a recognized standard of pitch.

Diatonic A scale or musical passage staying strictly within the 7 notes of its key signature, thus without chromatically altered notes.

Diatonic scale Any scale of successive notes remaining within its key signature, just as major, natural minor, or any of the modes, as illustrated in the entry for *Mode.*

Didgeridoo A wind instrument used by indigenous northern Australians, traditionally consisting of a hollow wooden tube with a beeswax mouthpiece on one end. It is played by buzzing lips into the tube and generally played with circular breathing.

Dièse (Fr., dee-ez) The sharp (#).

Dies iræ (Lat., dees ee-ray) "Day of Wrath," the Judgment Day. A principal movement in a requiem.

Diesis (It., dee-E-sis) **Diésis** (Fr., dee-ez-sis) The sharp (#).

Difficile (It., dee-FEE-chee-le, Fr. dee-fee-seel) Difficult.

Digital Information of any kind stored or conveyed by numerical description.

Digital audio The conversion of sound waves into numerical code.

Digital piano A keyboard instrument whose sounds are digitally stored and retrieved.

Dignità (It., deen-yee-TAH) Dignity, grandeur.

Dilettante (It., dee-le-TAHN-te) A lover of art; an amateur.

Diligenza (It., dee-lee-JEN-zah) Diligent.

Diluendo (It., dee-loo-EN-do) Diminishing, dying away.

Diminished chord See *Diminished seventh chord* and *Diminished triad.*

Diminished intervals Minor or perfect intervals lowered by a half step. These may occur either within a key signature or by alteration.

Diminished seventh chord A chord consisting of a root, minor third, diminished fifth, and diminished seventh. The E diminished seventh chord is E, G, B♭ and D♭. Because each interval is a minor third, inverting the chord will still sound like a root-position diminished seventh, with a different root.

Diminished triad   A triad consisting of the root, minor third, and diminished fifth. The E diminished triad is E, G, and B♭.

Diminuendo (It., dee-mee-noo-EN-do)   See *Decrescendo*.

Diminution   In counterpoint, the imitation of a given subject or theme, in notes of shorter length, having the effect of speeding up. The opposite is called augmentation.

Direct   A mark sometimes placed at the end of a staff to indicate the following note.

Direct motion   Similar or parallel motion; the parts rising or falling in the same direction.

Direttore (It., dee-re-to-re)   Conductor.

Dirge   Music for a funeral, or in commemoration of the dead.

Diritta (It., dee-REE-tah)   Direct; straight on in ascending or descending intervals.

Dis (Ger., dees)   The note D sharp.

Discant, Discantus (Lat., dis-KAN-tus)   See *Descant*.

Disciolto (It., di-SHOL-to)   Skillful, dexterous.

Disco   Dance music popular in the 1970s, often characterized by string backing, prominent hi-hat parts driving in 16th notes, and sometimes featuring novel electric guitar effects.

Discord   A dissonant combination of sounds, in contrast to consonant resolution. Traditional harmony requires resolution or concord to satisfy the ear; in post-traditional harmony, degrees of unresolved dissonance became a new element of style and syntax.

Discothèque (Fr., dis-ko-tek)   A place where people gather to dance, thus the origin of disco music.

Discreto (It., dis-KREH-to)   Discreetly.

Dis-dis (Ger., diss-diss)   D double sharp.

Disinvolto (It., diz-een-VOL-to)   Confident; nonchalant.

Disinvolturato (It., diz-een-vol-too-RAH-to)   Confidently; nonchalantly.

Disjunct   Intervals greater than stepwise adjacent notes.

Disjunct motion   Moving by intervals greater than stepwise adjacent notes.

Dis moll (Ger., dis-mol)   The key of D# minor.

Disperato (It., deez-pe-RAH-to)   With desperation.

Dissonance   See *Discord*.

Distinto (It., dees-TIN-to)   Clear; distinct.

Distortion   Audio effect that alters a sound by making it sound less clear; that is, distorting its audio wave shapes.

Divertimento (It., dee-ver-tee-MEN-to)   1. From the word "diversion," a short, light composition; sometimes a series of airs and dances introduced between the acts of an opera. 2. An instrumental composition like a suite, of several short movements.

Divertissement (Fr., dee-vehr-tees-MAHN)   1. A ballet, dance, or entr'acte in an opera that is not essential to the plot. 2. See *Divertimento*.

Divisi (It., di-VEE-zee)   Divided, separated. 1. In ensemble or choral parts, this word instructs performers within a section to divide and share multiple notes shown for that part. 2. When not specified otherwise, divisi means split into 2 parts, but one also sees "divisi a3," "divisi a4," or occasionally larger numbers.

Divotamente (It., dee-vo-tah-MEN-te) **Divoto** (It., dee-VO-to)   See *Devoto*.

Dixieland   One of the first genres of jazz, developed in New Orleans during the early 1900s, characterized by syncopated rhythms and multiple instruments improvising simultaneously.   The instrumentation typically included cornet, clarinet, trombone, piano, drums, banjo (or guitar) and tuba.

Dixième (Fr., deez-ee-em)   An interval at the tenth.

Dizi (Chin., dee-zee)   A transverse bamboo flute, with a buzzing membrane; used in traditional Chinese music.

DJ   Disk jockey. Originally referring only to a radio announcer who played LPs, the more recent use defines a performer who slides an LP back and forth under the needle, producing snippets of music or other sounds, as well as creating a percussive rhythm.

Djembe (JEM-be)   A skin-covered hand drum with a goblet shape that produces a deep, resonant sound; used in traditional West African music.

D moll (Ger., day-mol)   The key of D minor.

Do (Lat., do)   A syllable applied to the first note of a scale in solfège. In the "fixed Do" system, Do is always the pitch C, but in the "movable Do" system, it always represents the tonic note, regardless of pitch.

Dobro   See *Resonator guitar*.

Dodecaphonic (do-dek-ah-FON-ic)   Music organized through a "tone row" in which no pitch is repeated until all 12 pitches have been sounded. See *Twelve-tone music*.

Doigt (Fr., dwah)   Finger.

Doit (Eng., doyt)   A jazz technique where the main note is sounded, followed by an upwards glissando.

Dolcan   See *Dulciana*.

Dolce (It., DOL-che)   Sweet, soft, delicate.

Dolcezza (It., dol-CHET-zah)   Sweetness; softness of tone.

Dolciano (It., dol-chee-AH-no) **Dolcino** (It., dol-CHEE-no)   See *Dulcian*.

Dolent (Fr., do-lahn) **Dolente** (It., do-LEN-te)   Sorrowful, mournful, pathetic.

Dolentemente (It., do-len-te-MEN-te)   Sorrowfully, mournfully.

Dolore (It., do-LO-re)   Grief, sorrow.

Dolorosamente (It., do-lo-ro-zah-MEN-te)   Sorrowfully, sadly.

Doloroso (It., do-lo-RO-zo)   Sorrowful, sad.

Dominant   The fifth note of the diatonic scale.

Dominant chord   A chord founded on the fifth note of the diatonic scale. The dominant is of special importance to traditional harmony, because it most often leads to closure on the tonic chord.

Dominant harmony   Harmony based on the dominant chord of a key; the term can be used for an extended harmonic elaboration of the dominant, not just one chord.

Dominant seventh chord   A chord built on the fifth degree of a diatonic scale, consisting of a major triad and minor seventh. In the key of C, the dominant seventh chord is G-B-D-F. In any given key, a chord with the same structure starting on a different degree of the scale is called a secondary dominant.

Domra (Rus., DOM-rah)   A Russian stringed instrument similar to a balalaika, used during the 16th and 17th centuries.

Dona nobis pacem (Lat., DO-nah NO-bis PAH-chem)   The concluding section of the Mass, within the Agnus Dei movement.

Donna (It., DO-nah)   Lady; applied a principal female singer in an opera.

Doo wop   A popular song genre of the 1950s, generally sung by male a cappella groups interjecting nonsense syllables (such as "doo wop") between lyric lines.

Dopo (It., DO-po)   After.

Doppel (Ger., DOP-l)   Double.

Doppel-Be (Ger., DOP-l bay)   A double flat (♭♭); lowering a note two half-steps.

Doppelgriffe (Ger., DOP-l-gree-fe)   See *Double stop*.

Doppelkreuz (Ger., DOP-l-kroytz)   A double sharp (✕), raising a note two half-steps.

Doppio (It., DO-pee-o)   Double; sometimes indicating that octaves are to be played, or that a tempo should be doubled.

Doppio movimento (It., DO-pee-o mo-vee-MEN-to)   Double-time, twice as fast as the preceding tempo.

Doppio pedale (It., DO-pee-o pe-DAH-le)   Playing two notes on the pedals of organ at same time.

Dorian (DOR-ee-uhn)   A modal scale corresponding to D to D on the white keys of the piano. Also see *Mode*.

Dot   1. A rhythmic dot placed after a note or rest increasing the duration by one half. One may also place a rhythmic dot after a previous rhythmic dot to add half the value of the previous dot. 2. A dot placed over or under a note signifies staccato articulation; when these articulation dots are used within a slur or phrase mark, they may indicate a slight articulation within that phrase mark, or a short note at the end of the slur.

Double (Fr., doob-l)   1. An old name for a variation, particularly in the Baroque era. 2. To play or sing in unison, or in octaves, with another performer. 3. To play a second instrument. Playing a third or fourth instrument is also called doubling.

Double bar   Two vertical strokes through the staff, to divide or end a section or movement. Two thin barlines indicates a sectional division; a thin barline followed by a thick barline indicates a final ending. Also see *Repeat*.

Double bass   See *Contrabass*.

Double bassoon   1. See *Contrabassoon*. 2. A 16 or 32-foot organ reed-stop, of smaller scale and softer tone than the double trumpet.

Double concerto   A concerto for two solo instruments and orchestra.

Double counterpoint   See *Counterpoint, double*.

Double croche (Fr., doob-l krosh)   Sixteenth note.

Double diapason   An organ stop tuned an octave below the diapasons. It is called a 16-foot stop on the manuals; on the pedals it is a 32-foot stop.

Double dièse (Fr., doob-l dee-ayz)   A double sharp (×).

Double dot   Two dots placed after a note or rest, increasing its duration by three-fourths of its original value.

Double flat   A symbol (♭♭) indicating that a note is lowered two half-steps.

Double fugue   A fugue with two simultaneous subjects.

Double horn   A French horn with the tubing of both an F and B♭ horn. The different sets of tubing are selected by use of a fourth valve.

Double note   A breve; a note twice the length of a whole note.

Double quartet   A composition written for eight instruments or voices, grouped as two distinct quartets.

Double reed   The reed system of the oboe and bassoon families, formed of two pieces of cane tied together; there is no separate mouthpiece for these instruments other than the double reed itself.

Double sharp   A symbol (×) indication that a note is raised two half-steps.

Double stem   When two vocal or instrumental parts share one staff, they are often notated with the higher part upstemmed, and the lower part downstemmed. When these parts share a common pitch, that notehead receives both an upstem and a downstem, and is said to be double stemmed.

Double stop   Two notes played simultaneously by one player on bowed string instruments.

Double-stopped diapason   An organ stop of 16-foot tone on the manuals; the pipes are stopped or covered at the top.

Double tierce   An organ stop tuned a tenth above the diapasons, or a major third above the principal.

Double time   A new tempo at twice the pulse of the preceding music.

Double tonguing   A method of articulating quick notes on woodwind and brass instruments, rapidly alternating the front and back of the tongue, as if saying ta-ka-ta-ka.

Doucement (Fr., doos-mahn)   Sweetly, softly, pleasingly.

Douleur (Fr., doo-ler)   Grief, sorrow, pathos.

Doux (Fr., doo)   Sweet, soft, gentle.

Downbeat   1. The first beat of a measure. 2. The downward motion of a conductor's hand or baton to indicate the first beat of a measure.

Down bow   Moving the bow "downward" from the frog to the tip, indicated by the symbol ⊓.

Doxology   1. A form of praise sung in a church service, usually at the close of a prayer, psalm, or hymn. 2. The Gloria Patri, used at the end of the psalms in church.

Drag   In drum technique, a stroke consisting of two grace notes leading to the main note.

Dramatic soprano   A soprano with a slighty lower tessitura and darker timbre than other sopranos; the voice of a dramatic soprano is often powerful enough to cut through a full orchestra.

Dramatic tenor   A tenor with a ringing and powerful voice that can be heard above a full orchestra; heroic opera roles are frequently written for dramatic tenors.

Drammatico (It., drah-MAH-tee-ko)   Dramatic.

Drawbars, Drawstops   Organ stops placed on each side of the rows of keys, with which the player opens or closes the stops.

Drei (Ger., drigh)   Three.

Dreifach (Ger., DRIGH-fakh)   Three times, triple.

Dreist (Ger., drighst)   Brave, bold, confident.

Dritta (It., DRI-tah) **Dritto** (It., DRI-to)   Right, as in "mano dritta," the right hand.

Dritte (Ger., DRI-te)   Third.

Droite (Fr., drwaht)   Right, as in "main droite," the right hand.

Drone   1. A continuously-sounding sustained pitch, the term being used in folk music from many cultures around the world, and in Western art music when the goal is to evoke the static harmony of folk or world music. In traditional harmony, a sustained bass note over which much music progresses is often called a pedal tone, analogous to the effect of holding down an organ pedal. 2. One or more non-fingered tubes on a bagpipe, sounding a static note in unison or octaves and serving as a perpetual bass.

Drum   A percussion instrument formed of a cylinder made of thin wood or metal, over each end of which is drawn a tight membrane. Drums may either be pitched (such as the timpani and rototoms) or unpitched (such as the snare drum and bass drum), and may be struck by hand or a wide variety of beaters.

Drum and bugle corps   An ensemble of brass and percussion players, marching as they play.

Drum head   The membrane stretched over the top of a drum to be struck by a mallet, brushes or drumstick. Originally animal skin, drum heads are now more typically made of plastic or other synthetics.

Drum, kettle   See *Timpani*.

Drum kit   See *Drum set*.

Drum machine   A digital sequencer with percussion sounds stored, that may be programmed to play a pre-composed drum set part.

Drum roll   The technique of creating a sustained sound on a percussion instrument, particularly the snare drum. The closed (or "buzz") roll involves applying pressure to each stroke to produce multiple bounces; the open (or double-stroke) roll involves two rapid strokes alternating between the left and right hands.

Drum set   A set-up of various-size drums and cymbals (and sometimes extra percussion), arranged for one person to play all instruments simultaneously.

Drumstick   A wood stick with a special tip, used to strike a drum.

D.S.   See *Dal segno*.

Dub   In audio engineering, to make a copy of a complete recording, or of isolated tracks.

Due (It., DOO-eh)   Two.

Due corde (It., DOO-e KOR-de)   Two strings.

Due pedali (It., DOO-e pe-DAH-lee)   Two pedals.

Duet   1. A composition for two voices or instruments. 2. It is considered correct to use the term "piano duo" when two pianists play together at separate pianos, and "piano duet" when they share a piano.

Due volte (It., DOO-e VOL-te)   Twice.

Dulcian   1. A small bassoon, no longer in common use. 2. A reed-stop (8- or 16-foot tone) in the organ.

Dulciana principal   A 4-foot organ stop of delicate tone.

Dulciana stop   An 8-foot organ stop with soft and sweet tone.

Dulcimer   1. A plucked-string instrument with frets, belonging to the zither family, used in Appalachian folk music. 2. See *Hammered dulcimer*.

Dumka (Cz., DOOM-kah)   A dirge, elegy, or funeral song. It possibly gave rise to the early English slow dance called the *dump* or *dumpe.*

Dump, Dumpe   The name of a slow old English dance with a peculiar rhythm, usually in 4/4 meter.

Duo (It., DOO-o)   1. A composition for two voices or instruments. 2. An ensemble of two performers. 3. It is considered correct to use the term "piano duo" when two pianists play together at separate pianos, and "piano duet" when they share a piano.

Duodecima (It., doo-o-DE-chee-mah)   The twelfth note from the tonic; also an organ stop tuned a twelfth above the diapasons.

Duolo (It., DWO-lo)   Sorrow, sadness, grief.

Duple meter   A time signature with two pulses per bar.

Duplet   A "tuplet" in which two notes are played in the time of three notes (or five or any other odd number).

Duplication   When one or more pitches of a chord are repeated in different parts.

Dur (Ger., door)   Major, as in a key, scale, or chord.

Dur (Fr., dür)   Hard; harsh of tone.

Duramente (It., doo-rah-MEN-te)   Harshly, roughly, played in a firm, bold style.

Duration   1. The length of a composition. 2. In synthesized music, the length of a tone or timbre.

Durchführung (Ger., DOORSH-für-oong)   See *Development.*

Durchkomponiert (Ger., DOORSH-kom-po-nee-airt)   Through-composed. See *Song.*

Durchspielen (Ger., DOORSH-shpeel-n)   To play to the end.

Duro (It., DOO-ro)   Rude, harsh.

Düster (Ger., DÜS-ter)   Gloomy.

Dyad   A pair of notes, usually played simultaneously.

Dynamics   Relative degrees of loudness, as illustrated in detail on page 10.

E   1. The 3rd note of a C scale, called *mi* in most countries. 2. The major scale with four sharps in its signature.

E (It., e)   And (used before a consonant).

Ed (It., ed)   And (used before a vowel).

Ear training   The discipline of learning to recognize melodic and harmonic intervals.

Ebollimento (It., e-bo-lee-MEN-to)   Boiling over, passionate.

Ebollizione (It., e-bo-lee-tsee-O-ne)   A sudden boiling passion.

Eccheggiare (It., e-ke-JAH-re)   To resound, to echo.

Ecclesia (It., e-KLE-zee-ah)   Church.

Ecclesiastical modes   See *Church modes*.

Échappée (Fr., ay-shah-pay)   See *Escape tone*.

Échelle (Fr., ay-shell)   The scale.

Écho (Fr., ay-ko) **Eco** (It., AY-ko)   1. In acoustics, the repetition of a sound's entrance. This is distinct from reverberation which is the extension of the end of a sound. 2. In music composition, echo refers to an imitative entrance, often at a quieter dynamic level or by an antiphonal answering ensemble.

Echo cornet   An organ stop, the pipes of which are of small scale, with a light, delicate tone. It is usually placed in the swell.

Echoplex   An audio device from the 1960s that could be used in live performance to instantly record a phrase and play it back to create echo effects.

Éclat (Fr., ay-klah)   With dash or brilliance; an outburst.

Eclogue, Eglogue   A pastoral, poem, or song about shepherds and/or shepherdesses.

École (Fr., ay-kol)   1. A school or conservatory. 2. A method or course of instruction. 3. A style formed by an eminent artist.

École de chant (Fr., ay-kol duh shahn)   A singing school.

Écossaise (Fr., ay-ko-sayz)   1. Scottish. 2. A dance or tune in Scottish style. 3. A contradance of lively tempo in 2/4 rhythm.

Edel (Ger., AY-del)   Noble and distinguished.

E dur (Ger., ay door)   The key of E major.

Effetto (It., ef-FET-to)   Effect; the effect of music upon an audience.

Eguale (It., e-GWAH-le)   1. Equal, even, alike. 2. A composition for several matching voices or instruments (such as 3 tenor trombones).

Egualmente (It., e-gwahl-MEN-te)   Equally, evenly.

Eighth note   A note whose value is one-eighth that of a whole note. Also see page 4.

Eighth rest   A pause equal in duration to an eighth note.

Eight to the bar   A rhythmic accompaniment style, often on a piano within a rhythm section, based on 8 eighth notes in a 4/4 measure.

Eilen (Ger., IGH-len)   To accelerate; go faster.

Eilend (Ger., IGH-lend)   Hastening

Eilig (Ger., IGH-leesh)   Hasty, hurried.

Ein (Ger. Masc., ighn) **Eine** (Ger. Fem., IGHN) **Einen** (Ger., IGHN-en) A, an, one.

Einfach (Ger., IGHN-fakh)   Simple, plain.

Eingang (Ger., IGHN-gahng)   Introduction, lead-in, prelude.

Einhalt (Ger., IGHN-hahlt)   A pause.

Einheit (Ger., IGHN-hight)   Unity.

Einigkeit (Ger., IGH-neesh-kight)   Concord, harmony, unity.

Einklang (Ger., IGHN-klang)   Consonance, harmony.

Einlage (Ger., IGHN-lahge)   An inserted piece, an interpolation.

Einleitung (Ger., IGHN-ligh-toong)   Introduction, prelude.

Einmal (Ger., IGHN-mahl)   Once.

Einsatz (Ger., IGHN-zahts)   Entrance, attack.

Einschlafen (Ger., IGHN-shlahf-n)   1. To die away, to slacken the time and diminish the tone. 2. To fall asleep.

Einschmeichelnd (Ger., IGHN-shmigh-khelnd)   Flattering, insinuating.

Einstimmen (Ger., IGHN-shtim-n)   1. As one voice. 2. To agree in tuning. 3. To join in.

Eintönig (Ger., IGHN-te[r]-neesh)   Monotonous.

Eintracht (Ger., IGHN-trahkht)   Concord, unity.

Eintretend (Ger., IGHN-tre-tend)   Entering, beginning.

Eintritt (Ger., IGHN-trit)   Entrance, beginning.

Eis (Ger., ighs)   The note E sharp.

Éisis (Fr., igh-sees)   E double-sharp.

Electric bass   See *Bass guitar.*

Electric guitar   A guitar that is directly amplified through a pickup. While some may be acoustic guitars fitted with the pickup, the standard electric guitar is a solid-body instrument designed only for amplified use. The six strings are tuned to the same E-A-D-G-B-E as the conventional guitar, and may be retuned easily.

Electric piano   A keyboard instrument whose hammers strike tines connected to audio pickups.

Electromagnetic pickup   A metal transducer attached to any musical instrument to convert its acoustical sounds into electrical signals for amplification.

Electronic instrument   An instrument whose sound is generated by electronic circuitry. Note this term refers to actual electronic generation of the sound, not just electrical amplification. Therefore instruments such as electric guitar and electric piano are *not* electronic instruments.

Electronic music   Music partially or completely created or processed by electronic technologies. This term is generally used for exploratory art music but not as much for electronically-generated pop music.

Elegante (It., e-le-GAHN-te)   Elegant, graceful.

Eleganza (It., e-le-GAHN-zah)   Elegance, grace.

Elegia (It., e-le-JEE-ah)   See *Elegy.*

Elegiaco (It., e-le-JEE-ah-ko)   Mournful, plaintive.

Elegy   A mournful or plaintive poem or musical composition.

Elevation   A motet or organ piece played or sung in the Catholic Mass during the elevation of the Host.

Elevato (It., e-le-VAH-to)   Elevated, exalted, sublime.

Elevazione (It., e-le-vah-tsee-O-ne)   Elevation, grandeur.

Eleventh   A compound interval measuring eleven scale degrees, or an octave plus a fourth.

Embellishments   Any types of grace notes or melodic ornaments, generally notated through symbols rather than full standard notation.

Embouchure (Fr., ahm-boo-shür)   1. The facial, muscle, lip, and jaw positioning involved in producing sound on a woodwind or brass instrument. 2. Occasionally used in referring to a mouthpiece.

E moll (Ger., ay mol)   The key of E minor.

Emozione (It., e-mo-tsee-O-ne)   Emotion, agitation.

Empfindung (Ger., emp-FEEN-doong)   Emotion, passion, feeling.

Emphase (Ger., em-FAH-ze)   Emphasis.

Emphatique (Fr., am-fah-teek)   **Emphatisch** (Ger., em-FAH-teesh)   Emphatic.

Empty fifth   See *Open fifth*.

En (Fr., ahn)   In.

Encore (Fr. ahn-kor)   1. Again; a demand for the reappearance of a performer. 2. The piece performed on the reappearance of the performer.

End-blown flute   A recorder or flute that is blown vertically from the top; the modern flute, whose headjoint is blown across, is described as a transverse flute.

Ende (Ger., END-e)   End; conclusion.

Energicamente (It., e-nair-jee-kah-MEN-te)   Energetically, forcibly.

Energico (It., e-NAIR-jee-ko)   Energetic, vigorous, forcible.

Énergique (Fr., ay-nair-zheek)   Energetic, vigorous, forcible.

Energisch (Ger., en-AIR-gish)   Energetic, vigorous, forcible.

Enfatico (It., en-FAH-tee-ko)   Emphatic.

Enfler (Fr., ahn-flay)   To swell, to increase the tone.

English horn   See *Cor Anglais*.

Enharmonic   An equivalent re-spelling, using a different pitch name and different accidental. For example, G# and A♭ are enharmonic equivalents of each other.

Enharmonic change   A switch from "flat spellings" to the enharmonic equivalent in "sharp spellings," or vice versa.

Ensemble (Fr., ahn-SAHM-bl)   From the word "together." 1. Any group of musicians playing together. 2. Sometimes used referring to the actual togetherness of musicians, such as uniform style or intonation, or rhythmic accuracy.

Entr' acte (Fr., ahn-trahkt)   Music played between the acts of a ballet, opera, or other theater piece.

Entrada (Sp., en-TRAH-dah)   An overture or introduction, often festive.

Entscheidung (Ger., ent-SHIGH-doong)   Decision, determination.

Entschlafen (Ger., ent-SHLAHF-n)   See *Einschlafen*.

Entschlossen (Ger., ent-SHLOS-n)   Determined, resolute.

Entschluss (Ger., ent-SHLOOS)   Resolution.

Entusiasmo (It., en-too-zee-AHZ-mo)   Enthusiasm.

Entwurf (Ger., ent-VOORF)   1. Sketch or outline of a composition. 2. The exposition of a fugue.

Enunciare (It., e-noon-CHAH-re)   To enunciate, declare, proclaim.

Envelope   The shape of a sound's amplitude over time, whether acoustic or electric. See *ADSR*.

Epico (It., E-pee-ko)   Epic, heroic.

Epilogue   A concluding piece or section.

Episode   1. A portion of a composition digressing from the principal theme.   2. Part of a fugue that intervenes between statements of the subject.

EQ   See *Equalization*.

Equabile (It., e-KWAH-bee-le)   Equal, alike, uniform.

Equabilmente (It., e-kwah-beel-MEN-te)   Equally, smoothly, evenly.

Equal counterpoint   Counterpoint pairing notes of equal duration against each other.

Equale   See *Eguale*.

Equalization   The controlled balancing of various frequency bands in recorded or amplified sounds, such as increasing or decreasing highs, middles, or lows.

Equalizer   Any tool or software that controls equalization.

Equal temperament   The tuning system that divides an octave into twelve truly equal semitones, not favoring one pitch as a foundation. Also see *Temperament*.

Erhaben (Ger., er-HAHB-n)   Elevated; sublime; in an exalted style.

Erhu (Chin., ur-hoo)   A two-string fiddle used in Chinese music.

Erklingen (Ger., er-KLING-en)   To ring; to resound.

Erleichterte (Ger., er-LIGH-shter-te)   In a relieved manner.

Ermattet (Ger., er-MAH-tet)   Wearied, exhausted.

Ermunterung (Ger., er-MOON-te-roong)   Animation, excitement.

Ernst (Ger., ernst)   Earnest; serious;

Ernsthaft (Ger., ERNST-hahft)   Serious.

Erntelied (Ger., ERN-te-leed)   Harvest song.

Eroica (It., e-RO-ee-kah)   Heroic.

Erst (Ger., erst)   First.

Erweckung (Ger., er-VEK-oong)   Animation, excitement.

Erweitert (Ger., er-VIGH-tert)   Expanded, developed, extended.

Es (Ger., es)   The note E flat.

Escape tone   A non-chord tone approached by a step and resolved by a leap in the opposite direction.

Es dur (Ger., es door)   The key of E flat major.

Eses (Ger., ess-ess)   The note E double-flat.

Esitamento (It., e-zee-tah-MEN-to)   Hesitation.

Es moll (Ger., es mol)   The key of E flat minor.

Espagnol (Fr., es-pan-YOL)   In Spanish style.

Espagnuolo (It., es-pahn-yoo-O-lo)   In Spanish style.

Espirando (It., es-pee-RAHN-do)   Breathing deeply; gasping.

Espressione (It., es-pre-see-O-ne)   Expression, feeling.

Espressivo (It., es-pre-SEE-vo)   Expressive.

Estampie (Fr., e-stahm-pee)   Dance music from the 13th and 14th centuries.

Estinto (It., es-TEEN-to)   Becoming extinct, dying away.

Estravagante (It., es-trah-vah-GAHN-te)   Extravagant.

Estremamente (It., es-tre-mah-MEN-te)   Extremely.

Esultazione (It., e-zool-tah-tsee-O-ne)   Exultation.

Et (Lat. et; Fr. ay)   And.

Ethnomusicology   From the perspective of traditional European art music and mainstream Western culture, the study and scholarship of other musical cultures and traditions.

Ethos (Gr., EE-thos)   The ancient Greek concept that individual modes embody different characters or moods.

Étouffé (Fr., ay-too-FAY)   Muted, damped; generally used for harp.

-etta (It., E-tah), **-etto** (It., E-to)   An Italian diminutive suffix, for example to describe a light opera as an operetta, or a short fugue as a fughetta.

Étude (Fr., ay-TÜD)   1. A study or exercise, generally designed to focus on one specific skill or musical focus. 2. A concert piece of etude-like nature.

Etwas (Ger., ET-vahs)   Somewhat; a little.

Etwas frischer (Ger., ET-vahs FRISH-er)   Somewhat faster (*più mosso*).

Euphonium   A brass instrument with conical tubing and valves, with a range similar to the trombone. It is often confused with the baritone, which has a smaller bore and curved bell.

Euphony A very subjective term for agreeable sounds.

Eurhythmics (yoo-RITH-miks) A system of teaching rhythm through body movement, developed by Emile Jaques-Dalcroze; sometimes called the Dalcroze method.

Evaded cadence See *Deceptive cadence*.

Exercise See *Etude*.

Exposition The initial section of a sonata form movement, fugue, or other composition, in which most or all the thematic material is introduced. The exposition of a large work may be quite long and include many themes.

Expression 1. That quality in a composition or performance which elicits or communicates feelings or moods. 2. Expression marks are signs, words, or phrases, written in the music to direct the performer in style and mood.

Expressionism An attitude and approach in certain 20th-century music whereby composers expressed intense gestures and feelings through very striking music, generally focusing on strong unresolved dissonance, and tragic stories or images. This was in stark opposition to the gentle style of Impressionism.

Extemporization See *Improvisation*.

F 1. The fourth note in the C scale, called *fa* in most countries. 2. The major scale with one flat in its signature. 3. F was the note first used as a clef to assign pitch in medieval neume notation because F below middle C was a good medium note for baritone voice, which was generally in the middle range of plainchants. 4. f is the abbreviation for the dynamic marking forte.

Fa (Lat., fah) In many countries, the note F; in solfège, the fourth note of the scale.

Fabliau (Fr., fah-blee-o) A fable.

Faburden A 15-century English genre where chains of first inversion chords harmonize a plainchant in the middle voice. See *Fauxbourdon*.

Facile (Fr., fah-seel) (It., FAH-chee-lay) Light, easy.

Facilità (It., fah-chee-lee-TAH) Facility.

Facing The cut or angle on the opening of a mouthpiece for clarinet or saxophone; the angle of the facing determines how much room the reed has to vibrate.

Fackeltanz (Ger., FAH-kl-tahnts) A dance with torches.

Fado (Port., FAH-do) A Portuguese song and dance.

Fagott (Ger., fah-GOTT) Bassoon.

Fagotto (It., fah-GOT-to) 1. Bassoon. 2. An organ stop.

Fagotto contra (It., fah-GOT-to KON-trah) See *Contrabassoon*.

Faiblement (Fr., fay-bl-mahn) Feebly, weakly.

Fake To play a song, or its accompaniment, generally without advance knowledge or preparation, especially of the chords.

Fake book A sheet music songbook with only melody, lyrics, and chord symbols, for musicians to "fake" the accompaniment.

False accent An accent creating the impression of a downbeat anywhere other than on a strong pulse.

False cadence See *Deceptive cadence.*

False relation See *Cross relation.*

Falsetto 1. A false or artificial voice. 2. The head-voice as distinguished from the chest-voice, specifically above the break from the naturally-sounding vocal register.

Fancy See *Fantasy.*

Fandango (Sp., fahn-DAHN-go) A Spanish dance in 4/4, generally accompanied with castanets and having a strong emphasis upon the second beat of each measure.

Fanfare A short, lively, and loud and piece of music, traditionally composed for trumpets and kettledrums, used as a musical herald. More recent music also has developed the concept to apply to any music evocative of the mood and style of a fanfare.

Fantaisie (Fr., fan-tay-zee) **Fantasia** (It., fahn-tay-ZEE-ah) **Fantasie** (Ger., fahn-tah-ZEE) See *Fantasy.*

Fantasiren (Ger., fahn-tah-ZEE-r'n) To improvise; to play extemporaneously.

Fantastico (It., fahn-TAHS-tee-ko) Fantastical; whimsical; capricious.

Fantasy Fancy, imagination, caprice; music whose form is free and unique, rather than cast in a traditional model.

Farandole (Fr., fa-rahn-dol) A lively dance in 6/8 or 4/4 time, peculiar to Provence.

Farsa (It., FAHR-sah) Farce.

Fastosamente (It., fah-sto-zah-MEN-te) Pompously, proudly.

Fastoso (It., fah-STO-zo) Proudly; stately; in a lofty and pompous style.

Fauxbourdon (Fr., foh-boor-DUN) A 15-century Burgundian genre where a cantus firmus is harmonized by parallel first-inversion chords.

F clef Bass clef; a symbol on the fourth line of the staff indicating the position of F below middle C. See the clef diagram on page 3.

F dur (Ger., f door) The key of F major.

Feedback The sound created when a loudspeaker's output is picked up by a microphone or transducer on an instrument, creating a continuous howling. Although it originally was an accident to be avoided with microphones, it has become an important resource for electric guitarists.

Feier (Ger, FIGH-er) Festival, celebration.

Feierlich (Ger, FIGH-er-leesh) Solemn, grave.

Feminine cadence. The gentle and unresolved effect of a cadence reaching the tonic on a weak beat. See *Masculine cadence.*

Fender Bass Originally the Fender brand of electric bass guitar, which at one point was the first and only brand pioneering this instrument, the term gradually became a generic description of any electric bass guitar.

Fender Rhodes An electric piano introduced in the mid-1960s; its bell-like sound, resulting from hammers striking metal tines, has become a staple of popular music.

Ferma (It., FAIR-mah) Firm, resolute, steady.

Fermamente (It., fair-mah-MEN-te) Firmly, steadily.

Fermata (It., fair-MAH-tah) A hold of indefinite length marked by the ⌢ symbol over notes and rests. Occasionally modifiers are placed over the symbol, such as poco (short), lunga (long), or other terms. In the 20th century, some composers also evolved a squared fermata for long or measured holds and often indicated a precise duration in seconds.

Fermato (It., fair-MAH-to) Firmly, steadily, resolutely.

Fermo (It., FAIR-mo) Firm, resolute.

Feroce (It., fe-RO-che) Fierce; with an expression of ferocity.

Ferocità (It., fe-ro-chee-TAH) Fierceness, roughness.

Fertig (Ger., FAIR-teesh) Quick, nimble, dexterous.

Fervente (It., fair-VEN-te) Fervent, vehement.

Fervido (It., FAIR-vee-do) Fervent, vehement.

Fes (Ger., fes) The note F flat.

Fest (Ger.) 1. A festival, such as a Musikfest, or music festival. 2. Firm,steady.

Festiglich (Ger., FES-tig-leesh) Firmly, steadily.

Festivamente (It., fes-tee-vah-MEN-te) Festively, brilliantly.

Festivo (It., fes-TEE-vo) Merry, cheerful.

Festlich (Ger., FEST-leesh) Festive, solemn.

Festoso (It., fes-TO-zo) Merry, cheerful.

Feuer (Ger., FOY-er) Fire, ardor, passion.

Feurig (Ger., FOY-reesh) Fiery, ardent, passionate.

Fg. German abbreviation for Fagotto, or Bassoon.

F holes Sound holes on a bowed string instrument, which resemble an *f*.

Fiacco (It., FEE-ah-ko) Feeble, weak, languishing.

Fiato (It., FYAH-to) Breath, voice.

Fiddle Violin; the term is commonly used among folk musicians, and as slang among classically-trained musicians.

Fiducia (It., fee-DOO-chee-ah) Confidence.

Field music Music for military instruments, or martial music such as fife and drum.

Fieramente (It., fee-er-ah-MEN-te) Proudly, vehemently, boldly.

Fiero (It., FYE-ro) Bold, energetic, proudly.

Fife A small, shrill flute, typically used in martial music, together with drums. It has six holes and from one to six keys. The fife is also used as a student instrument in preparation for flute playing.

Fifteenth 1. An interval measuring fifteen scale steps, or two octaves. 2. An organ stop two octaves above the diapasons, of 2-foot pitch.

Fifth An interval measuring five scale degrees.

Figuration 1. See *Figured bass*. 2. A melodic elaboration of a chord.

Figurato (It., fee-goo-RAH-to) Figured, florid.

Figure 1. See *Motif*. 2. See *Figured bass*.

Figured A free and florid melody.

Figured bass A system of harmony involving a bass line notated with numerals (called figures) that indicate chords for a keyboard player to add above the bass. The numerals indicate an interval from the bass note to a significant note in the harmony; for example 6 indicates that the chord's root is a 6th above the bass, while a 7 indicates that the bass note is the root and a 7th should be added to the chord. Slashes on the figures signify chromatic alteration. When there is no figure, it is understood that the common chord of the bass note is to be used as its harmony. Originating as a form of musical shorthand employed in the 17th and 18th centuries, it is used in the present day primarily for the study of harmony. Also see *Basso continuo*.

Filar la voce (It., fee-LAHR lah VO-che) To spin out, to prolong the tone, gradually augmenting and diminishing the sound of the voice.

Filter An audio device that decreases or boosts certain frequency ranges. This can be used in sound synthesis, and is frequently used in audio production to eliminate hiss or ambient noise.

Finale (It., fi-NAH-le) 1. The last section or movement of an extended work. 2. By analogy, any big ending, which can be the end of a movement or act of a theater work.

Fine (It., FEE-ne) The end of a movement or composition.

Finement (Fr., feen-mahn) Finely, acutely.

Fingerboard The neck-like part of a string instrument on which the fingers press down on the strings to produce different pitches. The term is used both for the violin family and for guitar-like instruments.

Finger cymbals Very small cymbals that come in pairs and are strapped to two fingers to click against each other.

Fingering 1. The act of applying fingers to keys, strings, or holes, on any instrument. 2. Numerals written in music to show which finger to use. 3. Occasionally used to describe a fingering system related to the construction of a wind instrument, such as the Boehm fingering system.

Fingerpick A pick placed on an individual finger to articulate individual strum patterns on guitar or banjo. See *Fingerpicking*.

Fingerpicking A method of guitar or banjo playing using fingerpicks on individual fingers (or using the fingers themselves) for fast and ornate picking patterns with the strumming hand. This fingerpicking style is in strong distinction to the plectrum (flatpick) style of strumming or melody playing with one larger pick.

Fingersatz (Ger., FING-er-zahts)   Fingering.

Fioriture (It., fee-o-ree-TOO-re)   Literally, little flowers; graces and embellishments in singing.

First-movement form   See *Sonata form.*

First Viennese school   The term used to identify the three primary composers of the late Classical style in Vienna: Haydn, Mozart and Beethoven; this label was coined in the 20th century to differentiate these composers from the Second Viennese school.

Fis (Ger., fis)   The note F sharp.

Fis dur (Ger., fis door)   The key of F sharp major.

Fis moll (Ger., fis mol)   The key of F sharp minor.

Five-string banjo   See *Banjo.*

Five, mighty   See *Russian Five.*

Five, Russian   See *Russian Five.*

Fixed-do   A system of solfège in which C is always called *do*; the opposite of moveable-do in which the tonic note is always called *do* regardless of letter name. Also see *moveable-do* and *solfège.*

Fixed syllables   See *Fixed-do.*

Flag   The hook-like curve that may be placed on the stem of a note, indicating an eighth note. Multiple flags may be added to further halve rhythmic values, therefore 2 flags indicates a 16th note, 3 flags indicates a 32nd note, and so on.

Flageolet (Fr., flah-zhe-o-lay, Ger., flah-ge-o-LET)   1. See *Recorder.* 2. An organ stop of 2-foot tone and wooden pipes. 3. See *Harmonic.*

Flageolet tones   See *Harmonic.*

Flam   A drum figure consisting of a short grace note leading to the main note.

Flamenco (Sp., flah-MEN-ko)   1. A rhythmic dance style of Andalusian (Spanish) origin. 2. A style of guitar playing to accompany Flamenco dance which features both strong rhythmic strumming and freer improvisatory passages.

Flanging   A time-based audio effect related to phase-shifting, where the original signal is mixed with a variably delayed copy.

Flat (Ger., *Be*; Fr., *Bémol*; It., *Bemolle*)   The symbol ♭, lowering the pitch of the following note by a half step. It came originally from the letter b, as its shape and its foreign names indicate.

Flat, double   See *Double flat.*

Flatpicking   In guitar music, using a single plectrum (pick) to strum chords or articulate a melody. Not to be confused with *Fingerpicking*.

Flatterzunge See *Fluttertongue*.

Flauto (It., FLOW-to) 1. Flute. 2. Flauto coupled with amabile, amoroso, di Pan, dolce, grave, etc., constitutes names of various organ stops of generally soft and agreeable tone.

Flautone (It., flow-TO-ne) A 16-foot pedal stop in an organ, of soft tone.

Flauto piccolo (It., flah-OO-to PIK-ko-lo) See *Piccolo*.

Flauto transverso (It., flow-to trahns-VAIR-so) Flauto traverso (It., flow-to trah-VAIR-so) 1. An old designation of the modern flute (held and blown crosswise from the body) in contrast to the earlier flutes played like the modern recorder. 2. An organ stop.

Flebile (It., FLE-bee-le) Mournful, sad, doleful.

Flemish school A group of composers from the Netherlands and Belgium who developed the polyphonic style of the Renaissance, including Johannes Ockeghem and Josquin des Près.

Flessibile (It., fle-SEE-bee-le) Flexible.

Flexatone A pitched percussion instrument consisting of a thin strip of spring steel and two wooden knobs attached to springs. When shaken, the knobs strike the steel, creating a glissando-like pitch controlled by bending the steel with the thumb.

Florid Flowery and ornamental, embellished, as in the melody in Baroque-era music.

Florid counterpoint Free and ornate counterpoint.

Flourish 1. A short fanfare of trumpets or other brass instruments. 2. A brisk heralding gesture.

Flüchtig (Ger., FLÜKH-teesh) Lightly, nimbly.

Flue pipes Organ pipes that create sounds without the use of reeds.

Flue stop See *Stop, flue*.

Flügel (Ger., FLÜG-l) From the word for "wing," a grand piano, so called because of its wing-like shape.

Flügelhorn A conical brass instrument similar to the cornet, but of larger dimensions. The tone is mellow and used more in jazz than in concert music.

Flute 1. The only family of woodwind instruments played without a reed, the tone produced by blowing across a transverse headjoint. Historically flutes were most often made of wood, but modern flutes are made of metal, except for the piccolo which is more often wood. Being a popular instrument in many cultures, there is a tremendous legacy of flutes of other materials and designs, and in many sizes and fingering systems. The flute was transformed from a fairly simple instrument into a sophisticated agile one by Theobald Boehm in the 1830s, with his introduction of new fingering mechanisms. The C Flute is the standard instrument, and a staple of band and orchestra, with the C Piccolo also being standard in orchestra and band. Alto Flute, Bass Flute, and lower instruments are rarely used outside of chamber music and flute ensembles. See *Piccolo, Alto Flute, Bass Flute*. 2. An organ stop of the diapason species, the tone of which resembles that of the flute.

Flûte à bec (Fr., flüt ah bek) Literally "flute with a beak," referring to the mouthpiece, the term refers to the recorder family.

Flute work In organ music, the flute work includes all flue stops not belonging to the principal work and gedackt work, as well as various modifications of these two groups.

Fluttertongue A technique on wind instruments where a tremolo is created by fluttering of the tongue, much like rolling an r in speech.

FM See *Frequency modulation.*

F moll (Ger., ef mol) The key of F minor.

FM synthesis See *Frequency modulation.*

Fois (Fr., fwah) Time, as in the number of repetitions.

Folgt sogleich (Ger., folkt so-GLIGHSH) Continue immediately.

Folio A collection of songs or other sheet music.

Folk music Music of any culture passed down by vernacular tradition; generally of spontaneous composition and evolution for the general population, in distinction to erudite and studied styles of art music.

Foot 1. A pattern of syllables with a distinct metrical count; the term is more prevalent in poetry than music, but it is directly related to music that follows text rhythm, such as hymns and simple songs. 2. Part of an organ pipe, below the mouth. 3. A term used to label stops on an organ, based on the approximate length of the longest pipe in each rank. Any rank sounding at its actual notated pitch (matching the octave of a piano keyboard) is called "8-foot." If sounding an octave higher, "4-foot," two octaves higher, "2-foot," an octave lower, "16-foot," etc.

Forlana (It., for-LAH-nah) **Forlane** (Fr., for-lahn) A lively Venetian dance in 6/8 time, used by gondoliers.

Form 1. Any conventional structural pattern used to build a piece of music, such as Fugue, Sonata, Ternary, or other established and traditional patterns. 2. The general term for any composition's structure, even if it does not easily fit a description.

Formants The various materials and factors of an instrument or performance space that affect its acoustic resonance.

Formes fixes French poetic structures developed during the 14th and 15th centuries, eventually being used for the musical structure of songs. Also see *Ballade, Rondeau, and Virelai.*

Forte (It., FOR-te) Loud, strong, typically notated as f.

Fortean analysis See *Set theory.*

Fortement (Fr., for-te-mahn) **Fortemente** (It., for-te-MEN-te) Loudly, powerfully, vigorously.

Fortepiano (It., FOR-te-pee-AH-no) 1. A dynamic marking to attack a note strongly, then diminish instantly, typically notated *fp*. 2. The main keyboard instrument of the Classical period, celebrated for its new ability to distinguish dynamics and voicing, and therefore leading to the repertoire of classical-era piano music exploiting dynamics. The fortepiano is a close relative to the modern piano (formerly called a pianoforte) but not as fully resonant. The importance of the new ability to play both loud and soft is the reason for the instrument's name, meaning loud-quiet.

Forte possible (It., FOR-te po-SEE-bee-le) As loud as possible.

Fortezza (It., for-TE-tzah) Force, power, strength.

Fortissimo (It., for-TEE-see-mo) Very loud, notated *ff*.

Fortississimo (It., for-tee-SEE-see-mo) Extremely loud, notated *fff*.

Fortsetzung (Ger., FORT-set-soong) A continuation.

Forza (It., FOR-tsah) Force, strength, power.

Forzando (It., for-TSAHN-do) **Forzato** (It., for-TSAH-to) Forced; laying a stress upon one note or chord, often notated *fz*.

Four-part harmony Chorale harmony, or instrumental harmony resembling a chorale, most typically voiced as Soprano, Alto, Tenor, and Bass parts.

Fourth An interval measuring four scale degrees.

Fox trot A relaxed American social dance in 4/4.

Frailich (Yid., FRAI-likh) A dance rhythm in Klezmer music.

Française (Fr., frahn-sez) A graceful 3/4 dance in French style.

Franchezza (It., frahn-KE-tzah) Freedom, confidence, boldness.

Freddamente (It., fre-dah-MEN-te) Coldly; without animation.

Freddezza (It., fre-DE-tsah) Coldness, frigidity.

Free composition Composing in a free style, or not in accordance with the rules of a musical form.

Free reed A reed stop in an organ, in which the tongue produces the sound by a rapid vibratory motion. The tone of a free reed is smooth and free from rattling, but not usually so strong as that of the beating reed.

Frei (Ger., frigh) Free; unrestrained as to style.

French horn See *Horn.*

French overture A form developed in the 18th century that has three sections: the first is slow and characterized by dotted rhythms, the second is fast, and the third is a return to the opening material.

French Sixth One type of "augmented sixth" chord, so called for the chromatically-spelled interval that resolves outward; the "French sixth" chord is distinguished from other augmented-sixth chords by its conspicuous flatted fifth, creating a chord reminiscent of the whole-tone scale. One example of a French sixth would be G-B-D♭-E#. This chord sounds like an altered G dominant-seventh chord that should resolve "inward" to G-C-E, but in 19th-century harmony the emancipation of leading tones led to new thoughts on harmony whereby this chord could equally lead to several chords: F#-B-D-F# or F#-B-D#-F# or F#-A#-C#-F#, all of which exhibit proper (though surprising) voice-leading and resolution of leading tones.

Frequency   The number of vibrations (also called cycles) per second created by a tone; the higher the number, meaning the faster the vibrations, the higher the pitch. Pitch and frequency are often labeled in Herz, or Hz, such as A=440 Hz, meaning 440 vibration cycles per second.

Frequency modulation   1. The primary means of radio broadcast technology, using frequency to modulate a "carrier" wave. 2. In synthesis and audio engineering, to vary the frequency of an electronic signal.

Frescamente (It., fres-kah-MEN-te)   Freshly, vigorously, lively.

Fresco (It., FRES-ko)   Fresh, outdoors.

Fretboard   A fingerboard with raised grids (frets) to help locate the proper spots for fingering.

Fretless   An instrument whose fingerboard has no frets, often used to describe those bass guitars that by exception are not fretted.

Fretta (It., FRE-tah)   Increasing the time; accelerating.

Frets   Narrow strips of wood, ivory, metal, plastic, or other materials, set across the fingerboard of a guitar, mandolin, banjo, or similar instruments, to mark exact points on the fingerboard for stopping the strings, also serving as temporary bridges to render the tone of plucked strings more brilliant.

Freude (Ger., FROY-de)   Joy.

Freudig (Ger., FROY-dig)   Joyfully.

Frisch (Ger., frish)   Fresh, brisk, lively.

Friss   The quick second section of a csárdás.

Frog   The "heel" of a string player's bow, where the hair is closest to the grip held in the player's hand. The proximity to the wrist allows bowing at the frog to have much force and grit.

Fröhlich (Ger., FRE[R]-leesh)   Joyous, gay.

Frottoir (Fr., frah-TWAHR)   See *Washboard.*

Frosch (Ger., frosh)   See *Frog.*

Frühlingslied (Ger., FRÜ-lings-leed)   Spring song.

F-schlüssel (Ger., ef SHLÜS-l)   The F or bass clef.

Fuga (It., Lat., FOO-gah)   Fugue.

Fugara (Lat., foo-GAH-rah)   An organ stop of the gamba species.

Fugato (It., foo-GAH-to)   In the style of a fugue, a short fugue passage within a larger work.

Fuge (Ger., FOO-ge) **Fugha** (It., FOO-gah)   Fugue.

Fughetta (It., foo-GET-tah)   A short fugue.

Fugitive pieces   Ephemeral compositions.

Fugue (Eng., fyoog)   A term derived from the Latin word fuga, "a flight," denoting a contrapuntal discipline of composition in which a subject is introduced by one "voice" and answered by others, according to stylized traditional rules. Fugues vary greatly in construction and inventive freshness, but every fugue is necessarily a contrapuntal development of the Subject announced as an unaccompanied statement at the beginning. The exposition comprises this Subject, which is a conspicuously memorable phrase; upon finishing the Subject, the "voice" (or instrumental part) leads into a Countersubject which serves as contrapuntal accompaniment to the Answer. This Answer is actually a transposed restatement of the Subject, up a perfect fifth or down a perfect fourth. Subsequent statements of Subject and Answer complete this initial section. The remainder of the fugue consists of statements of the Subject in various keys alternating with modulatory, often sequential, episodes.

Fugue, double   See *Double fugue.*

Full anthem   An anthem in four or more parts, without verses or solo passages; to be sung by the whole choir in chorus.

Full orchestra   A slightly vague term referring to an orchestra with a full complement of players. Since there is no exact definition of an orchestra's size, the term is generally used only in distinction to string orchestra or chamber orchestra.

Full organ   An organ with all its registers or stops in use.

Full score   A complete score of all parts of a composition, vocal or instrumental, or both combined, written on separate staves placed under each other.

Fundamental   1. In acoustics, any sounded note's primary pitch and sound, in distinction to the overtones it produces. All sounds (other than pure sine waves) consist of a blend of this fundamental and some proportion of its overtones. 2. The root pitch on which any chord is built. 3. See *Harmonic series.*

Fundamental position   Describes any chord when the root is the lowest note sounded. See *Inversions.*

Funèbre (Fr., foo-nebr)   Funereal, mournful.

Funerale (It., foo-ne-RAH-le)   Funereal, mournful.

Fünf (Ger., fünf)   Five.

Fünf-fach (Ger., fünf-fahk)   Fivefold; five ranks, when referring to organ pipes.

Funk   A strongly rhythmic, driving, syncopated style that evolved from R&B, often with songs remaining on one chord without changes, the shape of the song being built on rhythmic tension.

Fuoco (It., foo-O-ko)   Fire, energy, passion.

Fuocoso (It., foo-o-KO-zo)   Fiery, energetic, passionate.

Furia (It., FOO-ree-ah)   Fury, passion, rage.

Furiant   A quick Bohemian dance characterized by alternations between 6/8 and 3/4 groupings.

Furiosamente (It., foo-ree-o-zah-MEN-te)   Furiously, madly.

Furioso (It., foo-ree-O-zo)   Furious, vehement, mad.

Furniture stop   An organ stop consisting of several ranks of pipes, of very acute pitch; a mixture stop.

Furore (It., foo-RO-re)   Fury, rage, excitement.

Fusion   A form of jazz with strong rock influence.

Fuzz box   A small sound processor that introduces fuzzy-sounding distortion into an amplified instrument's signal, most typically for electric guitar or bass guitar.

Fuzz pedal   A continuous controller in the form of a variable pedal by which a guitarist (or other amplified performer) can control the degree of fuzzy distortion.

G   1. The fifth note of the C scale, called Sol in most countries. 2. The major scale with one sharp in its signature. 3. The lowest or fourth string of a violin, the third of the viola and violoncello. 4. See *G clef.*

G. (Fr., abbr. for *gauche*)   Left; as in m.g., with the left hand.

Gagaku (Jap., gah-gah-koo)   Traditional music of the Japanese court.

Gagliardamente (It., gahl-yahr-dah-MEN-te)   Briskly, gaily.

Gai (Fr., gai)   Gay, merry.

Gaiement, Gaiment (Fr., gai-mahn)   Merrily, lively, gaily.

Gaio (It., GAH-ee-o)   With gaiety and cheerfulness.

Galant   See *Style galant.*

Galante (It., gah-LAYN-te)   Gallant.

Galantemente (It., gah-lahn-te-MEN-te)   Gallantly

Galliard   A lively and popular Renaissance dance in 3/4 time.

Galop   A quick dance, generally in 2/4 time.

Gamba   The family of various-size string instruments that gave rise to the modern orchestral string instruments.

Gamba-bass   A 16-foot organ stop, on the pedals.

Gamba, viola da   See *Viola da gamba.*

Gamelan (Javanese, GAHM-e-lahn)   An ensemble of Indonesian origin consisting of gongs, drums, cymbals, and pitched percussion. Strings, flutes, and vocalists may also be included.

Gamme (Fr., gahm)   Scale.

Gang (Ger., gahng)   Pace; rate of movement or motion.

Ganz (Ger., gahnts)   Whole, entire.

Gaohu (Chin., gow-hoo)   A two-stringed fiddle, higher in pitch than the erhu; used in traditional Chinese music.

Gapped scale   A scale, such as the pentatonic scale, with at least one interval greater than a whole step.

Garbatamente (It., gahr-bah-tah-MEN-te)   Gracefully.

Garbato (It., gahr-BAH-to)   Graceful.

Garbo (It., GAHR-bo)   Simplicity, grace, elegance.

Gato   A popular dance of Argentina in 3/4 or 6/8.

Gauche (Fr., gosh)   Left.

Gaudioso (It., gow-dee-O-zo)   Merry, joyful.

Gavot (Eng., ga-VAHT)   **Gavotta** (It., gah-VOT-tah)   **Gavotte** (Fr., gah-VOT)   A graceful dance of even rhythm, generally in 2 or 4, with a half-bar pickup to each phrase.

G clef   Treble clef, representing an ornate letter G which curls around the second line of the staff, indicating that notes on that line are the G above middle C. See page 3.

G dur (Ger., gay door)   The key of G major.

Gebrauchsmusik (Ger., ge-BROWKHS-moo-zik)   Useful music; music with a function or for the enjoyment of amateur players.

Gebrochen (Ger., ge-BRO-kh'n)   Broken, as in arpeggiated chords.

Gebunden (Ger., ge-BOON-d'n)   Connected, legato.

Gedackt (Ger., ge-DAHKT)   Stopped organ pipes; in opposition to the open pipes.

Gedämpft (Ger., ge-DEMPFT)   Muted.

Gedehnt (Ger., ge-DAYNT)   Lengthened.

Gefällig (Ger., ge-FE-leesh)   Pleasingly, agreeably.

Gefühl (Ger., ge-FÜHL)   Sentiment, expression.

Gehalten (Ger., ge-HAHL-ten)   Sustained.

Gehaucht (Ger., ge-HOWCHT)   Whispered, sighed.

Gehend (Ger., GAY-end)   Moving, andante.

Geige (Ger., GIGH-ge)   Violin.

Geistlich (Ger., GIGHST-leesh)   Holy, spiritual.

Geistvoll (Ger., GIGHST-fol)   Full of spirit.

Gelassen (Ger., ge-LAHS-s'n)   Calmly, quietly.

Geläufig (Ger., ge-LOY-feesh)   Easy, fluent, rapid.

Gelinde (Ger., ge-LIN-de)   Softly, gently.

Gemächlich (Ger., ge-MESH-leesh)   Leisurely.

Gemählig (Ger., ge-ME-leesh)   Gradually; by degrees.

Gemässigt (Ger., ge-ME-sikt)   Moderate.

Gemendo (It., je-MEN-do)   Lamenting.

Gemisch (Ger., ge-MEESH)   Mixed, or compound stops in an organ.

Gemshorn (Ger., GEMS-horn)   On organ, a metal flue stop having tapering pipes of 8-, 4-, or 2-foot pitch on the manuals and 16-foot pitch on the pedal, with a mellow horn-like timbre. The tone is light, but very clear.

Gemüt(h) (Ger., ge-MÜT)   Mind, soul.

Gemüt(h)lich (Ger., ge-MÜT-leesh)   Agreeable, expressive, genial.

General bass   See *Basso continuo*.

General MIDI   The most standard organization of numeric instrument assignments for MIDI sounds. See *MIDI*.

General pause (Ger., ghay-ner-AHL POW-ze)   See *G.P.*

Generoso (It., je-ne-RO-zo)   Generous.

Genre (Fr., zhahn-ruh)   Style, idiom, category.

Gentile (It., jen-TEE-le)   Pleasing, graceful, elegant.

Gentilezza (It., jen-tee-LE-tzah)   Grace; elegance; refinement of style.

Gentilmente (It., jen-teel-MEN-te)   Gracefully, elegantly.

German sixth, German augmented sixth   One type of "augmented sixth" chord, so called for the chromatically-spelled interval that resolves outward. An example of a German sixth would be Ab-C-Eb-F#. This chord sounds like a simple Ab dominant-seventh chord that should resolve "inward" to Ab-Db-F, but in 19th-century harmony the emancipation of leading tones led to new thoughts on harmony whereby this chord could equally lead to G-C-E-G or G-C-Eb-G, thus the spelling of F# rather than Gb to justify the motion to G.

Ges (Ger., ges)   The note G flat.

Gesamtkunstwerk (Ger., ge-zahmt-KOONST-verk)   Literally, "unified art work"; the term was coined by Richard Wagner to describe his unification of mythological drama, music, and visual art in his operatic works. Also see *Music drama*.

Gesang (Ger., ge-ZAHNG)   1. A song. 2. Singing.

Gesangvoll (Ger., ge-ZAHNG-fol)   In a singing manner (*cantabile*).

Geschick (Ger., ge-SHIK)   Skill, dexterity.

Geschleift (Ger., ge-SHLIGHFT)   Slurred, legato.

Geschwind (Ger., ge-SHVINT)   Quick, rapid.

Ges dur (Ger., ges door)   The key of G flat major.

Ges moll (Ger., ges mol)   The key of G flat minor.

Gestopft (Ger., ge-SHTOPFT)   1. Stopped (in general). 2. The "stopped" hand-muting of a horn that produces a brilliant tinny sound; such notes are marked by a + sign above the notes.

Gestossen (Ger., ge-SHTOS-n)   Separated, detached.

Getheilt (Ger., ge-TIGHLT)   1. Divided, separated. 2. Partial organ stops (organ).

87

Getragen (Ger., ge-TRAHG-n) Well-sustained; carried.

Gewiss (Ger., ge-VISS) Firm, resolute.

Ghost note In jazz or jazz-inspired styles, any note within a phrase that is barely heard, although the surrounding notes of the phrase are given a full tone. This uneven support of certain notes can also be called "ghosting" a note.

Gig Short for "engagement," American slang for a job, used in all genres of music.

Gigue (Fr., zheeg) **Gige** (Ger., gee-geh) **Giga** (It., JEE-gah) Jig, a lively species of dance in a fast triple meter, generally notated as 3/8, 6/8, 12/8, or occasionally 4/4 with triplet subdivisions. The exuberant Gigue is often the last movement in a dance suite. The name was probably derived from the small 12th-century French fiddle of the same name.

Giochevole (It., jo-KE-vo-le) Merry, sportive.

Giocondo (It., jo-KON-do) Cheerful, merry.

Giocosamente (It., jo-ko-zah-MEN-te)

Giocoso (It., jo-KO-zo) Humorously, sportively.

Gioioso (It., jo-YO-zo) Joyous.

Gioia, gioja (It., JO-yah) Joy, gladness.

Gioioisamente, giojosamente (It., jo-yo-zah-MEN-te) Joyfully.

Gioioso, Giojoso (It., jee-o-YO-zo) Joyous.

Gioviale (It., jo-vee-AH-le) Jovial.

Giovialità (It., jo-vee-ah-lee-TAH) Joviality.

Gis (Ger., gis) The note G sharp.

Gis dur (Ger., gis door) The key of G# major.

Gis moll (Ger., gis mol) The key of G# minor.

Gitana (It., jee-TAH-nah) A Spanish dance.

Giubilazione (It., joo-bee-lah-tsee-O-ne) Jubilation.

Giubilio (It., joo-BEE-lee-o) **Giubilo** (It., JOO-bee-lo) Jubilation.

Giubiloso (It., joo-bee-LO-zo) Jubilant, exulting.

Giustamente (It., joo-stah-MEN-te) Evenly; with precision.

Giustezza (It., joo-STE-tzah) Precision.

Giusto (It., JOO-sto) Performed in steady and exact time.

Glass harmonica A collection of tuned glasses rotating on a spindle in keyboard-like order, to be played by wet fingers rubbing against the spinning glasses. Mozart composed original music for this uncommon 18th-century instrument which was invented by Benjamin Franklin.

Glee A British vocal composition in three or four parts, generally consisting of more than one movement, the subject of which may be grave or gleeful. The glee was less intricate than the madrigal, and was frequently accompanied, while the madrigal was always sung *a cappella*.

Glee club   A men's chorus; while the name implies either light or British musical genres, the term is used by all kinds of men's choruses.

Gleich (Ger., glighsh)   Equal, alike, consonant.

Gleiten (Ger., GLIGHT-n)   To glide the fingers, as in a glissando.

Gli (It. pl., lyee)   The (masc. plural), as *gli strumenti*, the instruments.

Glide   Sliding pitch, portamento.

Glissando (It., gli-SAHN-do)   Sliding in pitch. Note that portamento always means a totally smooth slide, as on a violin or voice, with no increments within the slide. Glissando can refer to both this pure portamento, or to its best approximation on other instruments, such as piano or harp, where only specific pitched notes may be played.

Glocke (Ger., GLOK-e)   Literally, "bells"; in Mahler symphonies, Almglocke implies the use of Alpine cowbells.

Glockenspiel (Ger., GLOK-en-shpeel)   1. A set of small steel bars laid-out in keyboard style to be struck with mallets; generally assembled in a small box to be placed on a table. Glockenspiel is frequently used in the orchestra and in concert band, whereas smaller lighter bells are more appropriate for marching bands. 2. An organ stop in imitation of bells.

Gloria (Lat., GLO-ri-a)   The second movement of the Mass.

Glottis (Gr., GLO-tis)   The narrow opening in the larynx, forming the mouth of the windpipe, which by its dilation and contraction contributes to the modulation of the voice.

G moll (Ger., ge mol)   The key of G minor.

Goat Trill   1. A vocal ornament introduced by Monteverdi, consisting of rapid and detached repetitions of the same note. 2. A derogatory Italian term for an overly-wide vocal vibrato *(Trillo caprino)*.

Gold record   A recording that has been certified by the RIAA to have sold over 500,000 copies.

Gondellied (Ger., GON-d'l-leed)   A gondolier song.

Gong   A Chinese instrument consisting of a large, circular plate of metal, mounted in a frame, capable of producing sounds of great dynamic range. Gongs are generally considered to be pitched instruments, although the pitch is often unclear due to the strong overtones over the fundamental pitch. There are many types of gongs exhibiting different shapes and degrees of pitch clarity; those with "buttons" in the middle often are clearest in pitch. The large, flat-shaped gong most commonly used in orchestras is called a *Tam-tam*.

Gopak   A Ukrainian folk dance in a quick 2/4 time, also called a Hopak.

Gospel   Although the term literally refers only to the first four books of the New Testament, the musical use of this word refers to an exuberant style of highly-spirited singing characteristic of some African-American churches, and subsequently to non-religious popular music in which love ballads are sung with a style and fervor similar to the gospel style of church music.

Gospel choir   The choir forming the heart of gospel music.

G.P.   Grand pause or general pause. An ambiguous term connoting either a silence in strict tempo or holding a silent beat or measure out of tempo. Since both interpretations are in common usage, with opposite meaning, conductors and performers must be aware that composers might have meant either.

Grace notes   Ornamental embellishment notes indicated by small noteheads, generally played before the true rhythmic placement of the note to which they are attached. In the baroque and classical eras, this notation indicated an on-the-beat appoggiatura when the stem had no slash, and before-the-beat grace note when the stem was slashed. Grace notes from the romantic era through the present are played before the beat (regardless of whether a slash is shown), except in rare instances when a composer specifically indicates to play on the beat. Grace notes carry no specific rhythmic value and are usually played as fast as possible, subject to artistic interpretation and discretion.

Gradevole   (It., grah-DE-vol-e)   Graceful, pleasing.

Gradevolmente   (It., grah-de-vol-MEN-te)   Gracefully, pleasingly.

Grado   (It., GRAH-do)   A degree, or single step on the staff.

Gradual   1. That part of the Roman Catholic service sung between the Epistle and the Gospel. The name comes from Gradus, a step. 2. A cantatorium (book of chants) containing the graduals, introits, and other antiphons of the Catholic Mass.

Gradualmente   (It., grah-doo-ahl-MEN-te)   Gradually; by degrees or steps.

Grammy   A recording-industry award earned through peer-based voting.

Gramophone   An old form of phonograph.

Gran   (It., grahn)   Great, grand.

Gran cassa   (It., grahn CAHS-sah)   Bass drum.

Grand-barré   (Fr., grahn bah-ray)   See *Barré*.

Grand bourdon   Great or double bourdon; an organ stop of 32-foot tone in the pedal.

Grand choir   In organ playing, the union of all the stops of the choir organ.

Grandezza   (It., grahn-DE-tsah)   Grandeur, dignity.

Grandioso   (It., grahn-dee-O-zo)   Grand, noble.

Grand opera   See *Opera*.

Grand orgue   (Fr., grahnd org)   Great organ.

Grand pause   See G.P.

Grand piano   A piano built with its strings and soundboard suspended horizontally, in distinction to upright or spinet pianos whose soundboard is vertical. The term "grand" generally is used for pianos longer than 6 feet, whereas shorter pianos with horizontal soundboards are called baby grands.

Grand staff   The two-staff combination common to piano notation, with a treble clef for the right hand and bass clef for the left.

Grave (It., GRAH-ve)   1. A very slow tempo marking, or a slow and solemn movement. 2. A low pitch.

Gravicembalo (It., grah-vee-CHEM-bahl-o)   Harpsichord.

Gravità (It., grah-vee-TAH)   Gravity, majesty.

Grazia (It., GRAH-tsee-ah)   Grace, elegance.

Graziosamente (It., grah-tsee-o-zah-MEN-te)   Gracefully.

Grazioso (It., grah-tsee-O-zo)   In a graceful style.

Great octave   See *Tablature*.

Great organ   In an organ with three rows of keys, the middle row is often the Great containing the most important stops and having its pipes voiced louder than those in the Swell or Choir organ.

Great pause   See *G.P.*

Great staff   See *Grand staff*.

Gregorian chant   A form of highly-developed plainchant codified by Pope Gregory. A Gregorian chant consists of five parts: the intonation, the first reciting note or dominant, the mediation, the second reciting note or dominant, and the cadence. Also see *Plainsong* and *Church modes*.

Gregorian modes, Gregorian tones   See *Church modes*.

Grobgedackt (Ger., GROB ghe-dahkht)   An organ stop. Large stopped diapason of full tone.

Groove   1. A regular beat or feel, the term is primarily used in rock music and those genres of jazz where regular rhythm is desirable. It is always a positive description to be "in a groove." 2. The fine path or channel on a phonograph record in which the needle sits and picks up the sound information.

Grossartig (Ger., GROS-ahr-teesh)   Grand.

Grosse caisse (Fr., gros kais)   Bass drum.

Gross gedackt (Ger., gros ge-DAHKHT)   Double stopped 16-foot diapason in an organ.

Grosso (It., GRO-so)   Full, great, grand, large.

Grottesco (It., gro-TES-ko)   Grotesque.

Ground bass   See *Chaconne*.

Growl   An animal-like sound played on a brass (or woodwind) instrument to imitate the growl of an animal, most often in jazz or blues.

Grunge   A grungy tangent related to garage and heavy metal rock styles.

Gruppetto (It., groo-PE-to)   See *Turn*.

G-schlüssel (Ger., ge-shlüs-l)   G clef.

Guanzi (Chin., gwahn-zee)   A cylindrical double-reed instrument; used in traditional Chinese music.

Guaracha (Spa., gwahr-AH-chah)   A Spanish dance.

Guarnerius (gwahr-NAI-ri-us)   A top-line violin manufacturer of historical vintage.

Guerriero (It., gwe-ree-E-ro)   Martial, warlike.

Guidonian syllables   The original set of Latin syllables assigned to notes for pedagogical purposes; attributed to Guido d'Arezzo, who took these syllables from a plainchant whose phrases started successively on C, D, E, F, G, and A. These syllables, *ut, re, mi, fa, sol,* and *la,* served as the original solfège scale, with the addition shortly thereafter of *si* for the note B.

Güiro (Sp., gwee-ro)   A hollowed gourd with a notched surface used as a percussion instrument in Latin-American music; it is played by scraping across the notches with a wooden stick.

Guitar (gi-TAHR)   1. A plucked string instrument of great resonance, evolved from the lute family. The body and neck are somewhat similar to the violin though considerably larger, the top and back however being flat, and much deeper. The six strings vibrate over a circular sound-hole. Of Spanish invention, the guitar was originally most popular in that country, primarily for folk and dance music rather for serious recital compositions. However in the 20th century, the modern guitar became a standard instrument in the classical concert world, spawning a wealth of original music as well as transcriptions. 2. Les Paul's introduction of the electric guitar in the 1950s radically transformed American popular music, creating an instrument with the same tuning and fingering yet a totally different approach to sound and style. The guitar, both acoustic and electric, is generally tuned as shown below, sounding an octave lower. It is not uncommon to retune individual strings for individual songs' or compositions' needs within a performance.

Guitarron (Sp., gee-tar-RON)   A large, deep bodied 6-string bass used in Mexican mariachi bands. The instrument is fretless, and the strings are tuned to A, D, G, C, E and A (one octave above the lower A).

Gusto (It., GOOS-to)   Literally taste, and often meaning exuberance or expression.

H   1. The German indication for B-natural, whereas Germans use theletter B to indicate what Americans call B♭. 2. Also stands for heel in organ music.

Habanera (Sp., hah-bahn-YE-rah)   A slow Spanish dance in 4/4, best known in concert music through an aria in Bizet's opera *Carmen*.

Hairpin   Commonly-used slang for a crescendo ($<$) or diminuendo ($>$) symbol, due to its hairpin-like shape.

Halb (Ger., hahlb)   Half.

Half cadence   See *Imperfect cadence.*

Half note   A note whose value is one-half that of a whole note.

Half rest   A pause equal in duration to a half note.

Half step   The smallest interval in traditional tuning systems, such as the relationship between E and F, or between A and B♭.

Hallelujah (Heb., hal-le-LOO-yah)   1. A word meaning "Praise the Lord." 2. A musical composition based on this text.

Hammer   A small felt-covered piece of wood connected to a piano's keyboard mechanism to strike the strings.

Hammered dulcimer   An instrument usually of a triangular shape, the strings of which are struck with small rods held in each hand.

Hammerklavier (Ger., HAH-mer-klah-veer)   A 19th-century term for piano, describing the hammer action, which contrasted with the previous plucking action on earlier keyboard instruments.

Hammer-on   A guitar technique where one note is played in traditional manner, and then a second pitch is produced by "hammering" down another finger on the fretboard (without re-plucking the string) to raise the pitch.

Hammond organ   An electric organ employing mechanical tonewheels to produce its sound; popular in homes and churches in the mid 20th century, this instrument was later widely adopted by jazz and rock keyboardists.

Handbell   A finely tuned bell with a handle and spring-action clapper. Handbells come in sets of great range and are usually played by ensembles (called handbell choirs) in which each player is assigned one or several bells, and the melodies and harmonies are created by the composite effect of many musicians smoothly connecting their notes into a whole.

Hand organ   See *Barrel organ.*

Hardiment (Fr., ahr-dee-mahn)   Boldly, firmly.

Harfe (Ger., HAHR-fe)   Harp.

Harmon mute   See *Wah–wah mute.*

Harmonic   1. A sound produced on any type of string instrument through stopping the pitch on the fingerboard with only light pressure, thereby "confusing" the string into producing an overtone rather than the fundamental tone. The specific overtone produced depends on the location of the lightly-stopped node. Harmonics produced by touching nodes at intervals above an open string are called "natural harmonics" and are only available for certain pitches, since they depend on open strings. When two fingers are used, one to correctly stop the string to a specified pitch, and another to lightly touch a harmonic node above the stopped pitch, the result is called an "artificial harmonic." 2. Also see *Harmonic series*. 3. A general term relating to harmony.

Harmonica   1. A set of graduated metal reeds mounted in a narrow frame, blown by the mouth, and producing different tones on inhalation and exhalation. Most harmonicas are tuned to a major scale, but some have fewer pitches, and more recently there are chromatic harmonicas. Sometimes called Mouth Harp, Mouth Organ, or Blues Harp. 2. Also see *Glass harmonica*.

Harmonic figuration   Broken chords.

Harmonic flute   An open metal organ stop, of 8- or 4-foot pitch; the pipes are of double length, that is, 16 or 8 feet, and the bodies have a hole bored in them, midway between the foot and the top; the tone is exceedingly full, flute-like, and powerful.

Harmonic minor   See *Minor scale*.

Harmonic rhythm   The pattern in time created by the rate of chord changes. If chords change every 4 beats throughout a musical passage, and then the next phrase has chord changes on every beat, one speaks of the harmonic rhythm getting faster because the pace of the harmony is accelerating even though the actual tempo or note rhythms are not changing.

Harmonic series   The series of sounds that is present when a note is sounded, consisting of a fundamental pitch and many barely-audible pitches called overtones occurring at mathematically regular distances above it, as shown in the example below. The fundamental is the note perceived by the listener, and the relative strength of the overtones affect the timbre of the instrument playing that sound. Note that the fundamental is called the "first partial," and the first overtone is called the "second partial."

Fundamental
(1st partial)

Harmonie (Ger., hahr-MO-nee-e)   A small wind ensemble intended for outdoor or recreational use, popular with the wealthy patrons of 18th-century Germany.

Harmonium   See *Reed organ*.

Harmonizer   An audio device that combines an incoming audio signal with time-stretched versions of itself, creating harmonies and other layered sounds.

Harmony   1. The use of simultaneous pitches to create a composite result of chords, and relationships between chords. In traditional harmony, and in most non-traditional harmony, these relationships create a musical syntax through which one pitch becomes a "home" pitch of repose or closure, and other pitches or chords have relationships to that point of repose, allowing a sense of traveling and returning. 2. The use of chords rather than just unaccompanied melody. 3. Those musical parts providing the accompaniment or otherwise supporting the lead melody.

Harp   1. A string instrument of ancient origin, consisting of a triangular frame with strings extended vertically, played with the fingers. The modern pedal harp was invented in 1810, when Sebastian Erard introduced a system of three-position pedals by which any note could be raised either a semitone or a whole tone, allowing for chromatic notes without retuning. There are 7 pedals, each corresponding to a letter name. Each pedal can slide into a flat, natural, or sharp position; therefore one may slide all A's to become A♭, A♮, or A♯ and likewise for each letter name. Note that all octaves of a given pitch must change together, and that enharmonic spellings are frequently used in chromatic music to accommodate pitches that wouldn't fit the harp otherwise. The harp has very nearly the compass of the piano, starting with the lowest C♭ of that instrument, and ending with its highest F♯. It is notated as the piano, on two staves, generally one treble and one bass. 2. Any simpler folk or ethnic instrument, such as the Irish Harp, built with strings suspended vertically on a triangular frame.

Harp, Aeolian   See *Aeolian Harp*.

Harpsichord   A keyboard instrument in standard use before the invention of the piano, of similar construction but without touch-sensitive dynamics, the wires being plucked by quills rather than struck by hammers. Harpsichords often had two keyboards with differing tone quality, which could be played separately or coupled, allowing for contrasting color and loudness at discrete levels.

Hastig (Ger., HAHS-teesh)   Hurrying.

Haupt (Ger., howpt)   Head, principal.

Hauptsatz (Ger., HOWPT-zahts)   Principal theme, motive, or subject.

Hauptstimme (Ger., HOWPT-shti-me)   The musical line of primary importance; this term is most commonly used in atonal music of the early and middle 20th century. The Hauptstimme is indicated in music notation as **H**

Hauptwerk (Ger., HOWPT-vayrk)   Chief manual, or Great organ.

Haut, haute (Fr., o, ot)   High.

Hautbois (Fr., o-bwah)   Oboe.

Hawaiian guitar   See *Steel guitar*.

H dur (Ger., hah door)   B major.

Head 1. The membrane stretched over a drum or tambourine. 2. The scroll and peg box of a violin. 3. The point of a violin bow. 4. The theme of a jazz chart.

Headmotive In polyphonic choral music of the Renaissance, the main motive of each section which is introduced by one voice part and then imitated by each successive entrance by other voice parts.

Head voice The upper register of the voice, resonant in the head rather than the torso.

Heavy metal A genre of hard rock, notable for loud and often distorted guitars.

Heckelphone (HEK-l-fon)   A successor to the bass oboe, this instrument is actually constructed more like a bassoon, a product of the Heckel bassoon manufacturers. The majority of its small repertoire comes from German composers of the 20th century.

Heftig (Ger., HEF-teesh)   Vehement, boisterous.

Heftigkeit (Ger., HEF-tig-keesht)   Vehemence, impetuosity.

Heldentenor (Ger., HEL-den-ten-or)   Heroic tenor.

Helicon See *Sousaphone*.

Hell (Ger., hel)   Clear, bright.

Hemidemisemiquaver The British term for a sixty-fourth note.

Hemiola (hee-mee-O-lah)   A grouping of 2+2+2 beats, when 3+3 is expected. For example, when 3/4 meter is clearly established, a half note, followed by tied quarter notes, and then a half note creates the illusion of a 3/2 measure in place of the two 3/4 measures. Used frequently in baroque music, the hemiola is also very common in South American folk music, often notated as 3/4 interjected into a 6/8 passage.

Herald trumpet A very long straight trumpet used for fanfares in the presence of royalty.

Hervortretend (Ger., HAYR-for-tre-tend)   Prominent, distinct.

Herz Cycles per second of sound waves, abbreviated Hz. The measurement 440Hz means 440 sound wave cycles per second.

Herzlich (Ger., HERTS-lish)   Tenderly, heartfelt.

Heterophony (Gr., het-er-AH-fo-nee)   The opposite of homophony, the term describes differing or independent streams of melody being heard simultaneously.

Hexachord A group of six notes; this term can be used to describe part of a scale and is often used to describe a six-note segment of a 12-tone row.

Hidden fifths, hidden octaves The term applied when two voice or instrument parts move in parallel motion into the interval of a fifth or octave. Unlike parallel fifths and octaves, hidden fifths and octaves are allowable within the rules of traditional voice-leading.

High fidelity A term describing natural quality of sound reproduction.

Now obsolete, this distinction was used in the 1950s through the end of the 20th century to distinguish low-quality playback systems from higher-end products.

High Mass   The Mass celebrated in Roman Catholic churches by choral singing, distinguished from the low Mass in which prayers are read without singing.

Hi-hat   A pair of small cymbals on a stand brought together by a foot pedal; through the combination of playing with drumsticks, varying the distance between cymbals via the pedal, and clapping the cymbals by pedal alone, the hi-hat is an extremely versatile source of many sounds and effects. It is a standard element of drum sets in most rock and jazz traditions.

Hilfslinie (Ger., HEELFS-lee-nee)   Ledger line.

Hilfsnote (Ger., HEELFS-not)   Auxiliary note.

Hintergrund (Ger., HEEN-ter-groont)   In Schenkerian analysis, the deepest structure within a piece of tonal music. Literally "background," it represents the ursatz (fundamental structure) of an entire movement or piece.

Hip hop   A primarily African-American cultural movement and musical genre that originated in New York City in the late 1970's; the music is characterized by rhythmic beats that are sampled and looped and rhythmic chanting called "rapping."

Hirtlich (Ger., HEERT-leesh)   Pastoral, rural.

His (Ger., hees)   The note B sharp.

H moll (Ger., hah-mol)   The key of B minor.

Hoboe (Ger., HO-bo-e)   Oboe.

Hochzeit (Ger., HOKH-tsight)   Wedding.

Hochzeitslied (Ger., HOKH-tsights leed)   Wedding song.

Hocket   A polyphonic technique from the Middle Ages and Renaissance, where one voice has short abrupt entrances during another voice's brief rests, creating a "hiccup" effect from alternating interjections.

Hohlflöte (Ger., HOL-fle[r]-te)   Hollow-toned flute; an organ stop producing a thick and powerful hollow tone.

Hohlquinte (Ger., HOL-kwin-te)   A quint stop of the hohl-flute species sounding a fifth higher.

Hold   See *Fermata*.

Holzflöte (Ger., HOLTS-fle[r]-te)   Wood flute; an organ stop.

Homophonic   See *Homophony*.

Homophony   Harmonized music in which all parts have the same rhythm, resulting in a "block chord" texture as in hymns and other simple chorales.

Homorhythmic   Music where all parts have the same rhythm.

Honky-tonk   1. An earthy percussive style of piano playing, evolved from ragtime. 2. A style of country music featuring frequently tragic themes of working-class life.

Hook   1. Obsolete term for the flag on eighth notes. 2. A catchy phrase in a pop song, designed to "hook" the listener.

Hopak   See *Gopak*.

Hoquet (Fr., o-KAY)   See *Hocket*.

Hora (Heb., HO-rah)   A Jewish folk dance in 2/4, similar to polka.

Horn   1. A modern brass instrument that is standard in orchestra and band, consisting of a conical tube approximately 12 feet long twisted into several circular folds. The modern horn has three valves and is always notated as a transposing instrument in F, meaning that a notated middle C played on horn will sound a fifth lower, as the F below middle C. 2. Historically, "natural" horns had no valves and therefore needed tuning crooks to be substituted for each key one needed to perform in, because pitches were limited only to those in the overtone series. Natural horns are commonly seen in music of the middle and late 19th century, and were transposing instruments in whatever key the tuning crooks were set for, to accommodate the needed pitches. In modern practice, horn players perform "natural horn" parts on the modern horn in F, re-transposing as needed. The instrument, both in the modern and natural mechanism, has often been called French Horn, although this term has now fallen out of favor. 3. A slang term among both classical and jazz musicians for any instrument, most typically used for woodwind and brass.

Horn, English   See *Cor Anglais*.

Horn, French   See *Horn*.

Hornpipe   An old British dance in triple time, supposedly named from the instrument played during its performance. Modern hornpipes may be in common time and of a more lively character than the earlier genre.

Hosanna (Lat., ho-ZAH-nah)   "Praise the Lord."

Humbucker   A pickup on electric guitars and basses that eliminates noise and hum.

Humoresque   A light, humorous instrumental piece.

Huqin (Chin., hoo-cheen)   A family of vertical two-stringed fiddles used in Chinese music.

Hurdy-gurdy   An old folk instrument consisting of four strings played by a wheel rubbed in resin powder, serving as a bow. Two strings are played by keys to produce different pitches, while the other strings act as a drone.

Hurtig (Ger., HOOR-teesh)   Quick; allegro.

Hydraulic organ   An ancient organ powered by water, said to be invented by Ctesibius, a mathematician of Alexandria.

Hymn   1. A sacred song; a short, religious set of stanzas intended to be sung in church. 2. Anciently, a song in honor of the gods or heroes.

Hymn, vesper See *Vesper hymn*.

Hypo- A prefix for church modes beginning a fourth below the tonic, or psalm tone. See the music examples under *Church modes*.

Hz See *Herz*.

I (It., masc. pl., ee) The.

Iambic; iambus A poetical and musical foot, consisting of one short unaccented and one long accented note or syllable. Also see *Foot*.

Ictus (Lat., IK-toos) 1. A mark originating in plainchant to indicate phrases of notes, later evolving into the barline. 2. An accent.

Idée fixe (Fr., ee-DAI feeks) A "fixed idea" or recurring motif through a long composition.

Idiophone A musical instrument that produces sound through the vibration of the instrument itself, such as a cymbal, xylophone, or triangle.

Idyl, idyll (Eng., igh-DIL) A short work in pastoral style.

Ilarità (It., ee-lahr-ee-TAH) Hilarity, cheerfulness, mirth.

Il più (It., eel pe-OO) The most.

Im (Ger., eem) In the.

Imitando (It., ee-mee-TAHN-do) Imitating.

Imitation The repetition of a motif or phrase, as introduced by one instrument or voice part, next echoed one or several times in other voiceparts. Canon and fugue are strict forms of imitation, however the term may be used in a freer general sense for any use of successive entrances on a similar motive.

Immer (Ger., IM-er) Always, ever.

Impaziente (It., im-pah-tsee-EN-te) Impatient, hurried.

Impazientemente (It., im-pah-tsee-en-te-MEN-te) Impatiently, hurriedly.

Imperfect cadence 1. An authentic (V-I) cadence weakened by inverted chords or the lack of a tonic in the top voice. Also see *Authentic cadence*. 2. *(archaic)* A cadential phrase ending on a dominant chord, therefore needing an answering phrase to cadence on the tonic. Since this typically closes the first half of a long melody, it is also called a half cadence.

Imperfect intervals See *Intervals*.

Imperioso (It., im-pe-ree-O-zo) Imperious, pompous.

Impeto (It., IM-pe-to) Impetuosity, vehemence.

Impetuoso (It., im-pe-too-O-zo) Impetuous, vehement.

Imponente (It., im-po-NEN-te) Imposingly, haughtily.

Impresario The manager of operas or concerts.

Impressionism A musical style most associated with Debussy, Ravel, and other French composers of the early 20th century, in which gentle moods and impressions are evoked by using sensual instrumentation and harmonies, often with textures evocative of the painters also called Impressionist. This term implies that the composer is responding to impressions of sensing the outer world, in contrast to Expressionism in which composers express their inner passions and angst.

Impromptu A composition meant to sound improvised.

Improperia In the Roman ritual, a series of antiphons and responses forming part of the solemn service substituted, on the morning of Good Friday, for the usual daily Mass.

Improvisation The art of singing or playing music without preparation; extemporaneous performance. The term may be used for any musical genre.

In (It. And Lat., een) In, into, in the.

-ina (It. Fem., EE-nah) An Italian final diminutive, as in *sonatina*.

In alt (It., een ahlt) See *Alt*.

Incalzando (It., een-cal-TSAN-do) With growing warmth and fervor.

Incarnatus (Lat., in-car-NAH-tus) Part of the Credo of the Mass.

Incidental music Descriptive music accompanying a spoken play, or an instrumental passage in an opera.

Incomplete cadence A tonic cadence whose melodic note is not the tonic pitch itself.

Inconsolato (It., een-kon-so-LAH-to) In a mournful style.

Incordamento (It., een-kor-dah-MEN-to) Tension of the strings of an instrument.

Incordare (It., een-kor-DAH-re) To string an instrument.

Indeterminacy See *Aleatoric music*.

Inflection Any change or modification to a pitch.

Ingenue (Fr., an-zhe-NOO) A stock character in opera, usually performed by a lyric soprano; the "ingenue" is a young, morally wholesome, and naive character.

Innig (Ger., IN-nish) Sincere, cordial, with depth of feeling.

Innocentemente (It., in-no-chen-te-MEN-te) Innocently; in an artless and simple style.

-ino (It. masc., EE-no) An Italian final diminutive as in Andantino.

Inquieto (It., een-kwee-E-to) Restless, uneasy, agitated.

Insensibile (It., een-sen-SEE-bi-le) Insensible, in small degrees.

Insensibilmente (It., een-sen-see-beel-MEN-te) Insensibly.

Instantemente (It., een-stahn-te-MEN-te) Vehemently, urgently.

Instrument A device designed to produce musical sounds.

Instrumentation Assigning notes of a musical composition to specific instruments; factors include the resulting composite sound and also what is practical for each instrument.

Interlude 1. A short musical work introduced between acts of an theatrical work, allowing time to change the mood or to change scenery. 2. A shorter transitional movement played between the verses of a hymn or between larger movements of a full-length work.

Intermezzo (It., een-ter-ME-tso) See *Interlude.*

Interpretation Nuances of style and expression, such as subtleties of tempo and articulation, that come from a performer rather than the composer.

Interrupted cadence. See *Deceptive cadence.*

Interval The distance between two notes, counted by steps of a scale. See page 7 for a full diagram of musical intervals and their terminology.

Interval vector In set theory, a numerical array that expresses the intervallic content of a pitch-class set. See *Set theory.*

Intimo (It., een-TEE-mo) Intimate.

Intonation 1. The precise rendering of a pitch so that it is heard as being in tune. 2. Any of several systems of defining tuning systems, such as mean intonation, or just intonation. 3. The chanting (intoning) of plainchant.

Intrada (It., een-TRAH-dah) A short prelude or introductory movement.

Intrepidamente (It., een-tre-pee-dah-MEN-te) Boldly, fearlessly.

Intrepidezza (It., een-tre-pee-DE-tsah) Boldness, fearlessness.

Intrepido (It., een-TRE-pee-do) Bold, fearless.

Introduction An opening section of a composition designed to prepare the music to follow. This may be as short as a phrase, or as long as several minutes.

Introduzione (It., een-tro-doo-tsee-O-ne) Introduction.

Introit 1. Entrance. 2. A hymn or antiphonal chant sung while the priest approaches the altar at the commencement of the Mass. 3. In the Anglican Church, a short anthem, psalm, or hymn, sung while the minister proceeds to the table to administer the Holy Communion.

Invention A short piece based on imitative counterpoint, primarily represented by Bach's *Two-part Inventions* and *Three-part Inventions.*

Inversion 1. A chord whose lowest pitch is not the root of that chord. For example, first inversion describes a chord whose bottom note is the third of the chord, and second inversion describes a chord whose bottom note is the fifth of the chord. 2. Any other switching of notes or lines to reverse high pitch and low pitch. 3. In music of the 20th century, particularly in the 12-tone tradition, a mirror image of the original melody created by reversing the direction of upward and downward intervals, sometimes called melodic inversion.

Inverted canon A canon that uses melodic inversion (see above).

Inverted mordent   See *Mordent* and *Signs*.

Inverted turn   A turn from the principal note to the lower neighbor and back, then to the upper neighbor and back. See *Turn*.

Invertible counterpoint   Contrapuntal writing that allows the lower part to be played as the upper part.

Invocazione (It., in-vo-kah-tsee-O-ne)   An invocation, or prayer.

Ionian (igh-O-nee-uhn)   A modal scale corresponding to C to C on the white keys of the piano. This mode is the same as a major scale. Also see *Mode* and *Major scale*.

Ira (It., EE-rah)   Anger, wrath. See *Dies Irae*.

Irato (It., ee-RAH-to)   Irate. Angrily, passionately.

Irish harp   See *Harp*.

Irlandais (Fr., eer-lahn-day)   A tune or dance in Irish style.

Ironicamente (It., ee-ron-ee-kah-MEN-te)   Ironically.

Ironico (It., ee-RO-nee-ko)   Ironical.

Irresoluto (It., ee-re-zo-LOO-to)   Irresolute, wavering.

Isometer   The use of a pulse without a regular meter.

Isorhythm   A medieval technique combining a repeating rhythmic pattern (called a talea) with a repeating pitch pattern (called a color) which do not necessarily coincide, thereby creating a long cycle of rhythmic pattern repetitions with different pitches each time, and pitch patterns with different rhythms each time.

-issimo (EE-see-mo)   An Italian final, superlative, as Fortissimo.

Istesso (It., ee-STES-o)   The same.

Italian sixth   One type of "augmented sixth" chord, so called for the chromatically-spelled interval that resolves outward; the "Italian sixth" chord is distinguished from other augmented-sixth chords by omitting the fifth degree of the scale. One example of an Italian sixth would be Ab-C-F#. This chord sounds like an Ab dominant-seventh chord that should resolve "inward" to Ab-Db-F, but in 19th-century harmony the emancipation of leading tones led to new thoughts on harmony whereby this chord could resolve outward to G-C-E-G or G-C-Eb-G.

Ita missa est (Lat., ee-ta mee-sa est)   The closing text of the sung Mass, meaning "Go, the Mass is ended."

Jack   The quill which strikes the strings of a harpsichord, or the upright lever in piano action.

Jagdhorn (Ger., YAHGD-horn)   Hunting horn.

Jagdstück (Ger., YAHGD-stük)   A hunting piece.

Jägerchor (Ger., YE-gher-kor)   Hunters' chorus.

Jaléo (Sp., hah-LAY-o)   A Spanish national dance.

Jam   To improvise as a group, originally a jazz term later used by rock bands. In contrast to one soloist improvising over a determine set of chord changes, jamming implies the whole group explores together.

Jam session   A concert, rehearsal, or other musical experience in which the group jams. This standard jazz term did not get picked up as standard rock vocabulary.

Janissary music   Music inspired by Turkish military bands.

Jarábe (Sp., hah-RAH-be)   A Spanish dance.

Jaw harp   See *Jew's harp*.

Jazz   A set of musical styles originating among African-American musicians in the early 20th century, and evolving in many directions since then. Some streams of jazz are dance-oriented, some center on singing and poignant lyrics, some are very free and artistically experimental, and some influenced by rock. Jazz can be played by one musician, small combinations, or large ensembles, with or without singing. Characteristic of many jazz genres are: origin in song, improvisation to develop the melody, flexibility of melodic rhythm over a firmly driving rhythmic accompaniment, spicy harmony, instrumental inflections resembling vocal slides and ornaments, and "blue notes" which are flatted tones on the 3rd and 5th degrees of the scales, creating an expressive friction against the expected chord tones.

Jazz band   See *Big band*.

Jazz combo   A small group of jazz musicians playing as an ensemble, often piano, string bass, and drumset, and often with trumpet and/or saxophone.

Jeté (Fr., zhe-TAY)   Bouncing the bow of a violin (or other string instrument) on the string during a downbow, to produce a series of repeated notes.

Jeu (Fr., zhu)   1. Play; the style of playing on an instrument. 2. A register in an organ or harmonium; also *Grand jeu, plein jeu,* full organ, full power; *demi-jeu,* half-power.

Jeu d'anche (Fr., zhu d'ahnsh)   A reed-stop in an organ.

Jeu de cloches (Fr., zhu d'klosh)   See *Chimes*.

Jeu de timbres (Fr., zhu d'tam-bruh)   Orchestra bells played by keyboard.

Jew's harp   A small instrument of brass or steel, shaped somewhat like a lyre, with a thin, vibrating metal tongue. It is played held between the teeth, with the metal tongue twanged by the forefinger. The tone may be varied according to the position of the mouth, acting as a resonance chamber that can change the relative strengths of the overtones.

Jig   See *Gigue*.

Jingle   1. Each of the small, paired cymbal-like plates attached to a tambourine. 2. A brief song or sung phrase designed to market a product through advertising on TV or radio, the goal being to create a catchy hook keeping the product's name or slogan in the listener's awareness.

Jodel   See *Yodel*.

Joropo (Sp., ho-RO-po)   A fast Venezuelan dance in 3/4.

Jóta (Sp., HO-tah)   A fast Spanish dance in 3/4.

Jovialisch (Ger., yo-fi-AH-lish)   Jovial, joyous, merry.

Jubellied (Ger., YOO-buhl-leed)   Song of jubilee.

Jubiloso (It., yoo-bee-LO-zo)   Jubilant, exulting.

Jug band   A small band, consisting of a jug player and a mixture of traditional and home-made instruments, with origins in vaudeville shows.

Just intonation   A tuning system in which all intervals are derived from the pure fifth and the pure third above a given fundamental tone, as opposed to equal temperament.

K.   1. The abbreviation for Köchel, the cataloguer of Mozart's works; rather than opus numbers, Mozart's compositions are often referred to by Köchel numbers, such as K. 622. 2. The abbreviation for Kirkpatrick, the cataloguer of Domenico Scarlatti's works, often referred to by K. numbers.

Kalimba   An African "thumb piano," consisting of a palm-size sound box with metal spring-like keys attached to the top; a modernized version of the African mbira, it is used in traditional Zimbabwean music.

Kammer (Ger., KAH-mer)   Chamber.

Kanon (Ger., KAH-non)   Canon.

Kapelle (Ger., kah-PE-le)   Chapel.

Kapellmeister (Ger., kah-PEL-mighs-ter)   The music director of a church choir or orchestra.

Karaoke (Jap., kah-rah-O-ke, though generally Americanized to ka-ree-O-kee)   A coordinated system of song accompaniment with lyrics displayed on a screen to faciliatate singing along.

Kazoo   A hand-size tubular instrument with a vibrating membrane designed to resonate when one hums into it.

Keck (Ger., kek)   Fearless, bold.

Keckheit (Ger., KEK-hight)   Boldness, vigor.

Kent bugle   A historical bugle having six keys (soundholes and pads), four of which are played by the right hand and two by the left hand.

Keraulophon (Ger., ke-ROW-lo-fon)   An 8-foot organ stop, of a reedy and pleasing tone, its peculiar character produced by a small round hole bored in the pipe near the top.

Kettle drum   See *Timpani*.

Key   1. The lever by which the sounds of a piano, organ, or other similar instruments are initiated. 2. Any lever or other mechanism by which holes are opened and closed on woodwind instruments. 3. The harmonic orientation of a piece of music consisting of a central "home" note and a relationship to other notes in the home scale, such as C Major or G

Minor. 4. Short for drum key, the device used for turning the tension screws on a drum.

Keyboard (Ger., *Klaviatur*; Fr., *Clavier*; It., *Tastatura*) 1. The row of keys (see above) on a piano, organ, or similar instrument. The standard arrangement of natural notes as a lower row with sharp/flat notes rising higher is very long-standing. The oldest actually existing keyboard of the present style is on a spinet in the Paris *Conservatoire*, which is dated 1523. It is probable that the shape of the piano keyboard has not materially changed in the last five hundred years. 2. A generic term originating in the late 20th century to describe any electronic keyboard instrument.

Key bugle Any bugle using keys to play various pitches, as opposed to the standard bugle which can only play the notes in its natural overtone series.

Key note The tonic, or first note of every scale.

Key signature The notated grouping of sharps or flats at the beginning of a staff, indicating notes that are to be played flat or sharp throughout the composition, thereby indicating the key.

Kirchenmusik (Ger., KIRKH-n-moo-zik) Church music.

Kit The name of a small pocket-size violin formerly used by dancing masters. Its length is about 16 inches, and its bow about 17 inches.

Kithara (Gr., KITH-ah-rah) An ancient Greek stringed instrument similar to a lyre.

Klagend (Ger., KLAHG-nd) Plaintive.

Klang (Ger., KLAHNG) Sound, tune, ringing.

Klangfarbe (Ger., KLAHNG-fahr-beh) Tone color, quality of tone.

Klangfarbenmelodie (Ger., klahng-fahr-ben-MEL-o-dee) A modern technique that breaks up a musical line and passes it between several instruments of varying timbre.

Klappe (Ger., KLAH-pe) A key on any wind instrument; a valve.

Klar (Ger., klahr) Clear, bright.

Klarinette (Ger., klah-ree-NE-te) Clarinet.

Klavier (Ger., klah-FEER) 1. Piano, harpsichord, or clavichord. 2. The keys or keyboard of these instruments.

Klavierauszug (Ger., klah-feer-OWS-tsoog) Piano reduction.

Klein (Ger., klighn) 1. Small. 2. Minor, in describing intervals.

Kleingedackt (Ger., KLIGHN-ge-dahkht) A small covered stop in an organ, a stopped flute.

Klezmer A secular music tradition with roots in Ashkenazic Judaism. The traditional Klezmer orchestra contained strings, cimbalom, and flute; some modern orchestras borrow instruments from jazz, including clarinet, cornet, piano, and drums. The titles and lyrics for Klezmer music are traditionally in Yiddish.

Klingbar (Ger., KLING-bahr) **Klingend** (Ger., KLING-end) Sonorous, resonant, ringing.

Knabenstimme (Ger., KNAHB-n-SHTI-me) A boy's voice; a counter tenor.

Knee-stop A knee-lever under the manual of the reed organ; there are three kinds, used (*a*) to control the supply of wind; (*b*) to open and shut the swell box; (*c*) to automatically pull out, or draw, all the stops.

Köchel See *K.*

Konzert (Ger., kon-TSAIRT) See *Concerto.*

Konzertmeister (Ger., kon-TSAIRT-migh-ster) See *Concertmaster.*

Konzertstück (Ger., kon-TSAIRT-shte[r]k) Literally "concertpiece." See *Concerto.*

Koto (Jap., ko-to) A plucked string instrument, with 13 strings and 13 moveable bridges, used in traditional Japanese music. The tuning is generally similar to the Phrygian mode in Western music.

Kräftig (Ger., KREF-teesh) Forceful.

Kreuz (Ger., kroyts) Sharp.

Kreuz-doppeltes (Ger., kroyts DO-pel-tes) Double sharp.

Kriegerisch (Ger., KREE-ger-eesh) Warlike, martial.

Krummhorn (Ger., KROOM-horn) A Renaissance capped double reed woodwind instrument with keyless holes and a J-like shape.

Kurz (Ger., koorts) Short, detached staccato.

Kyrie (Gr., KEE-ree-eh) Lord.

Kyrie eleison (Gr., kee-ree-ay e-lay-ee-son) "Lord have mercy upon us." The first movement in a Mass.

L Left hand. In piano music, notes to be played with the left hand are sometimes written with an L over them.

La (Lat., lah) 1. In many countries, the note A. 2. In solfège, the sixth note of the scale.

La (Sp., lah, Fr., lah) The.

Labial Organ pipes with lips, called also flue pipes.

Lacrimosa (Lat., lah-kree-MO-zah) A section of the Requiem Mass.

Lacrimoso (It., lah-kree-MO-zo) In a sad and mournful style.

Lage (Ger., LAH-ge) Position of a chord, or of the hand.

Lagrimoso (It., lah-gree-MO-zo) See *Lacrimoso.*

Laisser vibrer (Fr., le-say vee-bray) See *l.v.*

Lament A mournful or plaintive musical composition.

Lamentando (It., lah-men-TAHN-do) Lamenting, mourning.

Lamentevole (It., lah-men-TE-vo-le) Lamenting, mourning.

Lamentoso (It., lah-men-TO-zo) Lamentable, mournful.

Lancio (It., LAHN-shee-o) Vigor.

Landini cadence A cadence named after 14th-century composer Francesco Landini. The most conspicuous trait is the deflection of the leading tone to the 6th degree of the scale before resolving.

Ländler (Ger., LEND-ler) A rustic country dance in 3/4, inspiring concert music by composers including Schubert and Mahler.

Ländlich (Ger., LEND-leesh) Rural.

Landlied (Ger., LAHND-leed) Rural song, rustic song.

Lang (Ger., lahng) Long.

Langsam (Ger., lahng-zahm) Slowly; equivalent to Lento.

Langsamer (Ger., LAHNG-zah-mer) More slowly.

Languendo (It., lahn-GUEN-do) **Languente** (It., lahn-GUEN-te) **Languido** (It., LAHN-guee-do) Languishing.

Lap steel guitar See *Steel guitar*.

Largamente (It., lahr-gah-MEN-te) **Largamento** (It., lahr-gah-MEN-to) Broadly, slowly.

Largando (It., lahr-GAN-do) Gradually slowing down.

Larghetto (It., lahr-GE-to) The diminutive of largo, and not as slow.

Largo (It., LAHR-go) A slow and solemn tempo marking.

Larigot (Fr., lah-ree-go) 1. Shepherd's flageolet or pipe. 2. An organ stop tuned an octave above the twelfth.

Laryngoscope A scientific instrument for examining the larynx devised in 1854 by Manuel Garcia, the celebrated singing master.

Larynx The upper part of the trachea. It is composed of five annular cartilages, placed above one another and united by elastic ligaments, by which it is so dilated and contracted as to be capable of varying the tones of the voice.

Lassù See *Csárdás*.

Latin 1. The ancient language often used for choral music of the Catholic church. 2. Short for Latin-American, any genres of music using rhythms popular in South America, Central America, or the Caribbean.

Lauda (Lat., LOW-dah) Hymn of praise.

Läufer (Ger., LOY-fer) A flight or run of rapid notes, a roulade.

Launig (Ger., LOW-neesh) Humorous, capricious.

Laute (Ger., LOW-te) Lute.

Le (Fr., luh, It. pl., le) The.

Leader 1. The first or principal violin in an orchestra, more often called a concertmaster. 2. Conductor. 3. On open-reel and cassette audiotape, a blank non-recordable buffer segment of tape to allow threading to the reel with some safety distance before the recordable tape.

Leading note See *Leading tone*.

Leading tone The seventh note of the diatonic scale that leads by half-step up to the tonic note. In minor scales, this term applies only to the raised version of this note.

Lead sheet Printed music for a song or jazz tune, including only the melody, lyrics, and chord symbols.

Leaning note See *Appoggiatura*.

Leap Any interval greater than a second, so-called because there is a jump between the non-adjacent notes.

Leben (Ger., LAYB-n) Life, vivacity.

Lebendig (Ger., leh-BEN-deesh) Lively.

Lebhaft (Ger., LAYB-hahft) Lively, quick.

Leçon (Fr., le-son) A lesson; an exercise.

Ledger lines Short extra lines drawn above or below the staff, for the placement of notes too high or low to fit on the regular staff.

Legando See *legato*.

Legatissimo (It., le-gah-TEES-see-mo) Extremely smooth and connected.

Legato (It., le-GAH-to) In a smooth, connected manner, without space between notes.

Légende (Fr., lay-zhahnd) 1. Legend. 2. Music in a romantic, narrative style.

Léger (Fr., lay-zhay) Light, nimble.

Légèrement (Fr., lay-zhair-mahn) Lightly, nimbly.

Leggerezza (It., le-jer-E-tsah) Lightness and agility.

Leggero (It., le-JE-ro) See *Leggiero*.

Leger lines See *Ledger lines*.

Leggiadra (It., le-JAHD-rah) Graceful, elegant.

Leggiero (It., le-JE-ro) Light, swift, delicate. The proper Italian word is spelled *leggero*, but this variant spelling has been standard in music since the 19th century.

Legno (It., LEN-yo) Wood. See *Col legno*.

Leichenmusik (Ger., LIGHKH-n-moo-ZIK) Funeral music.

Leicht (Ger., lighkht) Light, easy, facile.

Leichtfertig (Ger., LIGHKHT-fayr-teesh) Lightly, carelessly.

Leidenschaftlich (Ger., LIGH-den-shahft-leesh) Impassioned, passionate.

Leise (Ger., LIGH-ze) Low, soft, gentle.

Leiser (Ger., LIGH-zer) Softer.

Leitmotif (Ger., LIGHT-mo-teef) An easily recognizable theme or phrase associated with a specific character or concept in opera, theater, film, or programmatic concert music. The device originated with Weber's operas and flourished through Wagner and other late Romantic composers as a means to follow and dramatize the development of a story line.

Leno (It., LE-no) Weak, feeble, faint.

Lent (Fr., lahn) Slow

Lent The 40 days preceding Easter, during which church music is traditionally focused on the Passion story, and not of a celebratory nature.

Lentamente (It., len-tah-MEN-te) Slowly.

Lentando (It., len-TAHN-do) With increased slowness.

Lentezza (It., len-TE-tsa) Slowness.

Lento (It., LEN-to) Slow.

Leslie speaker An amplification box, most often used with electric organs in the 1960s and 1970s, inside which the speaker rotates on a spindle very quickly, to create an odd phasing effect.

Les Six See *Six, Les.*

Lestamente (It., les-tah-MEN-te) Quickly, lively.

Lestezza (It., les-te-tsah) Agility, quickness.

Lesto (It., LES-to) Lively, nimbly, quick.

LFO Low-frequency oscillator, an early device for music synthesis.

L.H. Abbreviation for left hand.

Liberamente (It., lee-be-rah-MEN-te) Freely.

Libero (It., LEE-be-ro) Free, unrestrained.

Libretto (It., lee-BRE-to) 1. The text of an opera or other extended piece of music. 2. A book in which this text is printed.

Licenza (It., lee-CHEN-zah) License, freedom.

Lick A short catchy phrase, generally used only in rock music.

Lieblich (Ger., LEEB-leesh) Lovely, charming.

Lieblichgedackt (Ger., LEEB-leesh-ge-DAHKHT) A stopped diapason organ register of sweet tone.

Lied (Ger., leet) A song; a ballad; a lay.

Lieder ohne Worte (Ger., LEE-der o-ne VOR-te) Songs without words.

Lieto (It., lee-EH-to) Joyful.

Lievo (It., lee-EH-vo) Light.

Lift A short breath or caesura in choral or vocal music.

Ligado (Sp., lee-GAH-do) *See Legato.*

Ligature 1. An adjustable brace securing the reed to the mouthpiece on clarinets and saxophones. 2. In plainchant and early music notation, a symbol that encompassed several notes of one melisma. 3. Formerly used to describe a slur or group of notes executed in one breath or phrase.

Light opera See *Operetta.*

Limiter An electronic device capping peaks in volume.

Linke Hand (Ger., LIN-ke hahnt) The left hand.

Lion's roar See *String drum.*

Lip 1. In organ construction, the lips of a flue pipe are the flat surfaces above and below the mouth, called the upper and lower lip. 2. On woodwind or brass instruments, used as a verb to control the sound with the lip, such as "lipping up the pitch."

Lip trill A trill on a brass instrument made only by changing lip pressure, rather than trilling with a finger.

Lira (It., LEE-rah) See *Lyre*.

Liscio (It., LEE-sho) Simple, unadorned, smooth.

Lispelnd (Ger., LIS-pelnt) Lisping, whispering.

L'istesso (It., lee-STE-so) See *Istesso*.

Litany A solemn form of liturgical prayer.

Liturgy The ritual for public worship in churches.

Liuqin (Ch., lyoo-cheen) A small pear-shaped, fretted lute with 5 strings; used in traditional Chinese music.

Liuto (It., lee-OO-to) Lute.

Lobgesang (Ger., LOB-ge-zahng) A hymn or song of praise.

Loco (It., LO-ko) Literally "place," the term indicates a return to the written register following an *8va* or other octave-changing instruction. Since octave signs are traditionally drawn with a continuous bracket indicating their termination, this instruction is usually included only as a cautionary reminder.

Locrian (LOK-ree-an) A modal scale corresponding to B to B on the white keys of the piano. Also see *Mode*.

Long meter In hymnody, a stanza of four lines in iambic measure, each line containing eight syllables.

Long mordent See *Mordent (double)*.

Lontano (It., lon-TAH-no) Distant; remote; a great way off.

Loop A technique originating with open-reel music editing by which a musical passage is spliced into a circular loop of audiotape, allowing it to be played over and over incessantly. Popular in the 1960s in both pop music and avant-garde concert music, looping has become easier through audio software and is a major component of Hip-hop music.

Loudness The intensity of sound. Also see *Volume*.

Lourde (Fr., loord) Heavy.

Loure (Fr., loor) 1. A 17th-century dance in 6/4. 2. A bagpipe.

Louré (Fr., loo-RAY) Legato. A bowing that gives a slight separation to each note of a slurred passage.

LP The abbreviation for Long Playing, this described 33RPM phonograph records that typically provided 20-25 minutes on each side, which was a notable advance over the previous shorter durations of 78RPM records.

Luftig (Ger., LOOF-teesh) Light.

Luftpause (Ger., LOOFT-pow-ze) A pause to breathe.

Lugubre (It., loo-GOO-bre) Lugubrious, sad, mournful.

Lullaby   A cradle song.

Lunga (It., LOON-gah)   Long; generally used above fermatas to indicate a long hold.

Lusingando (It., loo-zeen-GAHN-do) **Lusinghevole** (It., loo-zeen-GE-vo-le)   Soothing, coaxing, persuasively, insinuatingly.

Lustig (Ger., LOOS-teesh)   Merry, cheerful.

Lute   A historical guitar-like instrument, very common in the Middle Ages and Renaissance.

Luthier (Fr., loot-YAY)   A maker of string instruments including guitars, lutes, and violins.

Luttuoso (It., loo-too-O-zo)   Sorrowful, mournful.

l.v.   Abbreviation for "let vibrate" or the French "laissez vibrer." This abbreviation is used for piano, harp, or any ringing instruments instructing the player to let the sound continue ringing beyond the notated value.

Lydian (LID-ee-an)   A modal scale corresponding to F to F on the white keys of the piano. Also see *Mode*.

Lyra, lyre (LEE-rah, LIGH-er)   1. An ancient Greek string instrument, similar to a small harp. 2. A small clip attached to band instruments acting as a small music stand for marching. 3. Owing to its lyre-like shape, a bell lyre is another name for a lightweight marching glockenspiel.

Lyric   1. The words to a song; in proper usage, the singular term "lyric" describes the whole sung text. 2. In a singing style.

Lyric soprano   A soprano with a warm, bright voice that can be heard over an orchestra; ingénue roles are frequently written for lyric sopranos.

Lyric tenor   A tenor with a warm and agile voice that is somewhat lighter than a dramatic tenor.

M   1. Abbreviation of mezzo, in conjunction with other words such as mezzo-forte, mezzo-piano, or mezzo-soprano. 2. Sometimes used as an abbreviation for metronome (see *Metronome*), main (French for hand), mano (Italian for hand), or manual.

Ma (It., mah)   But.

Madrigal   Any secular a cappella vocal or choral composition, generally in three, four, five, or six voice parts. The madrigal's golden period was during the Renaissance, primarily in England and Italy, although it was also popular in other European countries.

Maestevole (It., mah-e-STE-vo-le)   Majestic.

Maestoso (It., mah-e-STO-zo)   Majestic.

Maestra (It. Fem., mah-ES-trah)   Feminine form of maestro.

Maestro (It. Masc., mah-ES-tro)   Master, conductor, composer; an experienced, skillful artist.

Maggiore (It., mah-JO-re)   Major.

Magnificat (Lat., man-YEE-fee-kaht)   Part of the vespers, or evening service, at the Roman Catholic Church.

Main (Fr., ma)   The hand.

Main droite (Fr., ma drwaht)   Right hand.

Main gauche (ma gosh)   Left hand.

Majeur (Fr., mah-zhoor)   Major.

Major   1. A key, chord, or scale most notably characterized by the 3rd degree of the scale being a major 3rd above the root pitch. See the tables of scales and chords in the preface to this book. 2. The larger of two diatonic spellings for intervals of the 2nd, 3rd, 6th, 7th, and octave extensions of these intervals. See the table of intervals in the preface to this book.

Major chord   See *Major triad*.

Major scale   The scale in which half steps fall between the 3rd and 4th, and the 7th and 8th tones, and all other adjacent intervals are whole steps. See page 5.

Major triad   A three-note chord consisting of a root (the letter name of the chord), and notes a major third above and perfect fifth above. Any octave transpositions are equally acceptable; therefore the simple triad C-E-G may have its notes distributed or duplicated in any octaves or low-to-high order.

Malagueña (Sp., mah-lah-GWE-nyah)   A folk music genre from southern Spain.

Malincolico (It., mah-leen-KO-lee-ko) **Malinconia** (It., mah-leen-KO-ni-ah)   Melancholy.

Malinconico (It., mah-leen-KO-nee-ko)   In a melancholy style.

Mallet   1. A stick with a special head made of yarn, rubber (hard or medium), felt, plastic or other materials, used to play pitched keyboard-like percussion instruments such as xylophone, marimba, vibraphone, and glockenspiel. 2. Any beater for any percussion instrument.

Mambo (MAHM-bo)   A Cuban ballroom dance with very strong rhythm.

Mancando (It., mahn-KAHN-do)   Decreasing; dying away.

Mandocello (It., mahn-do-CHE-lo)   A large member of the mandolin family whose low C-G-D-A tuning matches the cello.

Mandola (It., mahn-do-lah)   A large mandolin whose C-G-D-A tuning matches the viola.

Mandolin   A pear-shaped instrument evolving from the lute, with four doubled strings tuned to G-D-A-E, matching the violin. The fingering is like violin, but the fingerboard is fretted. It is played with a pick or plectrum.

Maniera (It., mah-nee-E-rah)   Manner, style.

Mannheim school (Ger., MAHN-highm)   A pocket of 18th-century

German composers based in Mannheim who developed modern orchestra writing and were particularly known for using crescendos as an orchestral device.

Mano (It., MAH-no) Hand.

Mano destra (It., MAH-no DES-trah) Right hand.

Mano sinistra (It., MAH-no see-NIS-trah) Left hand.

Manual A keyboard, generally used only in organ music to distinguish from the pedal keyboard.

Manualiter (Ger., mah-noo-AH-li-ter) Organ music to be played by the fingers alone, without the pedals.

Maracas (Sp., mah-RAH-cahs) One (or two) pairs of gourds filled with seeds, with an attached handle, shaken as a percussion instrument in Latin American music.

Marcando (It., mahr-KAHN-do) Marked, accented.

Marcato (It., mahr-KAH-to) Marked, accented.

March Music composed to accompany marching, and therefore with a binary rhythm and brisk pace.

Marching band An ensemble of woodwind, brass, and percussion instruments, often with many players per part to remain loud outdoors. The marching band function is generally military or more recently for entertainment during school sports events.

Marcia (It., MAHR-chah) March.

Marcia funebre (It., MAHR-chah foo-NE-bre) Funeral march.

Mariachi (Sp., mah-ree-AH-chee) A Mexican traditional folk music style.

Marimba A keyboard-percussion instrument originating in Africa, with wooden bars and large tubular metal resonators under each one to prolong the sound of each note. Its tone is somewhat softer than that of the xylophone.

Mark tree A percussion instrument similar to wind chimes, but with a linear array of suspended metal tubes of cascading pitch and size.

Marqué (Fr., mar-KAY) Marked, accented.

Martelé (Fr., mar-teh-LAY) See *Martellato*.

Martellato (It., mar-tel-LAH-to) 1. A style of bowing string instruments to produce an accented staccato. 2. Short sharp accents in piano music.

Marziale (It., mahr-tsee-AH-le) Martial; in the style of a march.

Masculine cadence A phrase ending with a final chord on a strong beat. Also see *Feminine cadence*.

Mask, Maske (Ger., MAHS-ke) **Masque** (Fr., mahsk) A species of musical drama, or operetta, including singing and dancing, performed by characters in masks. The masque was the predecessor of the opera.

Mass A series of choral compositions performed during the celebration of High Mass in the Roman Catholic Church, often accompanied by instruments. In church function these are sung at different liturgical points of the mass and not as one continuous musical work. See *Ordinary* and *Proper*.

Mässig (Ger., ME-seesh) Moderate, moderately.

Master 1. In audio engineering, a mechanical or software device that controls other devices. 2. The final version of a recording or sheet music engraving that is used to reproduce further copies.

Matins Morning prayer.

Mazurka A lively Polish dance in 3/4 time, often characterized by dotted rhythms.

Mbira See *Kalimba*.

m.d. Abbreviation for *main droite* or *mano destra*, meaning right hand.

Mean temperament A tuning system used from the Renaissance until the early 19th century, providing pure intonation for the key of C major at the expense of many notes outside of that key being out of tune.

Measure A unit of division of musical time, typically shown in notation by barlines, and counted by regular musical pulse cycles. When music is in 4/4, one measure equals one series of 4 beats. In some traditions the term bar only refers to the barline itself, while other traditions use the term bar interchangeably with measure.

Mediant The third note of the diatonic scale.

Medieval Referring to the Middle Ages, a period spanning from ca. 450 through the beginning of the Renaissance, which is often dated as ca. 1450.

Medley A musical work, typically showcasing many melodies from one large theater work, or from any other unified source such as one composer or one tradition. Generally these consist of a string of somewhat unrelated segments and transitions.

Mehr (Ger., mayr) More.

Melisma The singing of more than one note to one syllable of text.

Mellophone A brass instrument derived from the French horn, with the bell facing forward.

Melodeon 1. See *Reed organ*. 2. A diatonic button accordion.

Melodia (It., me-lo-DEE-ah) Melody.

Melodica A free-reed instrument similar to a harmonica, but with a single mouthpiece and a small two- to three-octave keyboard on top.

Melodic minor See *Minor scale*.

Melodrama This term was occasionally used in the late 19th and early 20th century to describe music with a declaimed (not sung) text. Robert Schumann's *Manfred* and Richard Strauss's *Enoch Arden* are examples.

Melody A succession of tones perceived to be a single musical entity. While a theme may have any kind of musical profile or pattern, the specific term melody generally implies a theme of a singable nature.

Melos (Gr., ME-los)   Song; the name Wagner applied to his expanded concept of melody, with a free and motive-driven phrase structure.

Membranophone   Any percussion instrument whose sound is produced by striking a skin-like membrane, such as drums or tambourine.

Même (Fr., mem)   The same.

Meno (It., ME-no)   Less.

Mensural notation   A system of indicating rhythms during the late Middle Ages and Renaissance; often considered the first notation system in Western music to employ individual note shapes for temporal values.

Mensuration canon   A canon in which the successive voices restate the shared themes at different rhythmic values. For example, the first voice or instrument may state a theme in steady eighth notes, while the second voice answers with the same pitches at half the speed, in quarter notes.

Menuet (Fr., men-ü-et)   See *Minuet*.

Menuetto (It., me-noo-ET-to)   See *Minuet*.

Merengue (Sp., me-REN-ge)   A two-step Latin American dance originating in the Dominican Republic.

Messa (It., ME-sah)   **Messe** (Fr., mes; Ger., ME-se)   Mass.

Messa di voce (It., me-sah dee VO-che)   Gradual swelling and diminishing of the vocal tone thorough control of the breath.

Mesto (It., MES-to)   Sad, mournful, melancholy.

Mestoso (It., mes-TO-zo)   Sadly, mournfully.

Mesure (Fr., me-zür)   Measure, strict time.

Metallophone   Any percussion instrument with tuned metal bars, such as the vibraphone.

Meter   1. A regular pattern of strong and weak beats, usually represented by a *Time signature.* 2. The arrangement of poetical feet, or of long and short syllables, in verse. 3. Less commonly, the succession of accents shaping the rhythm of the phrase, not the measure.

Method   A text used to teach a musical instrument or technique.

Metronome   A machine invented in 1815 by Johann Maelzel to measure time by means of a graduated scale and pendulum, to be shortened or lengthened.   In a traditional metronome, the pendulum's movable counterweight can be set at any designated number of clicks per minute to swing back and forth producing an audible click.   Modern metronomes use electronic, rather than mechanical, means to produce clicks.

Metronome markings   From Beethoven's later years onwards, composers have found it useful to indicate tempos defined by beats per minute, which is more precise than Allegro or Adagio. While modern notation typically includes noteheads, such as ♩ =120, earlier tradition often indicated M.M. = 120, the initials standing for Maelzel's Metronome.

Mezza (It., ME-tsah) **Mezzo** (It., ME-tso)   Medium, half.

Mezzo forte (It., ME-tzo FOR-te)   Moderately loud, notated *mf*.

Mezzo piano (It., ME-tzo PYAH-no)   Moderately soft, notated *mp*.

Mezzo-soprano (It., ME-tso so-PRAH-no)   1. A female voice of lower range than a soprano, but higher than a contralto. 2. A rarely used C clef on the second line of the staff, as illustrated on page 4.

Mezza voce (It., ME-tsah VO-che)   Half the power of the voice.

m.g.   Abbreviation for *main gauche*, meaning left hand.

Mi (Lat., mee)   In many countries, the note E; in solfège, the third note of the scale.

Microtone   Any interval smaller than a half step.

Middle Ages   See *Medieval.*

Middle C   The pitch C notated on one ledger line below the treble-clef staff or one ledger line above the bass-clef staff.

MIDI   Musical Instrument Digital Interface. Originally created as a shared open standard between several manufacturers of electronic instruments and software, to allow competing brands' instruments and sound modules to work in tandem, this standard quickly became a universal means for all computers, software, and electronic instruments to coordinate in a common language.

MIDI channel   Within a MIDI environment, one information pathway that may be specific to one instrument or sound or other set of instructions.

MIDI controller   Any keyboard, pedal, wheel, or other triggering device that allows real-time performance to be captured in MIDI information.

MIDI file   A computer file, analogous to a player-piano roll, bearing information about pitch, rhythm, and other parameters, to convey instructions to any MIDI playback source.

Militare (It., mee-lee-TAH-re)   In a military style.

Military band   A group of woodwind, brass, and percussion players often used for military-related musical performance, but the term is often synonymous with concert band.

Minacciando (It., mee-nah-CHAHN-do) **Minaccievole** (It., mee-nah-CHEH-vo-le) **Minaccioso** (It., mee-nah-CHO-zo)   Threatening, menacing.

Mineur (Fr., mee-nür)   Minor.

Miniature score   See *Score, miniature.*

Minim   The British term for a half note.

Minimalism   A style concept of the late 20th century, characterized by extensive repetitions of simple percussive patterns or repetitive pitch patterns without harmonic development. Composers including Steve Reich and Philip Glass expanded on the concept of ostinato-based textures and very slow harmonic motion, adding their own new sophisticated methods of developing long works, and developing mass audiences for their new genres. The term "post-minimalism" has been used to describe the further developed works of John Adams and other composers who build music on ostinato-based textures with slow harmonic motion, but which otherwise is more like traditional Western art music than the original fringe avant-garde concept of pure minimalism.

Minnesinger (Ger., min-ne-SING-er)   A German troubadour or minstrel of the 12th or 13th century; they wandered from place to place singing a great variety of songs and melodies.

Minor   1. A key, chord, or scale most notably characterized by the 3rd degree of the scale being a minor 3rd above the root pitch. See the tables of scales and chords in the preface to this book. 2. The smaller of two diatonic spellings for intervals of the 2nd, 3rd, 6th, 7th, and octave extensions of these intervals. See the table of intervals on page 7.

Minor chord   See *Minor triad.*

Minor scale   Any of three specific scales most notably recognized by the minor 3rd interval from the tonic note to the 3rd degree. (a) The Natural Minor scale is diatonically true to the key signature, with the lowered 3rd, 6th, and 7th degrees of the scale; this is identical to the Aeolian mode. (b) The Melodic Minor scale is altered to produce a melodic "leading" tone; the ascending Melodic Minor therefore has a lowered 3rd degree, but raised 6th and 7th notes – while the descending Melodic Minor has lowered 3rd, 6th, and 7th degrees. (c) The Harmonic Minor scale accommodates chord progressions with the diatonically true minor IV chord, and the functional V chord which must be a major chord. Therefore to accommodate both chords, the scale has a lowered 3rd and 6th, but a raised 7th, causing an augmented second in the scale. These scales are presented on page 5.

Minor triad   A three-note chord consisting of a root (the letter name of the chord), and notes a minor third above and perfect fifth above. Any octave transpositions are equally acceptable; therefore the simple triad C-Eb-G may have its notes distributed or duplicated in any octaves or low-to-high order.

Minstrel   1. A troubadour, a traveling musician of the Middle Ages, most typically singing songs of courtly love. 2. See *Minstrel show.*

Minstrel show   A form of American entertainment popular primarily in the 19th century. Consisting of variety and comedy acts, most minstrel shows featured white performers in blackface. Black performers began to form their own minstrel troupes after the Civil War.

Minuet   A light German dance in 3/4; popular with 18th-century composers, the minuet became a standard inner movement in the symphony and other multi-movement forms. In this context, it served as the opening and close of an ABA (ternary) structure, with the middle section consisting of a lighter Trio.

Minuetto (It., mee-noo-ET-to)   A minuet.

Mirliton (Fr., meer-lee-TON)   A toy flute with a vibrating membrane, similar to a kazoo.

Mirror canon   A canon in which the second voice imitates the first voice in inversion.

Miserere (Lat., mee-ze-RE-re)   "Have mercy"; a psalm of supplication, especially used during Holy Week.

Missa (Lat., MEE-sah)   A Mass.

Misterioso (It., mees-tay-ree-O-zo)   Mysteriously; in a mysterious manner.

Misura (It., mee-ZOO-rah)   Bar, measure.

Misurato (It., mee-soo-RAH-to)   Measured; in strict, measured time.

Mit (Ger., mit)   With, by.

Mit Dämpfer (Ger., mit DEMP-fer)   With mutes.

Mit dem Bogen geschlagen (Ger., mit dem BO-gen ge-SHLAH-gen) Hitting with the bow (*col legno*).

Mittelgrund (Ger., MIT-el-grund)   In Schenkerian analysis, the immediate prolongations of the ursatz (fundamental structure).

Mix   To balance and combine multiple audio signals, or tracks.

Mixed folio   A collection of songs by various songwriters, grouped by instrumentation or topic.

Mixing board   An electronic device that enables mixing audio tracks. Also called a mixing console or mixer.

Mixolydian (mix-o-LID-ee-an)   A modal scale corresponding to G to G on the white keys of the piano. Also see *Mode*.

Mixture stop   An organ stop consisting of three or more ranks of pipes that are intended to sound together. This combination of pipes adds harmonics and volume to the sound.

M. M.   The abbreviation for *Maelzel's Metronome*.

Mobile (It., MO-bee-le)   Movable, changeable.

Modal   Involving or pertaining to modes.

Modality   Harmonies and/or melodies based on modes.

Mode   An ordered series of musical intervals, or scale. The term "mode" most often refers to a diatonic scale pattern beyond the conventional major and minor, as shown below. Also see *Aeolian, Church modes, Dorian, Ionian, Locrian, Lydian, Major scale, Minor scale, Mixolydian,* and *Phyrgian*.

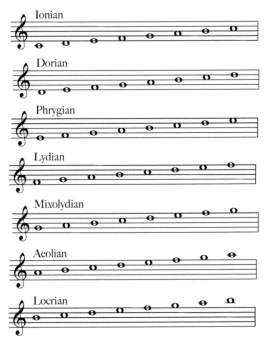

Mode, church   See *Church modes*.

Moderato (It., mo-day-RAH-to)   Moderately; in moderate time.

Modernism   An artistic and musical movement of the early- to mid-20th century, breaking with Romantic tendencies and instead emphasizing surrealism, abstraction, and expressionism.

Modulation   1. A transition of key; going from one key to another, by a certain succession of chords, either in a natural and flowing manner, or sometimes in a sudden and unexpected manner. 2. As applied to the voice, to accommodate the tone to a certain degree of intensity, or light and shade. 3. Also see *Tonicization*.

Modulation, direct   A sudden, unprepared shift into a new, often distantly-related, key.

Modulation, enharmonic   A modulation involving the altered notation of one or more notes belonging to a chord in the original key, thus allowing a resolution into an unexpected, often distantly-related, key.

Moll (Ger., mol)   Minor.

Molto (It., MOL-to)   Much; very much; extremely; a great deal.

Monochord   An ancient instrument with one string stretched over a sound box and a moveable bridge which is adjusted to produce different pitches.

Monody   A composition for a single voice with instrumental accompaniment. The term originally applied to those solos which were used in the operas of the early 1600's.

Monodic   For one voice; a solo.

Monophony   A single melodic line without any additional parts or accompaniment, as in plainchant.

Monothematic   A composition based on one theme.

Morbidezza (It., mor-bee-DET-sah)   Morbidity.

Morceau (Fr., mor-SO)   A musical piece, or composition.

Mordent   In Baroque music, a "shake" consisting of the principal note itself and the note above or below. The sign ♁ over the principal note calls for the upper auxiliary, and the same sign with a vertical line through it, ♁ for the lower auxiliary. The terms mordent and "inverted mordent" have both been used to indicate the upper or lower neighbor.

Morendo (It., mo-REN-do)   Dying away; expiring; gradually diminishing the tone and/or tempo.

Mormorando (It., mor-mo-RAHN-do) **Mormoroso** (It., mor-mo-RO-zo)   With a gentle, murmuring sound.

Mosso (It., MO-so)   Movement, or motion; *Meno mosso* means less movement, or slower; *Più mosso* means more movement, or faster.

Motet   A sacred vocal composition originating in the 13th century and flourishing through the Baroque period. Motets are generally contrapuntal, and it is possible that the word is derived from *moto* (motion), because of the constant motion of all the parts.

Motif (Fr., mo-TEEF)   A motive, or figure. Also see *Leitmotif.*

Motion   The progression of a melody, or part.

Motive   A small succession of notes, perceived as a meaningful musical entity within a composition.

Moto (It., MO-to)   Motion, movement; *con moto* means with motion, rather quick.

Moto perpetuo (It., MO-to pair-PAY-too-o)   Perpetual motion; a study in rapidity of execution and endurance.

Motown Sound   A style of popular music originating in 1960's Detroit, combining gospel, soul, and pop styles; Motown is often characterized by a driving quarter note feel, centered around black musicians performing and producing music for a mainstream audience.

Mouth organ   See *Harmonica.*

Mouthpiece   1. That part of a brass instrument which is applied to the lips.   2. That part of a single reed instrument that holds the reed and is inserted into the mouth.

Mouvement (Fr., moov-mahn)   **Movimento** (It., mo-vee-MEN-to)   Motion; movement; impulse; the time of a piece.

Movable-do   A system of solfege where the first note of any diatonic scale is called "do." Also see *Fixed-do* and *Solfège*.

Movement   The name given to any portion of a composition which is a complete structural unit with closure.

Mrdangam (Hindi, mr-DUHNG-uhm)   In traditional Carnatic music, a double-sided drum with each side varying in size and timbre.

m.s.   The abbreviation for *mano sinistra*, meaning left hand.

Multiphonics   The production of two or more notes simultaneously on a wind instrument.

Multitimbral   The ability to play more than one sound simultaneously on a synthesizer.

Multitracking   To record each voice, instrument or sound onto individual tracks which are to be mixed later.

Munter (Ger., MOON-ter)   Lively, sprightly.

Murmelnd (Ger., MOOR-melnd)   Murmuring.

Musetta (It., moo-ZE-tah)   **Musette** (Fr., mü-zet)   1. A small French bagpipe popular during the Baroque period.   2. An air or dance composed for the musette.   3. A composition, or movement in a composition, with a drone-bass. Also see *Oboe musette.*

Music   Organized sound.

Musica ficta   Presumed, and sometimes controversial chromatic alterations used in the performance of music from the 10th through the 16th centuries. In modern editions, they are shown as accidentals placed above the notes.

Musical   The common name for musical theater, the popular 20th-century American and British development of the operetta.

Musical saw   A large handsaw that is played with a violin bow and bent to change pitch.

Music box   A mechanical instrument consisting of a metal cylinder or disc fitted with pins that strike a steel comb with tuned teeth.

Music drama   A term used by music scholars and critics to describe Richard Wagner's unification of mythological drama, music, and visual art in his operas. Also see *Gesamtkunstwerk.*

Musicology   The study of music, frequently used in a less broad sense for the study of cultural music history.

Music theory   The study of the elements and parameters of music, shaped by the techniques and patterns developed by composers.

Music therapy   The use of music to improve or maintain the mental and/or physical well-being of a patient or client.

Musique concrète (Fr., moo-ZEEK kon-KRET)   Music created by the electronic manipulation of natural and man-made sounds.

Muta (It., MOO-tah)   Change; to change the note of a timpani or the key of a brass instrument.

Mutation   1. Organ stops which do not give a tone corresponding to the key pressed down, such as the quint, tierce, and twelfth; also called filling-up stops. 2. The transformation of the voice occurring at the age of puberty.

Mute   A device fitted to an instrument in order to alter its timbre and/or volume. Mutes are most commonly used on brass and string instruments. Also see *Con sordino* and *Senza sordino*.

Muthig (Ger., MOO-teesh)   Courageous, spirited.

m.v.   The abbreviation for mezza voce.

N   Abbreviation for niente.

Nacaire (Fr., nah-KAYR)   **Nacara** (It., nah-KAH-rah)   A brass drum with a loud metallic tone, formerly much used in France and Italy.

Nach (Ger., nahkh)   After.

Nachahmung (Ger., NAHKH-ah-moong)   Imitation.

Nachdruck (Ger., NAHKH-drook)   Emphasis, accent.

Nachdrücklich (Ger., NAHKH-drük-leesh)   **Nachdrucksvoll** (NAHKH-drooks-fol)   Energetic, emphatic, forcible.

Nachschlag (Ger., NAKH-shlahg)   Unaccented note at the end of a trill.

Nachthorn (Ger., NAHKHT-horn)   Night-horn; an organ stop of 8-foot tone, nearly identical with the Quintaton but of larger scale and more horn-like tone.

Nachtmusik (Ger., NAHKHT-moo-zik)   Night music; serenade.

Nach und nach (Ger., NAHKH oont NAHKH)   Little by little.

NARAS   Abbreviation for the National Academy of Recording Arts and Sciences. This organization is responsible for the Grammy awards.

Narrator   1. A speaker who recites a story to musical accompaniment, as in *Peter and the Wolf*. 2. A performer telling the story, generally in recitative, in an oratorio or passion.

Nationalism   The integration or infusion of one's nation or culture, often through music, art, and literature; a European social movement most prevalent in the 19th and 20th centuries. Nationalistic music features the use of folk melodies, dances, and stories.

Natural   The character ♮, used to cancel a sharp or flat.

Natural harmonic   A harmonic produced on an open string of a stringed instrument. Also called an open harmonic.

Natural horn   The old French horn, called also *Waldhorn*, without any keys.

Natural keys   Keys with no sharp or flat in the signature, such as C major and A minor.

Natural minor   See *Minor scale* and *Aeolian*.

N.C.   The abbreviation for "no chord."

Neapolitan chord   A major triad constructed on the lowered second scale degree, usually serving as a dominant preparation; this chord appears most often in first inversion, when it is called the Neapolitan sixth. In C major, the Neaopolitan sixth would be spelled F-A♭-D♭.

Nebenstimme (Ger., NE-ben-shti-muh)   The contrapuntal line of secondary importance; also used to label the secondary voice in a twelve-tone composition; indicated as **N**.

Neck   That part of a violin, guitar, or similar instrument, extending from the head to the body, and on which the fingerboard is fixed.

Negli (It. pl., NAY-lyee) **Nei** (It. pl., NAY-ee)   In the, at the.

Negligente (It., nay-lyee-JEN-te)   Negligent, unconstrained.

Negligenza (It., nay-lyee-JEN-tsah)   Negligence, carelessness.

Neighbor tone   A nonharmonic tone approached by step up or down from a chord tone, and resolved by returning to the same tone.

Nel (It., nel) **Nella** (It., NE-lah) **Nelle** (It. pl., NE-le) **Nello** (It., NE-lo) **Nell'** (It., nel)   In the, at the.

Neoclassicism   An early 20th century musical movement in which composers drew inspiration from the forms and ideas of the Classical period.

Neoromanticism   A musical movement of the mid- to late-20th century in which composers drew inspiration from the forms, melodies and harmonies of the Romantic period.

Netto (It., NE-to)   Neat, clear, quick, nimble.

Neu (Ger., noi)   New.

Neumes   Notational symbols used in Western music, primarily plainsong, during the Middle Ages.

New jack swing   A popular music style of the late 1980's and 1990's fusing rhythm and blues vocals with hip-hop rhythms and samples.

New Viennese school   See *Second Viennese school*.

Nicht eilen (Ger., neesht IGH-len)   Not rushing.

Nicht (Ger., neesht)   Not.

Nicht schleppend (Ger., neesht SHLEP-end)   Not dragging.

Niente (It., nee-EN-teh)   Nothing, silence. Abbreviated **n**.

Nineteenth   An organ stop, tuned a nineteenth above the diapasons. See *Larigot*.

Ninth   A compound interval consisting of an octave and a second.

Ninth chord   A chord consisting of a root, third, fifth, seventh, and ninth.

Nobile (It., NO-bee-le)   Noble, grand, impressive.

Nobilità, con (It., no-bee-lee-TAH kon) **Nobilmente** (It., no-beel-MEN-teh)   With nobility; dignified.

Nocturn, Nocturne   1. A composition describing or evoking the night, usually with a dreamy and romantic character. 2. A serenade meant to be played at night, often in the open air.

Nodal points, Nodes   Various stationary points dividing a vibrating string into segments that vibrate at different rates, producing overtones. See *Harmonics*.

Noël (Fr., no-el), **Nowell** (Eng., no-EL)   A Christmas carol, or hymn; the word had its origin in *Nouvelles* or *News (i.e.,* good tidings).

Non (It., non)   Not, no.

Nonchord tones, nonharmonic tones   Notes that are not part of the harmony at a given time; they are usually categorized by the manner in which they are approached and resolved.

Nonet   A composition for nine performers, or group of nine performers.

Non troppo (It., non TRO-po)   Not too much; moderately.

Non-transposing   A term used for any instrument whose pitches sound as written, such as a flute or violin.

Nose flute   A traditional flute originating in Hawaii, Polynesia, and other Pacific islands; a traditional Hawaiian belief states that air exhaled through the nose is purer than that exhaled through the mouth.

Notation   The representation of musical information by written characters.

Note   1. A musical sound. Also see *Pitch*. 2. The written representation of duration and/or pitch.

Notehead   The *head* or principal part of the written note as distinguished from the stem.

Note on, note off   The portions of the MIDI code that instruct when a note begins and ends.

Notturno (It., no-TOOR-no)   A nocturne.

Novelette   A name bestowed by Schumann (Op. 21) on instrumental compositions free in form, romantic in character, and characterized by a variety of contrasting themes.

Novelty song   A term coined by Tin-pan Alley composers to describe comic or nonsense songs, such as "Mairzy Doats" and "Yakety Yak."

Nuances (Fr. pl., nü-ahns)   Lights and shades of expression; variety of intonation.

Nuovo (It., noo-O-vo)   New; *di nuovo*, newly, again.

Nut   The small bridge at the upper end of the fingerboard of a guitar or violin, over which the strings pass to the pegs, or screws.

O before a consonant (It., o) **Od**, before a vowel (It., od) Or, as, either.

Obbligato (It., o-blee-GAH-to) **Obbligati** (It. Pl., o-blee-GAH-tee) **Obligé** (Fr., o-blee-zhay) **Obligat** (Ger., ob-li-GAHT) Obligatory, necessary; a part, or parts, which cannot be omitted, being necessary to a proper performance; a temporary solo in a concerted work, often misspelled *Obligato*.

Ober (Ger., O-ber) Upper, higher.

Ober-manual (Ger., O-ber mah-noo-AHL) The upper manual.

Oblique motion When one part ascends, or descends, while the others remain stationary. Also see *Contrary motion* and *Parallel motion*.

Oboe (Ger., O-bo-e, It., O-bo-ay) An instrument of great antiquity, consisting of a conical tube with various sound holes and keys, played with a double reed. The orchestra is almost always tuned to the "A" sounded by the oboe. A characteristic stop on the organ is called Oboe or Hautboy.

Oboe da caccia (It., O-bo-ay dah KAHT-chee-ah) A larger species of oboe, with the music written in the alto clef. Its place is taken in the modern orchestra by the English horn.

Oboe d'amore (It., O-bo-e dah-MO-re) A mellow-sounding double-reed instrument pitched a minor third below an oboe.

Oboe family A family of double-reed instruments that includes the Oboe, English horn, heckelphone, bassoon, and contrabassoon.

Oboe musette A sopranino oboe, pitched a minor third or perfect fourth above the standard oboe; also known as a piccolo oboe.

Ocarina A simple wind instrument made of terra cotta, shaped like an elongated egg, sharply pointed at one end. There are sound holes for fingers and thumbs, and the tone is produced through a whistle-like mouthpiece. It is limited to the diatonic scale and comes in various keys and sizes. Due to its shape, it is nicknamed the "sweet potato."

Octatonic scale An eight-note scale consisting of alternating whole steps and half steps; there are only three possible octatonic scales.

Octave 1. An interval measuring eight diatonic steps, or twelve half steps. 2. The name of an organ stop. Also see *Principal*.

Octave coupler A device used on organs to add the upper or lower octave to the notes actually played.

Octave fifteenth An organ stop of bright, sharp tone, sounding an octave above the fifteenth.

Octave flute See *Piccolo*.

Octave hautboy A 4-foot organ reed stop; the pipes are of the hautboy species.

Octave marks The abbreviation *8va* or *8*, followed by a dotted line, indicates that the note or notes over which it is placed are to be played an octave *higher* until the end of the dotted line, or until the word *loco* is reached. When the *lower* octave is desired, the dotted line, etc. is placed *under* the notes, sometimes with the addition of word "bassa." Occasionally, the higher or lower octave is to be played *with* the printed note, in which case the term *col 8va* or *col 8* is used.

Octavo (It., ok-TAH-vo) 1. A paper size typically used for choral publications, so called because large sheets are folded into eighths on the printing press. In recent years, octavo size is typically 7" x 10½" with some slight variation. 2. See *Octave*.

Octet A composition for eight performers, or a group of eight performers.

Ode 1. Lyrical verse with ancient Greek origins. 2. A musical setting of an ode.

Oder (Ger., O-der) Or.

Œuvre (Fr., ÜV-ruh) See *Opus*.

Off In organ music, a direction to push in a stop or coupler to discontinue that setting.

Offertory (Eng., OF-er-to-ry) A hymn, prayer, anthem, or instrumental piece sung or played during the collection of the offering. It follows the Credo in the Mass.

Off the string See *Spiccato*.

Ohne (Ger., O-ne) Without.

Ohne Dämpfer (Ger., O-ne DEMP-fur) Without mute.

Open 1. On stringed instruments, a string that is not fingered. 2. On brass instruments, not muted or stopped.

Open diapason An organ stop, generally made of metal, and thus called because the pipes are open at the top. It commands the whole scale, and is the most important stop on the instrument.

Open fifth A perfect fifth, notable for its hollow sound, used in place of a triad.

Open harmonic See *Natural harmonic.*

Open position Voicing of a chord in which the tones are spaced over more than an octave, also called open harmony. The opposite, with the notes as close together as possible, is called close position.

Open string The full, unstopped length of a string, or the note to which it is tuned.

Open unison stop See *Open diapason.*

Oper (Ger., O-per) **Opera** (It., O-pay-rah) 1. A drama set to music, for voices and instruments, with scenery, costumes, and staging. The chief parts of traditional opera, following the instrumental overture, are the recitative, aria, chorus, and the various kinds of ensemble (duet, trio, quartet, quintet, sextet, etc.) of which the finale is the most important.

2. The plural of opus, referring to the works of a composer. See *Opus*.

Opera buffa (It., O-pay-rah BOO-fah); **Opéra bouffe** (Fr., o-pay-RAH boof) See *Comic opera*.

Opéra comique (Fr., o-pay-rah ko-meek) See *Comic opera*.

Opera seria (It., O-pe-rah SE-ree-ah) A serious or tragic opera.

Operetta A short opera, generally with light and playful scoring and storyline.

Ophicleide (OF-i-klighd) A large conical brass instrument with metal keys, that served as the bass brass instrument of the orchestra until the invention of the tuba in the 1830's.

Ophicleide stop The most powerful manual reed-stop known in an organ; of 8 or 4-foot scale, it is usually placed upon a separate soundboard with great wind pressure.

Oppure (It., o-POO-ray) Or. See *Ossia*.

Opus (Lat., O-pus, Ger., O-poos) 1. Work, composition; an opus may include several numbers or may consist of a single piece. 2. Opus numbers are sometimes used to codify a composer's catalog of works.

Oratorio (It., o-rah-TO-ri-o) A musical drama, with similar musical components to opera, that is performed without the aid of scenery and staging. The libretto is usually based on scriptural narrative.

Oratorium (Lat., Ger., o-rah-TO-ri-oom) See *Oratorio*.

Orchestra (It., or-KAYS-trah) **Orchester** (Ger., or-KHES-ter) **Orchestre** (Fr., or-kes-tr) A body of performers on string instruments, generally in conjunction with various woodwind, brass, and percussion instruments. The modern orchestras consist of from 30 to over 100 performers.

Orchestration The arranging of music for an orchestra; also known as scoring.

Orchestrion A large mechanical instrument, similar in function to a player piano, consisting of various organ pipes and mechanical percussion instruments.

Ordinary The portions of the Roman Catholic Mass that remain the same from day to day, as opposed to the Proper. The Ordinary includes the Kyrie, Gloria, Credo, Sanctus and Agnus Dei. See *Mass* and *Proper*.

Organ 1. An instrument of ancient origin, originating as a bellows and fewer than a dozen pipes in a row. From the Middle Ages, it has grown into the massive instrument of the present day; utilizing windchests and blowers and containing thousands of open flue, stopped, and reed pipes of every conceivable tone color. The modern pipe organ ranges from the deep 64-foot tone to the highest harmonic, and varies in power from a thunderous fortississimo to a scarcely audible pianississimo. The organ is played from a keyboard, similar to that of a piano, but called a manual. On large organs there are three to five manuals, including the great, choir, swell, solo, and echo, beside a pedal keyboard played by the feet. The various ranks, or sets of pipes, are controlled by stops placed within reach. Also see *Pipe* and *Piston*. 2. A general term describing a keyboard instrument with sustained tone, such as a harmonium or electric organ.

Organetto (It., or-gahn-E-to) 1. A small, hand-pumped organ of the Middle Ages. 2. A modern free-reed instrument of Italy, similar to an accordion.

Organ point See *Pedal point*.

Organum (Lat., OR-gah-noom) 1. The Latin word for organ. 2. An evolution of plainchant originating in 9th century Europe and flourishing in 12th-century Paris; beginning as two-part chants moving in parallel motion, composers of organum gradually added voices that grew in independence, giving rise to polyphony in Western music.

Orgel (Ger., OR-gl) Organ.

Ornamental notes See *Ornaments*.

Ornamentation The embellishment of a melody.

Ornaments All notes not forming an essential part of the harmony, but introduced as embellishments. See *Mordent, Trill, Turn, Grace notes, Appoggiatura, Acciaccatura*.

Oscillator An electronic device that generates audio waveforms.

Oscilloscope An electronic device that displays the frequency and amplitude of an audio signal.

Osservanza (It., o-ser-VAHN-tsah) Observation; attention; strictness in keeping time.

Ossia (It., O-see-ah) Or; otherwise; indicating another way of playing a passage.

Ostinato (It., os-tee-NAH-to) Literally, "obstinate"; a motive or short phrase which is repeated persistently.

Ottava (It., o-TAH-vah) An octave; an eighth.

Ottava alta (It., o-TAH-vah AHL-tah) The octave above; an octave higher, commonly marked *8va*.

Ottava bassa (It., o-TAH-vah BAHS-sah) The octave below, commonly marked *8va bassa*.

Ottavino (It., o-tah-VEE-no) A piccolo.

Ou (Fr., oo) Or.

Oud (Arabic, ood) A pear-shaped, plucked string instrument used in traditional Middle Eastern music. It consists of a single low string, five doubled upper strings and a fretless fingerboard. The oud is often considered the predecessor to the European lute.

Outer voices The highest and lowest voices in a multi-part texture, especially four-part choral writing.

Ouvert (Fr., oo-vair) Open.

Ouverture   (Fr., oo-vair-TÜR)   **Overtura**   (It., o-ver-TOO-rah)
Ouvertüre (Ger., o-fer-TOO-re) An introductory instrumental movement in an oratorio, opera, or musical; also an independent piece for a full band or orchestra, in which case it is sometimes called a concert overture.

Overblow   To change the force of the airstream in a woodwind or brass instrument in order to alter the note or harmonic.

Overdrive   A type of audio distortion, created by overloading an amplifier; frequently used deliberately for effect in blues and rock music.

Overdubbing   The technique of adding a new audio signal to a previously recorded signal; a common technique used for recording popular music.

Overtone series   See *Harmonic series.*

P   1. Piano (***p***), pianissimo (***pp***), pianississimo (***ppp***) indicating a quiet dynamic level. 2. In French Organ music, P stands for Positif (choir organ).

Pacato (It., pah-KAH-to)   Placid; calm.

Pad   See *Synth pad.*

Palm mute   A technique used by guitarists to create a muted sound; the strings are dampened by the side of the hand near the bridge as the strings are plucked.

Pandiatonicism   The free use of diatonic notes without regard for traditional diatonic function; often used to describe the music of Aaron Copland and neo-classical works of Igor Stravinsky.

Panning   The left-right balance of an audio signal within a stereo field.

Panpipes   One of the most ancient and simple of musical instruments; it was made of reeds or tubes of different lengths fastened together and tuned to each other, stopped at the bottom and blown into by the mouth at the top.

Pans   Colloquial term for steel drums.

Pantomime   An entertainment in which not a word is spoken or sung, but the sentiments are expressed by mimicry and gesticulation accompanied by instrumental music.

Pantonality   A term used by Arnold Schoenberg to describe his twelve-tone serial technique in order to replace "atonality," a term he shunned.

Paradiddle   A drum rudiment involving a stroke with one hand, a stroke with the other hand, and two strokes with the first hand. This pattern then repeats, starting with the other hand.

Parallel chords   A technique in which chords progress in parallel motion, with the intervallic content remaining the same from one chord to the next.

Parallel fifths, parallel octaves   See *Parallel motion.*

Parallel keys   Major and minor keys that share the same tonic, for example C major and C minor.

Parallel motion   Two musical lines progressing up or down in the same direction, with their intervallic distance remaining the same from note to note. In Common Practice music, parallel motion involving fifths and octaves was considered objectionable (also called consecutive fifths or octaves). Also see *Contrary motion* and *Oblique motion*.

Paraphrase   A transcription or rearrangement of a vocal or instrumental composition for some other instrument or instruments, with more or less brilliant variations.

Parlando   (It., pahr-LAHN-do)   **Parlante**   (It., pahr-LAHN-te) Accented; in a declamatory style; in a recitative, or speaking style.

Part   The music for each separate voice or instrument.

Partials   See *Harmonic series*.

Partita   (It., par-TEE-ta)   1. An air with variations in the 16th and 17th centuries, or one of these variations. 2. A suite of dance-inspired movements in the 17th and 18th centuries. 3. A suite, with or without dance movements, from the 18th century to the present.

Partition   (Fr., pahr-tee-si-on)   **Partitur**   (Ger., pahr-tee-TOOR)

Partitura   (It., pahr-tee-TOO-rah)   Full score.

Part song   An unaccompanied choral composition for at least three voice parts. A melody harmonized by other parts more or less freely, but from which counterpoint is for the most part excluded.

Pas   (Fr., pah)   A step, or a dance in a ballet.

Paso doble   (Sp., PAH-so DO-ble)   A ballroom dance of Spanish origin in which the dancing couple imitates the motions and drama of a bullfight.

Passacaglia   (It., pah-sah-KAHL-yee-ah)   Similar to a chaconne, a passacaglia features a repeating phrase which may appear as melody and counterpoint as well as the ground bass; historically the passacaglia was in a slow 3/4 rhythm.

Passage   Any phrase, or short portion of an air or other composition. Every member of a strain, or movement, is a passage.

Passamezzo   (It., pah-sah-ME-tso)   An old slow dance in duple meter, similar to the Pavane, but somewhat more rapid.

Passecaille   (Fr., pas-kah-e)   See *Passacaglia*.

Passepied   (Fr., pas-pi-ay)   A lively old French jig in triple meter, almost like a quick minuet, with three or more strains, or reprises.

Passing tones   Notes which do not belong to the harmony, but which serve to connect those which are essential.

Passionatamente   (It., pah-see-o-nah-tah-MEN-te)   Passionately.

Passionato   (It., pah-see-o-NAH-to)   Passionate.

Passione   (It., pah-see-O-ne)   Passion; note that this term comes from the Greek word for suffering, hence its modern usage for romantic yearning as well as the Crucifixion.

Passion music, Passions-musik (Ger., pah-si-ons MOO-zik)   Music picturing the sufferings and death of Christ.

Pasticcio (It., pas-TI-chee-o) **Pastiche** (Fr., pas-teesh)   A medley made up of songs or pieces by various composers.

Pastoral, Pastorale (It., pahs-to-RAH-le)   1. A musical drama, the personages and scenery of which are chiefly rural. 2. An instrumental composition written in the pastoral style.

Patch   A sound in electronic music synthesis; the term derives from the patch cables used in early electronic music.

Patetica (It., pah-TAY-tee-kah) **Patetico** (pah-TE-tee-ko)   Pathetic.

Pateticamente (It., pah-tay-tee-kah-MEN-te)   Pathetically.

Pathétique (Fr., pah-tay-TEEK)   A descriptive term connoting passion and sorrow; occasionally used to label music evoking this mood, such as Beethoven's eighth piano sonata and Tchaikovsky's sixth symphony.

Patimento (It., pah-tee-MEN-to)   Affliction, grief, suffering.

Patter song   A song with a rapid, declamatory style, often found in operettas and musicals, in which alliteration and clever rhymes are used for comic effect.

Pauken (Ger. pl., POW-ken)   1. Timpani. 2. To beat the drums.

Pausa (It., pah-OO-zah)   A pause.

Pause (Ger., POW-ze)   A rest.

Pause (Eng.)   See *Fermata*.

Pavan (Eng.) **Pavana** (It., pah-VAH-nah) **Pavane** (Fr., pah-VAHN)   A grave, stately dance, which took its name from *pavano*, a peacock. It is in 4/4.

Paventato (It., pah-ven-TAH-to) **Paventoso** (It., pah-ven-TO-zo)   Fearful; timorous; with anxiety and embarrassment.

Pavillon chinois (Fr., pah-vee-yon shee-nwah)   An instrument with numerous little bells.

PCM   Short for pulse-code modulation, a technique of converting an analog signal into a digital representation; used for early digital keyboards and digital audio for computers and compact discs.

Peal   A set sequence of change-ringing on church bells. Also see *Change ringing*.

Pedal   1. Foot-operated levers on a piano. The sustain, or damper, pedal (on the right) raises the dampers from the strings for sustained sound; the soft, or *una corda*, pedal (on the left) shifts the mechanism so only one string is struck per note; the less common *sostenuto* pedal (in the middle) allows the performer to select specific notes to sustain. Various other pedals have been added through the years for color or novelty effects. 2.

On the organ, "pedal" can refer to the keyboard played with the feet, but also the swell and various pistons and couplers actuated by the feet. 3. The orchestral harp is equipped with seven pedals that raise and lower the seven diatonic notes by half steps. 4. The low foundation notes on brass instruments. 5. See *Pedal tone*. 6. The pedals on a drumset, typically on the bass drum and hi-hat cymbal. 7. Footswitches for electric guitar or bass which control amplifiers and tone effects.

Pedal keyboard   A keyboard played with the feet, commonly found on organs; also called the pedalboard.

Pedal tone   1. A bass note, sustained for several or many measures, while a variety of harmonies are introduced above it; named for the pedals of the organ. 2. Any sustained tone during which the harmony changes, also called pedal point. A sustained tone above the bass is called an inverted pedal point. 3. The fundamental note of a brass instrument, usually too low and soft to be musically useful.

Pedal steel guitar   See *Steel guitar*.

Peg   The devices on a string instrument that tighten and loosen the strings, thus affecting their tuning; also called tuning pegs.

Pegbox   That part of string instruments that houses the tuning pegs.

Pentachord   A five-note grouping, either a segment of a scale, a set of pitches in a tone row, or a pitch-class set.

Pentatonic scale   A scale of five notes; the most widely-known pentatonic scale is similar to a major scale with the fourth and seventh degrees omitted.

Per (It., pair)   For, by, from, in, through.

Percussion (Eng., per-KUSH-on) **Percussione** (It., payr-koo-see-O-ne)   A general name for all instruments that are struck; such as a gong, drum, bell, cymbals, triangle, or tambourine. Also see *idiophone* and *membranophone*.

Perdenosi (It., payr-den-DO-zee)   Literally, "becoming lost"; gradually decreasing the tone and the tempo.

Perfect   A term applied to certain intervals. See *Intervals*.

Perfect cadence   See *Cadence*.

Perfect pitch   Best described as "permanent pitch memory," the ability of some listeners to discern musical notes without external references; also called absolute pitch.

Performing rights organizations   Organizations that protect the musical copyrights of their members by monitoring live, recorded and broadcast performances, such as ASCAP, BMI, and SESAC.

Period   A complete musical sentence, containing at least two phrases and bringing the ear to a conclusion or state of rest.

Perpetual canon   See *Round*.

Personality folio A collection of songs composed by one songwriter, or performed by one recording artist or group.

Pesante (It., pe-ZAHN-te) Heavy, ponderous; with importance and weight, impressively.

Petit (Fr., pu-TEE) Little, small.

Peu (Fr., pü) Little, a little.

Peu à peu (Fr., pü ah pü) Little by little.

Pezzo (It., PE-tso) A separate piece of music, the plural form is pezzi.

Phantasie (Ger., fahn-tah-ZEE) See *Fantasia.*

Phonetic Referring to the sounds that occur in spoken language; the International Phonetic Alphabet (IPA) is the most widely-known universal system for transcribing these sounds into written symbols.

Phonograph An instrument using the vibration of a needle in a carved groove to record and reproduce analog sounds. Its prototype was invented by Thomas Edison in 1877.

Phrase A short musical statement, similar to a clause in language, often four or eight measures in length; open-ended and closed phrases are traditionally paired together to form complete musical statements, called periods.

Phrasing Dividing music into statements and/or sections; the grammar and punctuation of music.

Phrygian (FRIJ-ee-an) A modal scale corresponding to E to E on the white keys of the piano. Also see *Mode.*

Piacere (It., pee-ah-CHAY-re) Pleasure, inclination, fancy.

Piacevole (It., pee-ah-CHE-vo-le) Pleasing, graceful, agreeable.

Piagnevole (It., pee-ahn-YE-vo-le) Mournful, doleful, lamentable.

Piangendo (It., pee-ahn-JEN-do) Plaintively, sorrowfully, weeping.

Pianissimo (It., pee-ahn-I-see-mo) Extremely soft.

Piano (It., pee-AH-no) Soft.

Pianoforte or Piano A keyboard instrument in which felt-covered hammers strike steel strings and immediately drop back. The sound is transmitted via a bridge to an amplifying soundboard. The instrument was invented by Bartolomeo Cristofori at the opening of the 18th century. Many improvements, including the pedals, were made during the 19th century. Also see *Pedal.*

Piano Reduction A work for orchestra or other large ensemble condensed into two or four staves in order to be played by one or two pianists.

Piano roll 1. Rolls of paper with carefully-cut holes, designed to play songs on a player piano. The placement and length of the holes determine the pitch and duration of each note. Also see *Player piano.* 2. In MIDI sequencing software, a view showing a piano keyboard and MIDI notes, usually displayed as colored blocks; named for their visual similarity to player piano rolls.

Piano-vocal score   A score featuring a piano reduction of a full ensemble accompanying vocal and/or choral parts, often used for rehearsals. Also known as a piano score, or PV score; PVG stands for "piano-vocal-guitar" score.

Piano trio, Piano quartet, Piano quintet   Chamber music involving piano and strings. The piano trio usually involves a piano, violin, and cello; the piano quartet adds a viola, and the quintet adds an additional violin. One notable exception is Schubert's *Trout Quintet*, which adds a double bass in place of one of the violins.

Piatti (It. pl., pee-AH-tee)   Cymbals.

Pibroch (PEE-brok)   Highly complicated pieces of classical music from Scotland, traditionally played on bagpipes; the original Gaelic spelling is *piobaireachd*.

Picado (Sp., pee-KAH-do)   The rapid scale-like passages played by Flamenco guitarists.

Picardy third   The substitution of a major third for a minor third in the final tonic triad of piece or movement in a minor key.

Picchettato (It., pee-ke-TAH-to) **Picchiettato** (It., pee-kee-et-TAH-to)   Scattered, detached; in violin playing, the articulation indicated by dots under a slur.

Piccolo (It., PEE-ko-lo)   1. Small; little. 2. A small flute, sounding an octave higher than written, very common in the orchestra and band, with increasing presence in recent years in recital and chamber music. 3. A 2-foot organ stop of wood pipes, producing a bright and clear tone in unison with the fifteenth.

Pick   A device, constructed of wood, plastic, or metal, used to pluck the strings of a guitar, banjo, or other plucked-string instrument; also called a plectrum.

Pick scrape   The technique, common in rock music, of scraping the side of a pick down one of the wound-steel strings to produce a grating sound.

Pickup   A transducer, often found on electic guitars and basses, that converts vibrations into electric signals.

Piece   A musical composition.

Piena (It., pee-AY-nah) **Pieno** (It., pee-AY-no)   Full.

Pieta (It., pee-AY-tah)   Pity.

Pietosamente (It., pee-ay-to-za-MEN-te) **Pietoso** (It., pee-ay-TO-zo)   Compassionately; tenderly; pitifully.

Piezo-electric transducer   A small, highly-sensitive disc that uses the piezo-electric effect to detect vibrations and turn them into electric signals.

Pin bridge   A bridge designed to hold plastic, wooden, or metal pins;

these bridge pins serve to precisely control the height of the string.

Pincé (Fr., PAN-say)   Pinched. See *Pizzicato*.

Pipa (Chin., pee-pah)   A pear-shaped, fretted lute with 4 or 5 strings; used in traditional Chinese music.

Pipe   1. Any tube formed of a reed, metal, or wood which, being blown at one end, produces a musical sound. 2. The pipes on an organ. Organ pipes divide into two classes: the reed and the flue pipes. Reed pipes set a column of air in vibration by means of a reed which is set in a box or reservoir. Flue pipes sound by directing the wind against a thin edge in the mouth of the pipe, causing the column of air within to vibrate. Flue pipes may be stopped or open.

Pipe organ   See *Organ*.

Piston   1. A device which enables an organ player to activate the combination action of an organ to quickly change registration; pistons may either be activated by the hands or feet. 2. The up-and-down style of valve on most trumpets and some tubas, in contrast to rotary valves.

Pitch   A sound vibrating at a constant rate, generally described by a letter or solfège name, such as A or La, and in some contexts further defined by octave. The standard of pitch tuning has always been variable; for instance the A above middle C may be defined by current orchestras at 440~442 vibrations per second, but in Baroque times it was only 404, while Handel's tuning fork dated to 1740 gives the same note 416 vibrations.

Pitch bend   1. A guitar technique of sliding a string sideways with the left hand on the fretboard to bend a pitch upward and back. 2. An electronic function found on most MIDI controllers and synthesizers, that emulates portamento and glissando effects.

Pitch-class set   In set theory, a collection of pitches; they may be presented in any order as successive pitches and/or simultaneities (harmonic intervals and chords).

Pitch pipe   A breath-activated device that produces specific pitches to give musicians a standardized reference, particularly for singers to start an a cappella work.

Più (It., pee-OO)   More.

Più mosso (It., PEE-oo MO-so)   **Più moto** (It., PEE-oo MO-to) More motion, slightly faster.

Pivot chord   A chord that is shared by two keys, and therefore serves as the fulcrum in most traditional modulations; also called the common chord.

Pizzicato (It., pit-see-KAH-to)   Pinched; meaning that the strings of the violin, violoncello, etc., are not to be played with the bow, but plucked, with the right-hand fingers, producing a staccato effect.

Placido (It., PLAH-chee-do)   Placid, tranquil, calm.

Plagal cadence A cadence in which the final chord on the tonic is preceded by a subdominant chord. Because this progression is often used for the Amen at the end of a hymn, it is also called a church cadence or an "Amen cadence." See *Cadence*.

Plagal mode See *Church modes*.

Plainchant See *Plainsong*.

Plainsong Sacred monophonic vocal music, typically notated only in pitches, allowing the rhythm to follow the natural prosody of the liturgical words. Also called plainchant, this also includes the specific repertoires known as Gregorian, Ambrosian, and Byzantine Chant.

Plainte (Fr., plent) A moan or groan.

Platinum record A recording that has been certified by the RIAA to have sold over one million copies.

Player piano A mechanical piano that plays by itself with the aid of perforated piano rolls and a pneumatic mechanism.

Plectrum (Lat., PLEK-trum) See *Pick*.

Plectrum banjo A banjo with a longer neck and more frets than the tenor banjo, frequently preferred by soloists.

Plein jeu (Fr., plan zhu) Full organ; the term is also applied to a mixture-stop of several ranks of pipes.

Plötzlich (Ger., PLÜTZ-leesh) Abruptly.

Pluck To set a string in vibration by using a finger or pick.

Plunger mute An unused rubber toilet plunger, often with a hole in place of the removed shaft; manipulated over the bell by hand, this mute is capable of creating sounds similar to a muffled human voice.

Plus (Fr., plü) More.

Pochettino (It., po-ke-TEE-no) **Pochetto** (It., po-KE-to) Very little, slower.

Poco (It., PO-ko) Little.

Poco a poco (It., PO-ko ah PO-ko) By degrees, little by little.

Poi (It., PO-ee) Then, after, afterwards.

Poi a poi (It., PO-ee ah PO-ee) By degrees.

Poi a poi tutte le corde (It., PO-ee ah PO-ee TOO-te le KOR-de) Literally "little by little all the strings," this indicates a gradual release of the piano's una corda pedal.

Point (Fr., pwan) A dot.

Polacca (It., po-LAH-kah) See *Polonaise*.

Polka A lively Bohemian dance in 2/4 time.

Polka mazurka (Cz., POL-kah ma-ZUR-kah) A dance in triple time, played slow, and having its accent on the last part of the measure.

Polka redowa (Cz., POL-kah RED-o-wah) A dance tune in triple time, played faster than the polka mazurka, and having its accent on the first part of the measure.

Polonaise (Fr., pol-o-nez)   A Polish dance in triple time, with frequent runs and skips in the melody, and syncopation occurring freely in both the melody and the accompaniment.

Polychoral   A musical texture involving alternating groups of singers.

Polychord   A sonority consisting of two distinct, often contrasting, chords occurring simultaneously.

Polymeter   The use of different meters simultaneously, or in alternation.

Polyphony   A musical texture involving two or more independent musical lines; counterpoint.

Polyrhythm   The simultaneous use of two or more contrasting rhythms.

Polytonality   The simultaneous use of two or more different keys.

Pomposo (It., pom-PO-zo)   Pompous, stately, grand.

Ponderoso (It., pon-de-RO-zo)   Ponderously, massively, heavily.

Ponticello (It., pon-tee-CHE-lo)   1. The bridge of a string instrument. 2. The direction to bow near the bridge is *sul ponticello*, and the result is a nasal and scratchy, yet incisive tone.

Portamento (It., por-tah-MEN-to)   From *portare*, to carry. This indicates a carrying or gliding of the tone from one note to the next, but so rapidly that the intermediate notes are not defined, as would be the case in a legato passage between two principal notes. The expression occurs frequently in vocal music, but may also be found in instrumental music.

Portative organ   A small organ of the Middle Ages, consisting of a hand-operated bellows and one rank of flue pipes. Smaller than the positive organ, the portative organ was worn on a strap by the player.

Portato (It., por-TAH-to)   An articulated legato, notated by connecting notes with a slur and adding staccato marks.

Portunal-flaut (Ger., por-too-NAHL flowt)   An organ stop of the clarabella species, the pipes of which are larger at the top than at the bottom and produce a tone of clarinet quality.

Posaune (Ger., po-ZOW-ne)   1. A trombone. 2. A brassy reed stop on a pipe organ.

Positif (Fr., po-zee-TEEF) **Positiv** (Ger., po-zi-TIF)   The choir organ, or lowest row of keys with soft-toned stops in a large organ.

Position   1. A reference point taken by the left hand on the fingerboard of any string instrument. 2. A reference point on the trombone slide. 3. The voicing of notes in a chord. Also see *Close position* and *Open position*.

Positive organ   A small, single-manual organ originating in the Middle Ages and continuing in use through the Baroque era, when it was frequently used for basso continuo. The positive organ is somewhat larger than the portative organ, and is not worn by the player.

Possibile (It., po-SEE-bee-le)   Possible; as much as possible.

Posthorn   A valveless ancestor of the cornet and horn, used during the 18th and 19th century to announce postal riders or mail coaches; Gustav Mahler's 3rd symphony features an offstage posthorn solo, frequently played on flügelhorn.

Postlude (Lat., POST-lüde) **Postludium** (Lat., post-LÜ-di-um)   An after-piece; music intended to follow a sacred service or other ceremony.

Potpourri (po-poor-REE)   A medley, capriccio, or fantasy in which favorite airs and fragments of musical pieces are strung together.

Pour (Fr., poor)   For.

Poussé, poussez (Fr., poo-SAY)   Pushed.

Practice mute   A hollow-cone-shaped mute for trumpet or trombone that blocks and redirects the flow of air, similar to a wah-wah mute. Baffles and small air holes in the mute greatly reduce the volume of the instrument, allowing for quiet practice.

Praeludium (Lat., pray-LOO-dee-oom)   Prelude.

Pralltriller (Ger., PRAHL-TRI-ler)   An upper mordent. Also see *Mordent*.

Precentor   The appellation given to the master of the choir.

Precipitando (It., pray-chee-pee-TAHN-do)   Hurrying.

Precipitato (It., pray-chee-pee-TAH-to)   In a precipitate manner; hurriedly.

Precipitoso (It., pray-chee-pee-TO-zo)   Hurrying, precipitous.

Precisione (It., pray-chee-zee-O-ne)   Precision, exactness.

Preciso (It., pray-CHEE-zo)   Precise, exact, exactly.

Prelude   1. A short introductory composition, or extempore performance, to prepare the ear for the succeeding movements. 2. A composition of a free and improvised character.

Première (Fr., pre-mi-air)   1. First, used in any context. 2. The first performance of a new composition.

Preparation   The various methods of introducing non-chord tones and other dissonances into an otherwise consonant environment; these methods and the rules for their use have evolved and changed throughout music history.

Prepared piano   A technique made famous by avant-garde American composer John Cage, in which various objects are placed between or on the strings to create new, often percussive, timbres.

Presets   Default settings for keyboards, controllers, and computer music software.

Pressure sensitivity   The ability of a keyboard instrument to respond to finger pressure after a key is pushed down; a feature of the clavichord and some electronic keyboards.

Prestissimo (It., pres-TIS-see-mo) Very quickly; as fast as possible.

Presto (It., PRES-to) Quickly, rapidly.

Prima (It., PREE-mah) See *Primo*.

Prima donna (It., PREE-mah DO-nah) Principal female singer in a serious opera.

Prima volta (It., PREE-mah VOL-tah) The first time.

Prime The interval where two voices are on the same degree of the staff, a unison.

Primo (It., PREE-mo) 1. Principal, first. 2. The upper player in a four-hand piano composition. Also see *Secondo*.

Principal 1. The first-chair player in a band or orchestral section, or that instrument's section leader. 2. An important organ stop, tuned an octave above the diapasons, and therefore of 4-foot pitch on the manual, and 8-foot on the pedals. In German organs the term principal is also applied to all the open diapasons.

Principal bass An organ stop of the open diapason species on the pedals.

Processional Music intended for a gradual entrance into the performance space; the entrants may be officiants of the event to come, or the musicians themselves.

Process music Music whose development in composition and/or performance displays a discernable evolutionary process; the term is often used to describe the phasing and layering techniques used by composers such as Terry Riley and Steve Reich, as well as the electro-acoustic works of Karlheinz Stockhausen.

Program 1. A story or idea that serves as the basis for a piece of music. See *Program music*. 2. Printed information distributed at a concert to inform audience members.

Program music Instrumental music which either by its title, or by description printed upon the composition, gives a definite picture of events or objects. Famous examples include Vivaldi's *Four Seasons*, Beethoven's *Pastoral Symphony*, and the *Symphonie Fantastique* by Berlioz.

Progression Melodic progression is the motion from one tone to another. Harmonic progression is the motion from chord to chord.

Progressive jazz See *Cool jazz*.

Pronto (It., PRON-to) Quick.

Pronunziato (It., pro-noon-tsee-AH-to) Pronounced.

Proper The portions of the Roman Catholic Mass that vary depending on the specific occasion or time of year. See *Mass* and *Ordinary*.

Proportional notation A system of notation in which notes are visually lengthened or shortened depending upon their relative duration, often used for music that is measured in seconds, rather than traditional meters.

Proposta (It., pro-POS-tah)   Subject, or theme of a fugue.

Psalm   1. One of the 150 sacred song texts from the Biblical book of Psalms. 2. A musical setting of one of these texts.

Psalmody (SAHL-mo-dee)   The technique of singing psalms in a sacred service.

Psalter   A book containing the psalms and other devotional materials, often in musical settings; the Bay Psalm Book (1640) was the first book printed in the American colonies.

Psaltery   A stringed instrument much used by the Hebrews in ancient times, most likely an ancestor of the harp or zither families.

Pulgar (Sp., pool-GAR)   The thumb.

Pull-off   The technique of pulling off a finger stopping a string that is already vibrating; used on both bowed and plucked string instruments for grace notes, trills, and tremolos.

Pulse   A series of regular beats.

Pulse wave   A non-sinusoidal waveform that alternates irregularly between two levels; also known as a rectangular wave.

Pult (Ger., poolt)   See *Desk*.

Punk rock   A form of popular music in the 1970's, known for stripped-down instrumentation, fast tempos, and unsophisticated techniques.

Punta (It., POON-tah)   The point, the top; also a thrust, or push.

Purfling   Decorative inlaid strips of wood or abalone shell placed on the top (and sometimes bottom) plate of a stringed instrument.

PV, PVG   See *Piano score*.

Pythagorean scale   A logarithmic scale, doubling at each octave, in which string lengths correspond to the harmonic ratio of their pitches.

Pythagorean tuning   The system of tuning musical frequencies to emphasize the ratio of 3:2, or a perfect fifth. Devised by Pythagoras, it is the oldest method for tuning the chromatic scale.

Quadrat (Ger., quah-DRAHT)   Natural, ♮.

Quadrille (Fr., kah-DREEL)   A French dance, or set of five consecutive dance movements. Generally in 6/8 or 2/4 rhythm.

Quadruple counterpoint   See *Counterpoint, quadruple.*

Quadruple meter   A meter with four beats per measure.

Quadruplet   Four notes played in the space of three. Also see *Tuplet.*

Quality   1. The chromatic inflection of an interval or chord, signified with words such as major, minor, augmented and diminished. 2. The timbre of an instrument, often called tone quality.

Quantize   In MIDI sequencing, to rhythmically align selected notes to a specific value.

Quartal harmony   A harmonic technique utilizing vertical stacks of fourths, usually perfect fourths.

Quarter note   A note whose value is one-quarter of a whole note.

Quarter rest   A pause equal in duration to a quarter note.

Quarter-tone   A pitch whose frequency falls exactly halfway between two semitones.

Quartet, Quartett (Ger., quahr-TET) **Quartetto** (It., quahr-TET-to)   A composition for four performers, or a group of four performers.

Quasi (It., KWAH-zi)   In the manner of, in the style of, or somewhat.

Quaver (Eng., KWAY-vur)   The British term for eighth note.

Quickstep   A lively march, generally in duple meter.

Quieto (It., kwee-AY-to)   Quiet, calm, serene.

Quint (Lat., kwint) **Quinta** (It., KWIN-tah)   1. A fifth. 2. The name of an organ stop sounding a fifth (or twelfth) above the foundation stops.

Quintadena   An organ stop. See *Quintaton*.

Quintal harmony   A harmonic technique utilizing vertical stacks of fifths, usually perfect fifths.

Quintaton (Ger., quin-tah-TON)   A manual organ stop of eight-foot tone; a stopped diapason of rather small scale producing the twelfth, as well as the ground tone; it also occurs as a pedal-stop of 32- and 16-foot tone.

Quintet   A composition for five performers, or a group of five performers.

Qui tollis (Lat., quee TO-lis)   A part of the Gloria in the Mass.

Quintuple meter   An asymmetrical meter containing five beats per measure; often conducted as two beats plus three beats, or vice versa.

Quintuplet   Five notes played in the space of one beat or an otherwise-defined duration. Also see *Tuplet*.

Quodlibet (Lat., KWAHD-li-bet)   A light-hearted composition combining several melodies, often popular tunes, in counterpoint.

R   1. Right hand. In piano music, notes to be played with the right hand are sometimes written with an R over them. 2. *Ripieno*. 3. *Responsorium* in Catholic church music. 4. In French organ-music, "R" stands for *clavier de récit* (swell manual).

Rabbia (It., RAH-bee-ah)   Rage, fury, madness.

Rackett   A double-reed instrument used in the Renaissance and Baroque periods, consisting of a relatively small wooden cylinder with nine inter-connected chambers inside and finger holes in various places outside; it has a range similar to a Baroque bassoon, but has a softer sound.

Raddolcendo (It., rah-dol-CHEN-do) **Raddolcente** (It., rah-dol-CHEN-te)   With increasing softness; becoming softer by degrees;

gentler and calmer.

Raga 1. The melodic modes used in classical Indian music. 2. A set of rules for playing melodies with these modes.

Raganella (It., ra-ga-NE-la) See *Ratchet*.

Ragtime A style of instrumental music popular around the turn of the 20th century, combining the instruments, style, and form of band marches with the syncopations of African music. The term "rag" comes from the ragged (or syncopated) rhythm.

Rallentando (It., rah-len-TAHN-do) Gradually slowing; synonymous with ritardando.

R&B See *Rhythm and blues*.

Range The distance between the highest and lowest notes of a melody, or the compass of an instrument or voice.

Rap The technique of rhythmic chanting, most typically of urban-oriented couplets, over heavy rhythms, often with heavily produced percussion, pitched music, and samples of other music. Rap may be considered a musical development of streetcorner "dozens."

Rapidamente (It., rah-pee-dah-MEN-te) Rapidly.

Rasch (Ger., rahsh) Swift, spirited.

Rasgueado (Sp., rahz-gue-AH-do) A style of strumming in Flamenco guitar technique using the back of the fingernails in sequence for a rapid effect.

Ratamacue (RAT-a-mah-kyoo) A drum rudiment involving drag grace notes in the first hand, alternating triplet sixteenth notes starting with the second hand, and an accented eighth note with the first hand. This pattern then repeats, starting with the other hand.

Ratchet A percussion instrument consisting of a thin wooden tongue resting against a wooden wheel with teeth; as a crank is turned, the wheel rapidly scrapes against the tongue, creating a loud rattling sound.

Rattenuto (It., raht-te-NOO-to) See *Trattenuto*.

Rattle An ancient percussion instrument consisting of a hollow body filled with small solid objects.

Re (Lat., re) In many countries, the note D; in solfège, the second note of the scale.

Real answer In a fugue, an answer that transposes the entire subject up a perfect fifth or down a perfect fourth. Also see *Tonal answer*.

Realization The technique of improvising an accompaniment based on a bass line and figured bass symbols.

Rebab (Arabic, reh-BAHB) An ancient Arabic instrument consisting of a wooden body with skin stretched over the top, a thick neck, and three or four strings that may be plucked or bowed; spread through Islamic trading routes, rebabs can be found in traditional music from Spain to

Indonesia.

Rebec   A Medieval ancestor of the modern violin, of Arab-Islamic origin, with a wooden body and three bowed strings.

Recapitulation   The third and final section of a sonata-allegro form, in which all themes are traditionally restated in the home key.

Recessional   Music intended for a gradual exit out of the performance space; the entrants may be officiants of the concluded event, or the musicians themselves.

Recht (Ger., rekht)   Right.

Recital   A performance of music, often in a more intimate setting than a concert, featuring one soloist.

Recitative (re-si-tah-TEEV)   A declamatory style of singing, found in operas, oratorios, and cantatas. *Recitativo secco* (or "dry" recitative) is mostly syllabic and traditionally accompanied by continuo alone, while *recitative accompagnato* utilizes the full orchestra and is more melismatic.

Recorder   1. An end-blown flute of wood or plastic, using air directed against a thin lip to produce its tone. 2. See *Tape recorder.*

Redowa (Cz., RED-o-wah)   A Bohemian dance in alternating duple and triple meter.

Reduction   See *Piano Reduction.*

Reed   Thin strips of cane, wood, or metal which, when set in vibration by a current of air, produce a musical sound. Also see below.

Reed, double   Two reeds vibrating against eachother, used in oboes and bassoons. Capped reed instruments, such as bagpipes, crumhorns, and shawms, have a tube-shaped cap around the reeds to direct the flow of air in place of the lips.

Reed fifth; Reed nasat   A stopped-quint register in an organ, the stopper of which has a hole or tube in it.

Reed, free   A reed tuned to one pitch and fitted in an airway, such as the reeds in an accordion, organ, or Chinese sheng.

Reed organ   A small organ, equipped with a foot-operated bellows, designed for use in the home. The harmonium uses outward air pressure to activate the reeds, while the melodeon (or American reed organ) uses suction to pull air through the reeds.

Reed, single   A wide reed with tapered top, fitted to a mouthpiece against which it vibrates. Single reeds are found on clarinets and saxophones.

Reed stops   The stops in an organ whose tone is produced by the wind having to pass against a reed placed at the bottom of the pipe, putting the tongue into vibration.

Reel   A lively Scottish and Irish dance, most often in quadruple meter; originally the term Rhay, or Reel, was applied to a very ancient English dance, called the Hay.

Refrain   The repeating portion of a song. Also see *Burden.*

Regal   1. A small, portable reed organ of the late Middle Ages.   2. A German term for reed stops on an organ, especially the vox humana.

Reggae   A style of popular music originating in Jamaica, with a relaxed tempo and strong offbeats.

Register   1. The stops, or rows of pipes in an organ.   2. The high, low, or middle divisions of a voice or instrument.   3. The compass of a voice or instrument.

Registering; Registration   The management of the stops in an organ, either by hand or automatically.

Related   A term applied to those chords, modes or keys, which, by reason of their affinity and close relation of some of their component sounds, allow an easy and natural transition from one to the other.

Relative keys   Major and minor keys that share the same key signature, for example C major and A minor.

Relative pitch   The ability of a musician to determine the intervals between given notes.

Religiosamente (It., re-lee-jee-o-zah-MEN-te) **Religioso** (It., re-lee-jee-O-zo)   Religiously; solemnly; in a devout manner.

Remote keys   Those keys whose scales have few tones in common, for example the key of C and the key of Db.

Renaissance   From the French word for rebirth, a historical and artistic period, often dated from the Fall of Constantinople in 1453 to the beginning of the 17th century.

Repeat   A character indicating that certain measures or passages are to be sung or played twice. Written:

See also *Da Capo* and *Dal Segno*.

Replica (It., REH-plee-kah)   Repetition of a section of music.

Replicazione (It., ree-plee-kah-tsee-O-ne)   Repetition.

Reprise (Fr., ruh-preez)   In a musical work, the return of opening or early material at a later point; the term is often used for the return of an earlier song in a musical.

Requiem (Lat., RE-kwee-em)   A Mass, or musical service, for the dead. It traditionally contains the following sections: Requiem aeternam, Kyrie, Dies irae, Domine Jesu Christe, Sanctus, Benedictus, Agnus Dei, and Lux aeterna.

Resolution   The movement of music from dissonance to consonance.

Resonance   The ability of a performance space or instrument to boost the amplitude of certain frequencies.

Resonator   Devices added to some string and melodic percussion instruments to increase their amplitude.

Resonator guitar A type of guitar with one or more cone-shaped metal resonators on its belly.

Response 1. The answer given by the group following the leader in a call and response song. 2. In a fugue, the response is the repetition of the given subject by another part.

Responsorial A traditional call and response setting in Christian liturgy.

Rest 1. A measured silence. 2. The notated character indicating a specific duration of silence; a table of notated rests appears on page 4.

Retardation 1. Slackening or retarding the time. 2. Delayed ascent of a harmonic voice, the reverse of suspension.

Retrograde In twelve-tone serialism, the reversed ordering of the tone row.

Réveille (Fr., ray-vay-ye, Eng., RE-vuh-lee) Awakening, a military morning signal.

Reverb, reverberation The reflection and delay of a sound by various surfaces in a performance space; also, the replication of this effect through signal processing.

Reverse motion Imitation by contrary motion, in which the ascending intervals are changed into descending and vice versa.

R.H. Short for "right hand."

Rhapsody (Eng., RAP-so-dee) A free, ecstatic composition.

Rhodes piano See *Fender Rhodes*

Rhythm The variation of sounds by length and accentuation; in Western music, rhythm is traditionally the division of meters into various-sized portions of sound and silence.

Rhythm and blues Various styles of African-American popular music since 1948, when it replaced the term "race recordings"; over the years, R&B has included such styles as jump blues, gospel, funk, soul, and hip-hop.

Rhythm section The group of instruments in a jazz or popular music band that establishes the rhythmic and harmonic structure of each piece or song; this can include drumset, bass, piano, and guitar.

Ribs The side pieces of a bowed string instrument.

Ricercar, ricercare (It., ree-cher-KAHR, ree-cher-KAH-re) Literally, to search out or research; an instrumental composition of the late Renaissance and early Baroque, often considered a predecessor of the fugue.

Ricochet 1. The rebound of a drumstick or mallet off the surface of a percussion instrument. 2. A method of bowing in which the bow bounces off the string.

Ride cymbal A suspended cymbal, often found on a drumset, most often used for a steady rhythmic background pattern.

Riff A memorable, "catchy" phrase or ostinato pattern played by the

rhythm section in a jazz or popular music band; the pattern may be melodic, harmonic, or rhythmic.

Rigaudon (Fr., ree-go-don)   A lively French dance in duple or quadruple meter.

Rigore (It., ree-GO-re)   Rigor, strictness, usually referring to tempo.

Rigoroso (It., ree-go-RO-zo)   Rigorous, exact, strict.

Rinforzando (It., rin-for-TSAHN-do)   **Rinforzato** (It., rin-for-TSAH-to)   **Rinforzo** (It., rin-FOR-tso)   Strengthened; reinforced; a reinforcement of tone, or expression; indicating that either a single note or chord, or several notes, are to be played with emphasis, although not with the suddenness of a sforzando.

Ripieno (It., ree-pee-AY-no)   Tutti; a full mass of instruments as contrasted against the solo or principal instrument in each group.

Riposato (It., ree-po-ZAH-to)   Rested.

Riposo (It., ree-PO-so)   Rest.

Risoluto (It., ree-zo-LOO-to)   Resolved, resolute, bold.

Risonare (It., ree-zo-NAH-re)   To resound; to ring, or echo.

Risvegliato (It., rees-vayl-yee-ah-to)   Awakened, reanimated.

Ritardando (It., ree-tahr-DAHN-do)   Retarding; delaying the tempo gradually. Note the familiar ritard. is an abbreviation of this word. Ritardando is synonymous with rallentando.

Ritenuto (It., ree-te-NOO-to)   Detained; slower; kept back. Ritenuto indicates a more sudden change than ritardando.

Ritmico (It., REET-mee-ko)   Rhythmic.

Ritmo (It., REET-mo)   Rhythm, cadence, measure.

Ritornello (It., ree-tor-NEL-lo)   **Ritournelle** (Fr., ree-toor-nel)   A recurring instrumental passage played by the full orchestra, or *tutti*, in the first or last movement of a Baroque concerto.

Road map   A slang term referring to music notation involving many repeats and jumps to repeated sections, often involving segno and coda signs.

Rock, rock 'n' roll   A popular music genre that evolved from the jump blues and country music of the late 1940's; rock has progressed through many different styles and subgenres in the decades since its inception.

Rocksteady   A type of Jamaican dance music popular in the mid-1960's, evolving into reggae.

Rococo (Fr., ro-ko-KO, ro-KO-ko)   An artistic and musical movement of late Baroque, emphasizing lavish ornamentation. Also see *Style galant*.

Rohr-flöte (Ger., ROR-FLE[R]-te)   Reed-flute; a stopped diapason in an organ.

Rohr-quint (Ger., ROR-quint)   Reed-fifth; an organ stop, sounding the fifth above the diapasons.

Roll   See *Drum roll* or *Piano roll.*

Rolled chord   See *Arpeggio.*

Romance (Fr., ro-mahns) **Romanza** (It., ro-MAHN-tsah) **Romanze** (Ger., ro-MAHN-tse)   Formerly the name given to the long lyric tales sung by Medieval minstrels; now a term applied to an delicate and romantic composition with irregular form.

Roman school   A group of sacred composers in Rome during the late Renaissance and early Baroque.

Romantic period   An artistically diverse musical era, lasting from ca. 1820 to 1900, in which composers generally experimented with Classical forms, incorporated mystical and exotic themes, and utilized a highly expressive aesthetic. Personal expression and extramusical reference are typical of Romanticism.

Ronde (Fr., rond)   See *Whole note.*

Rondeau (Fr., ron-DO)   One of the French formes fixes of the late Middle Ages and early Renaissance, featuring rigid rules for the repetition of verse, refrain, and music. Also see *Formes fixes, Ballade,* and *Virelai.*

Rondo   A composition, vocal or instrumental, consisting of one prominent theme which reappears multiple times in alternation with other contrasting themes.

Root   The fundamental note of a chord.

Rosin   A block of solidified resin, frequently with additives, rubbed on the hairs of violin bows for a better grip on the strings.

Rotary valve   A valve directing the flow of air through a rotating passage, found on horns and some trumpets, trombones, and tubas.

Rototoms   Drums consisting of a single head in a metal frame; the pitch can be adjusted by rotating the frame.

Roulade (Fr., roo-lahd)   A florid vocal passage.

Round   A species of canon that can be reapeated *ad infinitum*, often in three or more parts imitating at the unison or octave; also called a perpetual canon.

Rounded binary   A predecessor to Sonata-Allegro form in which the opening material returns after a section of contrasting material, often represented as ABA; it differs from Ternary form in that the B section may not contain sharply contrasting material and is too inconclusive to stand on its own.

Roundelay, rondelet (Fr., ron-du-lay)   A short French poem or song with a regularly recurring refrain.

Row   See *Tone row.*

Rubato (It., roo-BAH-to)   Robbed or stolen time; irregular time; meaning a slight deviation to give more expression by retarding one note, and quickening another, but so that the time of each measure is not altered as a whole.

Rudiments   A common set of rhythmic patterns considered to be the basic vocabulary of drum technique. Also see *Drum roll*, *Paradiddle*, and *Ratamacue*.

Ruhig (Ger., ROO-ish)   Quiet.

Rumba   A moderato Cuban dance with Spanish and African influences.

Run   A rapid flight of notes introduced as an embellishment; a roulade.

Russian Five   The common English name of the *Moguchaya Kuchka* ("Mighty Little Handful"), a group of five Russian composers who wrote in a strongly nationalistic style in the late 19th century. The group consisted of Balakirev, Borodin, Cui, Mussorgsky, and Rimsky-Korsakov.

Rustico (It., ROOS-tee-ko)   Rural, rustic.

S   Abbreviation for *Segno*, *Sinistra*, *Subito*, *Soprano*, *Sul*, or *Senza*.

Sackbut   The Medieval ancestor of the modern trombone.

Sacred   Words or music intended for devotion.

Saddle   A small wooden piece on string instruments used to elevate the tailpiece.

Saite (Ger., ZIGH-te)   A string of a musical instrument.

Salcional (Fr., sal-see-o-nahl) **Salicet** (Fr., sah-lee-say) **Salicional** (sah-lee-see-o-NAHL)   An 8- or 16-foot organ stop of small scale and reedy tone.

Salsa   A style of Latin music and dance, developed in the 1960's and 1970's, with Puerto Rican and Cuban influences.

Saltando (It., sahl-TAHN-do)   Skipping the bow upon the strings.

Saltarella (It., sahl-tah-REL-lah)   A rapid Italian dance, skipping in character, usually in 6/8.

Samba   A Brazilian dance style, incorporating Portuguese harmonies and instruments with central African rhythms and dance steps.

Samisen (Jap., SAH-mee-sen)   See *Shamisen*.

Sampling   1. The technique of converting a continuous (analog) audio signal into a discrete (digital) signal. 2. The technique of incorporating pre-recorded sounds into a piece of music.

Sampler   A type of synthesizer that creates and plays digital samples of pre-recorded sounds, as opposed to an analog synthesizer.

Sämtlich (Ger., ZEMT-leesh)   Complete; as in complete works.

Sanctus (Lat., SANK-tus)   "Holy"; a principal movement of the Mass.

Sanft (Ger., zahnft)   Soft, mild, smooth; "mit sanften stimmen" means with soft stops.

Sans (Fr., sahn)   Without.

Sanza (SAHN-zah)   See *Kalimba* and *Mbira*.

Sanxian (Chin., sahn-shiahn)   A plucked, fretless lute, used in traditional Chinese music, with 3 strings and a body traditionally covered in snakeskin.

Saraband, Sarabande   A slow dance in triple meter, originating in Renaissance-era Spain; the dance has a characteristic rhythm of a quarter note followed by a half note.

Sarangi (Hin., sah-RAHN-jee)   A bowed string instrument used in traditional Indian music, consisting of a box-shaped body, three bowed strings, and approximately 35 sympathetic strings.

Sarrusophone   A brass instrument named after the Parisian bandmaster Sarrus, with a double reed like the oboe and bassoon. It resembles the saxophone, and is made in various pitches.

SATB   Shorthand for "Soprano, Alto, Tenor, and Bass," the basic voice parts of a mixed choir.

Satz (Ger., zahts)   Phrase.

Sautillé (Fr., so-tee-YAY)   Lightly bouncing the bow upon the string on a down-bow stroke.

Saw   See *Musical saw*.

Sawtooth wave   A non-sinusoidal waveform containing both odd and even harmonics; the tone is sharp and bright.

Sax-horns   See *Saxophone*.

Saxophone   A wind instrument invented in 1842 by Adolphe Sax, consisting of a conical brass tube, key mechanism based on the Boehm system, and a single-reed mouthpiece similar to that of the clarinet, to which it is closely allied. Saxophones are made in many sizes. The tone, while penetrating, is at the same time mellow and veiled in quality. They are most frequently used in wind and jazz ensembles, but also are used in orchestral settings and chamber and recital music.

Scale   1. A collection of notes arranged in ascending and descending order from a selected starting pitch. The most commonly-used scales are the diatonic scales, seven-note scales employing various patterns of half and whole steps. This includes the major scale, minor scale, and modes. Also see *Chromatic scale, Major scale, Minor scale, Mode, Pentatonic scale,* and *Whole-tone scale*. 2. In pipe organs, scale is the ratio between the length and width of the pipes. 3. In piano, scale is the ratio between length and thickness of strings and method of stringing.

Scale degrees   The component notes of a scale, often labeled by their location and function in the scale (supertonic, mediant, dominant, etc.); they may also be identified by numbers or solfege syllables.

Scat   A style of improvised vocal solo in jazz involving nonsense syllables and complicated musical lines that are instrumental in style.

Scena (It., SHAY-na)   The scena is the largest and most brilliant vocal solo form. It generally consists of recitative, cavatina and aria. It most often forms part of an opera, but it may be an independent composition.

Scenario A prose description of the plot and characters in an opera, oratorio, or other dramatic work.

Schalkhaft (Ger., SHAHLK-hahft) Roguish, playful.

Schalmei, schalmey (SHAL-mee) See *Shawm*.

Scherzando (It., sker-TSAHN-do) **Scherzhaft** (Ger., SHERTS-hahft) Playful, lively, sportive, merry.

Scherzo (It., SKER-tso) 1. Literally meaning "joke," a piece of a lively, sportive character, and marked, animated rhythm. 2. An inner movement in a symphony, from Beethoven onward, replacing the role of minuet in the symphonies of Haydn and Mozart. Scherzo movements are most often in triple meter and ternary form, with a trio as the B section.

Schietto (It., skee-E-to) Simple, plain, neat.

Schleppend (Ger., SHLE-pend) Dragging.

Schlicht (Ger., shleesht) Homely, plain.

Schluss (Ger., shloos) The end; conclusion.

Schmachtend (Ger., SHMAHKH-tend) Languishing.

Schmaltz (Yiddish, shmahlts) An slang term for overly sentimental music; the word literally describes rendered fat, especially from poultry.

Schmerzhaft (Ger., SHMERTS-hahft) Dolorous, sorrowful.

Schnell (Ger., shnell) Quick, rapid.

Schneller (Ger., SHNE-ler) More quickly; faster.

Schola cantorum (Lat., SKO-lah kahn-TO-room) 1. Literally, "school of singing"; the highly-trained papal choir specializing in plainchant during the Middle Ages. 2. A Parisian music academy founded at the end of the 19th century by Vincent D'Indy, Alexandre Guilmant, and Charles Bordes, in competition with the Paris Conservatory.

Schottische (Ger., SHOT-teesh) A moderate dance in duple meter, similar to a polka, with German origin; it was particularly popular in America during the early 20th century, when it was combined with ragtime music.

Schreiend (Ger., SHRIGH-end) Acute, shrill, screaming.

Schwach (Ger., shvahkh) Weak, soft.

Schweige (Ger., SHVIGH-ge) A rest.

Schwer (Ger., shvayr) Heavily, ponderously.

Schwermüthig (Ger., shvayr-MÜ-tish) In a pensive, melancholy, style.

Scioltezza (It., shee-ol-TE-tsah) Freedom, ease, lightness.

Sciolto (It., shee-OL-to) Free, light.

Scoop A jazz ornament, consisting of a short slide up to the written note.

Scordatura (It., skor-dah-TOO-rah) An altered tuning scheme for string instruments.

Score (Ger., *Partitur,* Fr., *Partition;* It., *Partitura.*) The written representation of a musical work, including all players' parts.

Score, condensed An abbreviated score typically in three staves, often used in band publications.

Score, full A complete score of all the parts of a composition, either vocal, instrumental, or both; each part is most often placed on a separate staff.

Score in C A score in which the notes for all transposing instruments have been written as they sound, in concert pitch.

Score, instrumental A score in which the instrumental parts are given in full.

Score, miniature A full score published in a small physical size for convenience and affordability, generally intended for study rather than performance. While the term "study score" only implies being smaller than optimum performance size, the term "miniature" describes scores that are quite small.

Score, piano-vocal See *Piano-vocal score.*

Score, short An abbreviated score of three or four staves, often sketched by composers prior to orchestrating a work.

Score, study A smaller, less-expensive orchestral score designed for study rather than conducting.

Score, transposed A score in which the notes for all transposing instruments remain transposed, as the performers see them.

Score, vocal See *Piano-vocal score.*

Scoring See *Orchestration.*

Scorrendo (It., sko-REN-do) Portamento, sliding from pitch to pitch.

Scotch scale An archaic term referring to the use of the pentatonic scale in Scottish and Irish folk melodies. Also see *Pentatonic scale.*

Scotch snap A rhythm common to Scottish music, especially the *Strathspey,* where a quarter note or beat is divided unevenly into a sixteenth followed by a dotted eighth note.

Scozzese (It., sko-TSE-ze) In the Scottish style.

Scraped instruments Percussion instruments that produce sound by scraping their components together. Also see *Güiro, Ratchet,* and *Washboard.*

Screw A metal knob at the frog end of a bow, serving to adjust the tension of the bow hair as it is turned.

Scroll The decorative carved spiral of wood at the top of the pegbox on a string instrument.

Scruggs style A three-fingered style of banjo picking popular in Bluegrass music; named after Earl Scruggs.

Sdegno (It., SDEN-yo) Anger, wrath, passion.

Se (It., say) If; as.

Sec (Fr., sek) **Secco** (It., SE-ko) Dry, detached.

Second An interval measuring two diatonic degrees, also called a step.

Secondary dominant In tonal music, a chord which has been chromatically altered to serve as a dominant in order to temporarily tonicize, and thereby emphasize, a note other than the tonic.

Secondo (IT., seh-KON-do) 1. The secondary player. 2. The lower player in a four-hand piano composition. Also see *Primo*.

Second Viennese school A term denoting Arnold Schoenberg and his pupils, most notably Alban Berg and Anton Webern; the music of this early 20th-century group exhibited atonal expressionism, organized by Schoenberg's system of 12-tone serialism.

Section 1. A discernable musical unit, with a certain degree of thematic and/or harmonic closure, within a larger movement or work; often represented by capital letters in descriptions of form. 2. A specified group of players in an ensemble, as in "flute section," or "second violin section."

Secular music Music which is intended for the concert hall or theatre; an expression used in contrast to sacred music.

Segno (It., SEN-yo) The symbol 𝄋 used as a landmark to jump back to. See *Dal Segno*.

Segue (It., SAY-gway) Continue immediately to the next movement.

Seguidilla (Sp., say-gwee-DEE-yah) A popular Spanish dance in triple meter.

Sehnsucht (Ger., ZAIN-zookht) Desire, longing, ardor, fervor.

Sehr (Ger., zair) Very, much, extremely.

Sel-sync Short for "selective-synchronous recording"; one of the earliest forms of multi-track recording, developed in the mid-1950's by Les Paul and the Ampex company.

Semibreve The British term for a whole note.

Semiquaver The British term for a sixteenth note.

Semitone A half-tone, or half-step.

Semplice (It., SEM-plee-che) Simple, pure, plain.

Sempre (It., SEM-pre) Always; often used to show that a dynamic or articulation continues for a long time.

Sensibilità (It., sen-see-bee-lee-TAH) Sensibility, expression, feeling.

Sentimento (It., sen-tee-MEN-to) Feeling; sentiment.

Senza (It., sen-tsah) Without.

Septet A composition for seven performers, or a group of seven performers.

Septolet See *Septuplet*.

Septuplet Seven notes played in the space of one beat or otherwise-defined duration. Also see *Tuplet*.

Sequence 1. A motivic or harmonic passage repeated and transposed multiple times, serving as an important component in thematic development and fugal episodes. 2. A chant traditionally sung prior to the reading of the Gospel in the Roman Catholic mass.

Sequencer   A device or software application designed to store and play back computer-generated music.

Sérénade (Fr., say-ray-nahd) **Serenata** (It., say-ray-NAH-ta) 1. A multi-movement work for an instrumental ensemble, similar to a divertimento. 2. A piece performed in a person's honor, traditionally under the window of the person to be entertained.

Sereno (It., say-RAY-no)   Serene, calm, tranquil, cheerful.

Serial music   Music whose pitches have been organized into an ordered series, or row, prior to its composition. Integral serialism involves the creation of rows for additional musical elements, such as rhythm, dynamics, and/or articulation. Also see *Twelve-tone technique*.

Serio (It., SAY-ree-o) **Serioso** (It., say-ree-O-zo)   Serious, grave; in a serious, sedate style.

Serpent   1. An ancient bass wind instrument, consisting of a metal mouthpiece and winding wooden body with finger holes and metal keys. Due to its difficulty and coarse tone quality, it was eventually replaced by first the ophicleide and then the tuba. 2. A reed-stop in an organ.

SESAC (SEE-sak)   Society of European Stage Authors and Composers; a performance-rights organization similar to ASCAP and BMI.

Sesquialtera (Lat., ses-qui-AL-te-rah)   An organ stop, comprising two or more ranks of pipes of acute pitch.

Sestet, sestetto (It., ses-TET, ses-TET-o)   See *Sextet*.

Set theory   A theory that defines collections of pitches (see *Pitch-class set*) and the various manipulations of those pitches through transposition, inversion, multiplication, and other means. This theory also describes the intervallic content and relative dissonance of a musical work through a numerical array called the interval vector. First mentioned by Howard Hanson in his book *Harmonic Materials of Modern Music* (1960), set theory was later codified by theorist Allen Forte in *The Structure of Atonal Music* (1973).

Seven-string guitar   A general term for a guitar with seven, rather than six, strings; Russian and Brazillian guitars traditionally have seven strings.

Seventeenth   An organ stop. See *Tierce*.

Seventh   1. An interval measuring seven diatonic degrees. 2. A note within a chord that is seven scale steps above the root.

Seventh chord   A chord composed of a root, third, fifth and seventh.

Severità (It., say-vay-ree-TAH)   Severity, strictness.

Sextet   A composition for six performers, or a group of six performers.

Sextolet   See *Sextuplet*.

Sextuplet   Six notes played in the space of one beat or an otherwise-defined duration. Also see *Tuplet*.

Sfogato (It., sfo-GAH-to)   A very high soprano or a direction to sing in a light manner.

Sforzando (It., sfor-TSAHN-do)   **Sforzato** (It., sfor-TSAH-to) Literally, "forced"; one particular chord, or note, is to be played with force and emphasis.

Sfumato (It., sfoo-MAH-to)   Vanishing, very lightly.

Shake   See *Trill*.

Shaker   An family of percussion instruments consisting of either a hollow body filled with small solid objects (such as a rattle), or a body on which loosely fixed objects collide (such as a tambourine).

Shakuhachi   A Japanese end-blown flute, traditionally made out of bamboo.

Shamisen (Jap., SHAM-i-sen)   A traditional three-stringed Japanese instrument, consisting of a skin-covered body and narrow, fretless neck. It is played with an ivory or wooden plectrum called a bachi.

Shanty   A worksong traditionally sung by sailors, particularly those from Europe and the Americas, in the 19th and early 20th centuries.

Shape-note   1. Sacred music in which each diatonic note is given a uniquely-shaped notehead, to facilitate performance by congregations who cannot read traditional notation. 2. The traditional style of singing shape-note music, especially popular in the American South.

Sharp   The sign # which, occurring either before a note or in the key signature, raises the pitch of a tone one chromatic half-step. See *Accidentals* and *Chromatic*.

Sharp, double   See *Double sharp*.

Shawm   A double-reed wind instrument of the Middle Ages and Renaissance; the immediate predecessor of the modern oboe.

Sheet music   Written or printed music.

Sheng   In traditional Chinese music, a mouth-blown free reed instrument consisting of bamboo pipes inserted into a gourd.

Shift   On a string instrument, the change of position of the left hand on the fingerboard.

Shivaree   The traditional wedding-night serenade of the newly-wed couple by a raucous band of family, friends, and neighbors.

Shō   A mouth-blown free reed instrument of Japan, descended from the Chinese *Sheng*.

Shofar (Heb., SHO-far)   An ancient ceremonial instrument of the Jewish faith, constructed from the hollowed-out horn of a ram or kudu.

Shuffle rhythm   See *Swing time*.

Si (It., see)   See *Ti*.

Siciliana (It., see-chee-lee-AH-nah)   **Siciliano** (It., see-chee-lee-AH-no)
Sicilienne (Fr. si-sil-yen)   A dance of the Sicilian peasants; a graceful

movement of a slow, soothing, pastoral character in 6/8 or 12/8.

Side drum   The common military drum so-called from its hanging at the side of the drummer when played upon; in modern practice it is generally synonymous with snare drum.

Sideman   A musician playing as an extra supporting an established group or soloist.

Sight-reading, sight-singing   The technique of performing a piece of music without studying or practicing it in advance.

Signal   The representation of sound waves in an alternate medium, such as electric voltage, radio frequencies, or pulses of fiberoptic light.

Signal processor   A device or software application that modifies audio signals through filtering, delay, equalization, and other processes.

Signature   See *Key signature* and *Time signature*.

Signs   Any symbol used to modify the performance of written music. See the music symbols listed on pages 10 and 11.

Sim.   Abbreviation for simile, an instruction to continue the immediate pattern of articulations, dynamics, or other nuances.

Similar motion   Two musical lines progressing up or down in the same direction, with their intervallic distance varying from note to note.

Simple meter   Any meter in which each beat is divided into two equal parts.

Sin' al fine (It., SEEN ahl FEE-ne)   To the end; as far as the end.

Sincopa (It., SIN-ko-pah)   **Sincope** (It., SIN-ko-pe)   See *Syncopation*.

Sine wave   In music, the simplest and "purest" form of sound wave, with no overtones; tuning forks and vibrating crystal glasses are both close in tone quality to a sine wave.

Sinfonia (It., sin-fo-NEE-ah)   **Sinfonie** (Fr., san-fo-nee)   1. An Italian opera overture, the ancestor of the symphony. 2. A term used by Bach and other Baroque composers for an instrumental prelude.

Sinfonietta (It., seen-fo-NYE-tah)   A diminuitive of "symphony," used by composers and ensembles to connote a smaller length or instrumentation than a symphony.

Single   An individual popular song released as a recording, video, or internet download.

Single-coil pickup   A magnetic transducer used on electric guitars and basses.

Single-reed instrument   An instrument that produces sound through one vibrating reed fitted into a mouthpiece, such as a clarinet or saxophone.

Singspiel (Ger., ZING-shpeel)   A popular style of German opera with simple, folk-like melodies and spoken dialogue replacing recitative; it was most popular from the mid-18th to mid-19th centuries.

Sinistra (It., SEEN-ees-trah)   Left. *Mano sinistra*; left hand.

Sino (It., SEE-no) **Sin'** (It., seen)   To; as far as; until. *Con fuoco sin' al fine*; with spirit to the end.

Sistrum   An ancient Egyptian percussion instrument, consisting of a handle topped with a metal loop and crossbars. Thin loops of metal were placed on the crossbars, producing a metallic tinkling when the instrument was shaken.

Sitar   A plucked string instrument, with 6-7 playable strings and 11-16 sympathetic strings, used in traditional Hindustani music.

Six chord   A first inversion triad, so called because of its figured bass symbol.

Six-four chord   A second inversion triad, so called because of its figured bass symbol.

Six, Les   Six diverse French composers who joined together for performances and publications in the first half of the 20th century. This group, consisting of Auric, Durey, Honegger, Milhaud, Poulenc, and Taillefaire, had few style traits in common.

Sixteenth note   A note whose value is a sixteenth of a whole note.

Sixteenth rest   A pause equal in duration to a sixteenth note.

Sixth   An interval measuring six diatonic degrees.

Sixth chord   A term that can refer to a first inversion triad, or a triad with an added sixth degree.

Sixty-fourth note   A note whose value is a sixty-fourth of a whole note.

Sixty-fourth rest   A pause equal in duration to a sixty-fourth note.

Sizzle Cymbal   A suspended cymbal with loose rivets (or taped-on coins) around the edge adding an extra sizzling effect when struck.

Ska   A style of popular music originating in Jamaica in the late 1950's, combining the walking bass of American swing music with the strong offbeats of Caribbean calypso.

Skala (Ger., SKAH-lah)   Scale.

Skiffle   A folk music style with blues and country influences, popular in the United States in the early 20th century; it is similar to jug band music, but uses primarily homemade instruments. Skiffle enjoyed a revival in Great Britain during the 1950's and early 1960's, where it served as a precursor to British rock music.

Skip   A term applied to any note motion exceeding that of a whole step.

Skirl   The collective noun for bagpipers.

Slancio, con (It., kon SLAN-chee-o)   With vehemence; impetuously.

Slargando (It., slahr-GAHN-do)   Extending, enlarging; becoming gradually slower.

Slave   The term for a MIDI device that is controlled by another.

Sleigh bells   A percussion instrument consisting of tiny metal bells affixed to a wooden handle.

Slentando (It., slen-TAHN-do)   Relaxing the tempo; becoming gradually slower.

Slide   1. A movable tube in the trombone, pushed in and out to alter the pitch of the tones while playing.   2. A glissando or portamento in which the pitch slides.

Slide guitar   A style of guitar playing in which a metal rod is slid along the strings, rather than fretting with the fingers, also known as bottlenecking. When the guitar is held flat on the lap, it is referred to as Steel guitar or Lap guitar.

Slider   A control on a mixing console or other device that can be shifted up or down to modify a musical parameter such as volume.

Slide trumpet   A trumpet that alters its pitches with a slide, rather than valves; also known as the piccolo trombone.

Slit drum   A traditional drum in several world cultures, consisting of a hollow piece of wood in which one or more slits have been cut.

Slur   A curved line drawn over or under two or more notes, signifying that they are to be executed legato. The slur is also used in piano music to indicate melodic phrasing. In wind instruments, slurs indicate tonguing articulation.

Small octave   The name given in Germany to the notes included between C on the second space of the bass staff and the B above, these notes sometimes expressed by small letters, as *a, b, c, d,* etc.

Smaniante (It., smahn-ee-AHN-te) **Smaniato** (It., smah-nee-AH-to)
Smanioso (It., smah-nee-O-zo)   Furious; vehement.

Smear   See *Glissando.*

Smorzando (It., smor-TSAHN-do) **Smorzato** (It., smor-TSAH-to)
Extinguished; put out; suddenly dying away.

SMPTE (SIMP-tee)   The Society of Motion Picture and Television Engineers; SMPTE time code is used to synchronize music with video.

Snare drum   A small drum commonly used in orchestras and wind ensembles, so named on account of the snares or strings (of raw-hide and metal coils) drawn over its lower head. The snares may be set to "on" to give the characteristic extra resonance, or "off" to behave as a typical drum.

Soave (It., so-AH-ve)   Played in a gentle, soft and engaging style.

Sock cymbal   See *Hi-hat.*

Soft pedal   See *Pedal.*

Sol (Lat., sol)   In many countries, the note G; in solfège, the fifth note of the scale.

Solenne (It., so-LE-ne)   Solemn.

Solfaing   Singing a scale to the monosyllables applied by Guido, *ut, re,* *mi, fa, sol, la, si;* using *do* in place of *ut* and sometimes replacing *si* with *ti*. See *Guidonian syllables.*

Solfège (Fr., sol-fezh) **Solfeggio** (It., sol-FE-jee-o)   Exercises for the voice according to the rules of *solfaing.*

Solmization   See *Solfège.*

Solo   1. A composition for a single voice or instrument, either with or without accompaniment. 2. A passage for a single voice or instrument introduced in an ensemble composition. In a score, this term may indicate "one player" rather than the ensemble, or it may indicate the featured melody.

Son (Fr., son)   Sound.

Sonabile (It., so-NAH-bee-lee)   Sonorous, resonant.

Sonare (It., so-NAH-re)   To sound; to have a sound; to ring; to play upon.

Sonata (It., so-NAH-tah) **Sonate** (Fr., so-NAHT, Ger., so-NAH-te)
An instrumental composition, usually of three or four distinct movements, each with a unity and closure of its own, yet all related so as to form a unified whole. A traditional Classical sonata commonly begins with an allegro movement, sometimes preceded by a slow introduction. This is followed by a slow and/or minuet movement, and then concluded with a fast movement frequently in rondo form.

Sonata da camera, Sonata da chiesa   See *Trio sonata.*

Sonata form   One of the most important and popular forms of Classical-era music, also known as sonata-allegro form. Several themes that differ in key and style are first presented in an exposition; one or more of these themes are then explored in a development section that often breaks them into smaller motives and moves through several key centers. Tonal resolution of these themes takes place in a concluding recapitulation section. Sonata form was traditionally used for the opening movement of a multi-movement instrumental work.

Sonata rondo form   A hybrid form, utilizing the ABACABA structure of a 7-part rondo, but inserting a development section in the C section; it can also be seen as a Sonata form with additional reiterations of the primary theme. Sonata rondo form was explored in several pieces by Mozart, Haydn, Beethoven, and Schubert.

Sonatina (It., so-nah-TEE-nah) **Sonatine** (Fr., so-nah-teen)   A short, easy sonata, generally in two or three movements. The sonatina movement differs from the sonata-allegro in having no development, or middle section, being merely an exposition, followed by a recapitulation.

Song   1. (Ger., *Gesang;* Fr., *chant;* It., *canto.*) Vocal musical expression or utterance. 2. (Ger., *Lied;* Fr., *chanson;* It., *canzone.*) A lyrical poem set to music. Traditionally, a song deals with emotions, while a ballad tells a story. The text of a song is frequently set to music in one of two styles:

strophic form, in which the music is repeated nearly verbatim for each stanza, and through-composed (Durchkomponiert) style, in which each stanza receives separate musical treatment according to its contents.

Song cycle A group of songs intended to be performed together as one multi-movement composition.

Song forms The standard forms traditionally used in folk and popular songs; these forms include strophic, verse and chorus, AABA, and 12-bar blues.

Song plugger The name given to early 20th-century piano players hired by music stores to promote sheet music by playing songs on an upper floor of the store; generally, customers could also request a song in order to hear it before making a purchase.

Song position pointer MIDI data in a synthesizer or sequencer application that keeps track of elapsed 16th notes in a sequence; this serves as a way to keep time in devices that are not equipped with SMPTE or MIDI time code.

Sono (It., SO-no) Sound, tone.

Sonore (Fr., so-nor) **Sonoro** (It., so-NO-ro) Sonorous, harmonious, resonant.

Sopra (It., SO-prah) Above, upon, over, before. See *Super*.

Sopranino saxophone The smallest member of the standard saxophone family, pitched in E♭ an octave higher than an alto saxophone.

Soprano (It., so-PRAH-no) 1. The highest class of female voice. 2. A singer with this voice range, normally extending from middle C to the G or A above the treble staff. 2. A rarely-used C clef on the first line of the staff, as illustrated on page 4.

Soprano saxophone A small saxophone, pitched in B♭ an octave higher than a tenor saxophone.

Sordamente (It., sor-dah-MEN-te) 1. Softly, gently. 2. Damped, muffled.

Sordine (Fr., sor-DEEN), **Sordino** (It., sor-DEE-no) Mute. Also see *Con sordino* and *Senza sordino*.

Sospirando (It., sos-pee-RAHN-do) Sighing; very subdued; doleful.

Sostenuto (It., sos-te-NOO-to) Sustaining the tone; holding the notes for their full duration.

Sotto (It., SO-to) Under, below.

Sotto voce (It., SO-to VO-che) Softly; in a low voice; in an undertone.

Soubrette (Fr., soo-BRET) A stock character in comic opera, usually performed by young sopranos with light voices; the soubrette is a mischievous, gossipy, and frequently flirtatious character who often accompanies the ingénue.

Soul   A genre of popular music combining elements from gospel and rhythm and blues, soul was highly popular in the 1960's and 70's.

Soundboard   The part of a string instrument, frequently made out of wood, that aids in transmitting the vibrations of the strings to the air, thus increasing the intensity of the sound; also called the sounding board.

Sound hole   One or more openings in the top soundboard of a string instrument, enabling the sound from the back soundboard to project more easily; also see *F holes*.

Sound post   A small wooden prop within a bowed string instrument, nearly under the bridge; it not only maintains the tension, but also carries the vibrations from the front soundboard to the back, thus making the whole sound-box vibratory.

Sousaphone   A tuba made in such a shape as to circle the body and rest on the shoulder, for marching band use.

Space   Any location on a staff between two lines.

Spanish guitar   See *Classical guitar*.

Spasshaft (Ger., SPAHSS-hahft)   Sportively, playfully, merrily.

Species counterpoint   A style of counterpoint developed in the 16th century for pedagogical purposes; students write musical lines against a given cantus firmus, progressing through various contrapuntal techniques, or species. The intended objective is to develop the ability to write free counterpoint.

Spezzato (It., spe-TZAH-to)   Split, or divided.

Spianato (It., spee-ah-NAH-to)   Smooth, even; legato.

Spiccato (It., spee-KAH-to)   Separated, pointed, distinct, detached; in violin music it means that the notes are to be played with the point of the bow, in an "off the string" style.

Spike fiddle   See *Rebab*.

Spinet (Eng., SPIN-et)   A word used for small keyboard instruments.

Spinto   A term used for Soprano and Tenor voice types that fall between lyric and dramatic; spintos possess a bright, but powerful sound that can cut through Romantic orchestras at dramatic climaxes.

Spirito (It., SPEE-ree-to)   Spirit, life, energy.

Spiritual   Sacred vocal music originated by African-Americans during slavery; the lyrics most often refer to Judeo-Christian theology, especially the story of Moses freeing the Israelites from Egyptian slavery.

Spitz-flöte (Ger., spitz-FLE[R]-te) **Spitz-flute** (Eng.)   Pointed-flute; an organ stop with a soft, pleasing tone, the pipes of which are conical and pointed at the top.

Splash cymbal   A small cymbal on a drumkit with a relatively quick attack and decay, used for accents.

Spoons   A percussion instrument, consisting of two or more spoons beaten together, popular in American and Russian folk music; the American technique evolved from Irish bones playing.

Sprechgesang (Ger., SHPRECH-ge-zahng) A term applied to recitative techniques used in Romantic German opera, in which the articulation is speech-like; also used in the early 20th century to describe Schoenberg's technique of *Sprechstimme.*

Sprechstimme (Ger., SHPRECH-shti-me) An expressionist vocal technique, attributed to Schoenberg, which is a hybrid of singing and speech.

Springend (Ger., SHPRING-end) Bouncing the bow on a string instrument.

Square wave A non-sinusoidal waveform that alternates regularly between two levels.

Squillante (It., squeel-AHN-te) Clear, plain, sounding, ringing.

Stabat mater (Lat., STAH-bat MAH-ter) "The Mother stood." The first words of a Latin hymn on the Crucifixion.

Stabile (It., STAH-bee-le) Firm.

Staccato (It., stah-KAH-to) Detached; distinct; separated from each other.

Staccato marks Small dots or placed over or under notes, to indicate separation from surrounding notes. Wedge-shaped marks indicate greater separation than dots.

Staff Five horizontal lines, on and between which notes are written.

Stanchezza (It., stahn-KE-tza) Weariness.

Standard In jazz, a tune that has an enduring place in the repertoire and is widely performed and recorded.

Ständchen (Ger., STEND-shen) A serenade.

Stanza A unit of text, usually consisting of four lines, within a hymn, ballad, or other strophic vocal work.

Stark (Ger., shtahrk) Strong, loud, vigorous.

Steel drum A pitched percussion instrument made from a 55-gallon oil drum and tuned chromatically. It is used in traditional Caribbean music. With an origin in the island nation of Trinidad and Tobago, it is also known as steelpans or pans.

Steel guitar A guitar designed to be played with a steel rod, rather than fretting with the fingers; the term can designate a resonator guitar, a slide guitar console, or the technique of playing in this manner; it is also known as lap steel guitar or Hawaiian guitar.

Steel-string guitar Any guitar designed to be strung with metal strings, giving a louder and brighter sound than nylon strings.

Steg (Ger., shteg) The bridge of a violin.

Steigerung (Ger., SHTIGH-ge-roong) An increase.

Stem   The thin vertical line attached to noteheads; it is placed on the right when pointing up, and on the left when pointing down.

Stentato, Stentando   (It., sten-TAH-to, sten-TAHN-do)   Forced, heavy, labored.

Step   The progression from one degree on the staff to the next above or below; the unit for measuring intervals. The whole-step or simply step is equivalent to a major second (or tone) and the half-step to a minor second (or semi-tone).

Step entry   In MIDI sequencing, the technique of entering pitch and rhythm information one note at a time; also known as step-time mode.

Steso   (It., STE-so)   Stretched out; slower.

Stesso   (It.)   The same; *l'istesso tempo*, in the same time.

Stick   Slang for a conductor's baton.

Stick, Chapman   See *Chapman stick*.

Stile antico   (It., STEE-le ahn-TEE-ko)   A style of composing that is conscious of the historical precedents for the treatment of consonance and dissonance. This broad term has been used to refer to musical conservatism from the Renaissance through the 20th century.

Stile concitato   (It., STEE-le kon-chee-TAH-to)   A Baroque vocal style, attributed to Monteverdi, in which emotional agitation is represented through long trills and rapidly repeated notes.

Stile moderno   (It., STEE-le mo-DER-no)   A term used for early Baroque music, such as that by Caccini and Monteverdi, in which there is a relative freedom in the treatment of consonance and dissonance.

Stimme   (Ger., SHTI-me)   1. Voice, or sound. 2. A part in vocal or instrumental music. 3. An organ stop, or register.

Stimmung   (Ger., SHTIM-oong)   Tuning, tune, tone.

Stirato   (It., stee-RAH-to)   Slowing down; dragging.

Stop   1. A register, or row of pipes in an organ. Organ stops consist of two kinds, flue and reed stops. For specific kinds of organ stops, see below. 2. On a string instrument, it means the pressure of the finger upon the string to determine pitch. Also see *Double stop*.

Stop, flue   The flue stops are subdivided into principal, or cylindrical pipes of diapason style; gedackt (or covered) pipes, which are stopped at the end and give a hollow tone; flute work, which includes narrow pipes that do not sound a fundamental tone, stopped pipes with chimneys, and three- or four-sided pipes.

Stop, reed   Stops consisting of pipes upon the end of which are fixed thin, narrow plates of brass, which, being vibrated by the wind from the bellows, produce a reedy thickness of tone. Also see *Pipe*.

Stop, salcional   A variety of Dulciana stop.

Stop, sesquilatera   A stop resembling the mixture, running through the scale of the instrument, and consisting of three, four, and sometimes five, ranks of pipes, tuned in thirds, fifths, and eighths.

Stop, solo   A stop which may be drawn alone, or with one of the diapasons.

Stop, tierce   A stop tuned a major third higher than the fifteenth, and only employed in the full organ.

Stop, treble forte   A stop applied to a melodeon, or reed-organ, by means of which the treble part of the instrument may be increased in power, while the bass remains subdued.

Stop, tremolo   A contrivance, by means of which a tremulous effect is given to some of the registers of an organ.

Stop, trumpet   A stop with a tone imitative of a trumpet. In large organs it generally extends through the whole compass.

Stop, twelfth   A metallic stop tuned twelve notes above the diapason. This stop, on account of its tuning, is never used alone.

Stopped diapason   A stop whose bass pipes are made of wood, and whose pipes above middle C are also generally of wood. They are only half as long as those of the open diapason, and are stopped at the upper end with wooden stoppers, or plugs, which lower the pitch an octave and render the tone more soft and mellow than that of the open diapason.

Stops, compound   An assemblage of several pipes in an organ, three or more to each key, adding additional harmonics. Also see *Mixture stop.*

Stops, draw   See *Drawbars.*

Stops, mechanical   Mechanical stops are those which do not give a tone, but work some mechanism (for instance, couplers).

Stops, mutation   In an organ, the twelfth, tierce, and their octaves.

Stradivari   The name of a very superior make of string instrument (especially violin) named after Stradivarius, who made them at Cremona, Italy in the first part of the eighteenth century.

Straight eighths   The technique of playing eighth notes evenly, as opposed to *Swing time.*

Straight mute   A hollow, cone-shaped mute that fits into the bell of a brass instrument; this mute creates a nasal, often metallic, timbre.

Strain   A section of music, often in a march or rag, usually set off by a double bar.

Strascinato   (It., strah-shee-NAH-to)   Dragged along; played slowly.

Strat, Stratocaster   A model of electric guitar made by Fender.

Strathspey   A moderate Scottish dance, slower than the reel, and in duple meter; it is characterized by sixteenth notes alternating with dotted eighth notes. Also see *Scotch Snap.*

Street organ   See *Barrel organ.*

Strepitoso   (It., stre-pee-TO-zo)   Noisy, boisterous.

Stretta (It., STRE-tah)   A concluding passage, coda, or finale, taken in quicker time to enhance the effect.

Stretto (It., STRE-to)   1. Literally, narrow or close; formerly used to denote that the movement indicated was to be performed in a quick, concise style. 2. In fugue writing, that part where the subject and answer overlap one another. 3. With growing excitement, as a stringendo.

Stride   A technique in jazz piano playing, in which the left hand plays bass notes (often doubled) on beats one and three and chords on beats two and four.

Stridente (It., stree-DEN-te)   Sharp, shrill, acute.

String bass   See *Contrabass*.

String drum   A long wooden box with 3 double courses of strings tuned to play a drone when struck with a stick; also known as a Psalterium or Tambourin a chordes.

String instruments   Instruments whose sounds are produced by striking or plucking strings, or by the friction of a bow drawn across them.

Stringendo (It., streen-JEN-do)   Pressing; accelerating the tempo.

String quartet   A composition for four string instruments, most often two violins, viola, and violoncello, or the ensemble itself.

Strisciando (It., stree-shee-AHN-do)   Gliding; slurring; sliding smoothly from one note to another.

Stroh violin   A violin that uses metal resonators and one or more metal horns to project its sound; also known as a violinophone, it was popular in the early years of recording for its increased carrying power.

Strophic   See *Song*.

Strum   To run the fingers across several strings on an instrument.

Strumenti a fiati (It., stroo-MEN-tee ah fee-AH-ti)   Wind instruments.

Strumento (It., stroo-MEN-to)   Instrument.

Stück(en) (Ger., SHTÜCK [-en])   Piece(s).

Stücken (Ger., SHTÜK-en)   Pieces.

Studien (Ger. pl., SHTOO-dee-en)   Studies.

Studio musician   See *Sideman*.

Study score   See *Score, study*.

Stufe (Ger., SHTOO-fe)   Step, degree.

Sturm und Drang (Ger., shtoorm oont drahng)   Literally, "storm and yearning"; a musical and literary movement in the 1760s through 1780s, characterized by strong emotions and subjectivity.

Stürmisch (Ger., SHTÜR-meesh)   Stormy.

Style galant (Fr., steel gah-LAHNT)   A musical style, part of the Rococo movement, emphasizing lavishly ornamented chamber music.

Styrienne (Fr., stee-ree-en)   An air or slow movement in duple meter, often in minor.

Su (It., soo)   Above, upon.

Suavità (It., soo-wah-vee-TAH)   Suavity, sweetness, delicacy.

Sub (Lat., sub)   Under, below, beneath.

Sub-bass (Ger., soob-bahss), **Sous-bourdon** (Fr., soo boor-DON)
1. Literally, "underbass"; an organ register in the pedals, usually a double-stopped bass of 32- or 16-foot tone. 2. The ground bass; see *Chaconne*.

Subdominant   The fourth note of the diatonic scale.

Subito (It., SOO-bee-to)   Sudden; immediate.

Subject   The theme of a fugue or similar contrapuntal work.

Submediant   The sixth note of the diatonic scale.

Suboctave   An organ coupler producing the octave below.

Subprincipal   Literally, "under principal"; below the pedal-diapason pitch. In German organs this is a double open bass stop of 32-foot scale.

Subtonic   Literally, "under the tonic"; the label commonly given to the lowered seventh scale degree in minor scales.

Subtractive synthesis   The electronic creation of complex sound waves by filtering white noise.

Suite (Fr., sweet)   1. A set of dances originating around 1600 as the freer *Partita*. The contrasts of the suite were well-established by Bach, and the movements gradually assumed the following order: a *prelude*, after which came the *allemande*, the *courante*, the *sarabande*, the *intermezzi*, and finally the *gigue*. The *intermezzi* were from two to four dances, or other movements, left to the choice of the composer (such as minuets or gavottes). Romantic and modern orchestral suites are generally of a much freer character, with music often taken from ballet or film scores. 2. A series, a succession; *une suite de pièces*, a series of lessons, or pieces.

Suite de Danses (Fr., sweet de[r] dans)   **Suivez** (Fr., swee-vay)   Follow, attend, pursue; the accompaniment must be accommodated to the singer, or solo player.

Sul (It., sool) **Sull'** (It., sool) **Sulla** (It., SOO-lah)   On, upon.

Sul ponticello (It., sool pon-tee-CHE-lo)   Bow near the bridge.

Sul tasto (It., sool TAHS-to)   Bow near the fingerboard.

Superoctave   1. An organ stop tuned two octaves, or a fifteenth, above the diapasons. 2. A coupler producing the octave above.

Supertonic   The second note of the diatonic scale.

Supplichevole (It., soo-plee-KEH-vo-le)   **Supplichevolmente** (It., soop-plee-keh-vol-MEN-te)   In a supplicatory manner.

Sur (It., soor; Fr., sür)   On, upon, over.

Suspension   A type of non-chord tone that retains a note, or notes, from the preceding chord into a new chord. This dissonance is resolved by a step down.

Süss (Ger., züs)   Sweetly.

Sussurando (It., soo-soo-RAHN-do)   Whispering, murmuring.

Sustain pedal   See *Pedal*.

Svegliato (It., svel-yee-AH-to)   Brisk, lively, sprightly.

Svelto (It., SVEL-to)   Free, light, easy.

Sweet potato   See *Ocarina*.

Swell   1. A gradual increase of sound. 2. See *Swell-organ*.

Swell-organ   In organs having three manuals, the third, or upper manual, controlling a number of pipes enclosed in a box, which may be gradually opened, or shut, and thus the tone increased, or diminished, by degrees. See *Organ*.

Swell-pedal   That which opens the shutters of the swell-organ, increasing the tone.

Swing   1. A style of big-band jazz popular in the 1930's and 1940's. 2. A term for the driving rhythm created by the interaction of musicians in a jazz ensemble.

Swing time   The technique of playing pairs of eighth notes unevenly, with the first note lengthened and the second shortened, sometimes approximating a triplet feel but less precise; also known as a shuffle rhythm.

Swung eighths   See *Swing time*.

Sympathetic string   A string designed to vibrate when a similar pitch is bowed or plucked on an active string.

Symphonic band   See *Band*.

Symphonic poem   An alternate term for tone poem. See *Program music*.

Symphonie (Fr., sam-fo-nee)   **Symphonie** (Ger., SIM-fo-nee) **Symphony** (Eng.)   In the first half of the eighteenth century, symphony meant an instrumental prelude, interlude, or postlude. After that time, it became the term for a large-scale composition of several movements for full orchestra. The symphony in its mature form is often attributed to Haydn, and generally consisted of an allegro movement (sometimes with a slow introduction), a slow movement, a minuet or scherzo, and a finale, often in rondo form. In recent years, composers have used the term both for conventionally-formed symphonies and for major works with different structures.

Synchronize   To coordinate two or more elements in time, such as music and video, or an acoustic performer with electronic sounds.

Syncopation   A temporary displacement of the natural accent in music. For instance, making the note attacks fall between the pulses or beats, or shifting the accent from the naturally strong first or third beat to the weak second or fourth beat. There are various forms of syncopation, but the principle is the same in all. The syncopation cannot be continued for too long a period without danger of entirely supplanting the original beat or pulse, especially when no part is sustaining the original accent against it.

Synthesis The creation of new sounds or timbres, especially through electronic means. Also see *Additive synthesis* and *Subtractive synthesis*.

Synthesizer A device, often equipped with a keyboard, that creates various electronic sounds or timbres.

Synth pad A smooth, sustained sound on a synthesizer, designed for sustained harmonic backgrounds. Synth pads are often designed to emulate the timbre of strings, organs or voices.

Syrinx Another word for Panpipes, named after the mythological nymph who was turned into musical reeds by Pan.

System A synchronized unit of simultaneous staves on a page of sheet music.

T An abbreviation of *Talon, Tasto, Tempo, Tenor, Toe* (in organ music), *Tre,* and *Tutti.*

Tab Evolved from tablature, a term specific to pop music for guitar or bass in a tablature notation style.

Tabla In traditional Hindustani music, a pair of hand drums with differing sizes and timbres.

Tablatura (It., tah-blah-TOO-rah) **Tablature** (Fr., tah-blah-tür) **Tablature** (Eng.) **Tabulatur** (Ger., tah-boo-lah-TOOR) A style of notation, usually written for plucked string instruments such as lute and guitar, in which a table is used to assign specific fingers to specific strings and frets.

Tabor A large, flat drum originating in the Middle Ages; held with a leather strap and played with a single beater, the tabor is often equipped with a gut snare.

Tacet (Lat., TAH-set) **Tace** (It., TAH-chay) **Taci** (It., TAH-chee) **Taciasi** (It., tah-chee-ah-zee) Be silent; a term found in vocal or instrumental parts to indicate that the particular voice or instrument has nothing to sing or play during a certain movement or period.

Tactus (Lat., TAHK-toos) An ancient term for the beat, or pulse, in a piece of music.

Tag The popular music equivalent of a coda; a repetitive section at the end that often fades out.

Takt (Ger., tahkt) Time, measure, beat.

Talea (Lat., TAH-le-ah) The term used to describe the fixed series of rhythmic durations in isorhythmic music.

Talking drum An hourglass-shaped drum with two heads whose pitch can be regulated by squeezing and releasing strings along its sides;

traditionally used by West African Griot musicians.

Tambour (Fr., tahm-BOOR) Drum.

Tambourin (Fr., tahm-boo-ran) 1. A tambourine. 2. A species of dance accompanied by the tambourine.

Tambourine A small, shallow drum with a single head; around the narrow shell are metal jingles. It is beaten by the hand.

Tambura (Hin., tahm-BOO-rah) A type of fretless lute from India, with a long neck and four to six wire strings.

Tamburo (It., tahm-BOO-ro) Drum.

Tam-tam See *Gong*.

Tangent The sharp-edged metal points that hit the strings on a clavichord. Also see *Clavichord*.

Tango A slow, sensuous dance in 4/4, with origins in Argentina and Uruguay, often characterized by melodies full of chromatic scale passages, dramatically swelling dynamics.

Tanto (It., TAHN-to) So much, as much; allegro non tante, not so quick; not too quick.

Tantum ergo (Lat., TAN-tum ER-go) A hymn sung at the benediction in the Roman Catholic service.

Tanz (Ger., tahnts) A dance.

Tape Electronic music from roughly 1950 through 1990 was stored for playback on magnetic film; in live performance music including playback of prerecorded sounds, Tape was often labeled as one of the ensembles instruments, as in: for Violin, Piano, and Tape.

Tape recorder An electronic device for recording analog signals on magnetic film.

Tapping The technique of tapping the fingers of both hands on the fingerboard of a guitar to produce rapid musical lines.

Tarantella (It., tah-rahn-TE-lah) A swift, delirious Italian dance in 12/8 time. The form has been adopted by many composers, for piano compositions.

Tardamente (It., tahr-dah-MEN-te) Slowly.

Tardo (It., TAHR-do) Tardy, slow.

Taste (Ger., TAHS-te) A key on a keyboard.

Tasto (It., TAHS-to) The fingerboard of a string instrument; sul tasto, bow near the fingerboard.

Tasto solo (It., TAHS-to SO-lo) One key alone; in organ or pianoforte music, this means a note without harmony; the bass notes over or under which it is written are not to be accompanied with chords.

Te The solfège syllable for the lowered seventh scale degree occurring in natural minor.

Tedesca (It., te-DES-kah) **Tedesco** (It., te-DES-ko) German: alla tedesca, in the German style.

Te Deum laudamus (Lat., te-DAY-um lou-DAH-mus)   "We praise Thee, O God"; a canticle, or hymn of praise.

Tell-tale   A movable piece of metal, bone, or ivory, attached to an organ, indicating by its position the amount of wind supplied by the bellows.

Tema (It., TAY-mah)   A theme, or subject; a melody.

Temperament   The division of the octave into twelve equal semi-tones, in defiance of the law of nature, which demands a different proportion. The introduction of equal temperament was a modification of the scale of nature that alone made music on keyed instruments practicable.

Tempestoso (It., tem-pes-TO-zo)   Tempestuous, stormy, boisterous.

Temple blocks   A percussion instrument originating in Asia consisting of several hollow wooden blocks of varying sizes, each of which has a slit in the middle.

Tempo (It., TEM-po)   The Italian word for time; tempo is generally defined as the speed of the music. The chief terms used for speed are (from slowest to quickest) *grave, largo, larghetto, adagio, lento, andante, andantino, moderato, allegretto, allegro, presto,* and *prestissimo. A tempo* means return to the original speed after a temporary variation. More contemporary music may have tempo instructions written in the composer's own language.

Tempo giusto (It., TEM-po jee-OOS-to)   In just, exact strict time.

Tempo markings   See *Tempo.*

Tempo ordinario (It., TEM-po or-dee-NAH-ree-o)   Ordinary, or moderate time.

Tempo primo (It., TEM-po PREE-mo)   First, or original time; after a middle section of a piece has been in a different tempo.

Temps (Fr., tahm)   Time.

Teneramente (It., te-ne-rah-MEN-te)   Tenderly, delicately.

Tenerezza (It., te-ne-RE-tsa)   Tenderness, softness, delicacy.

Tenor   A male voice whose range is above the baritone, normally extending from the C on the second space in bass to G on the second line in the treble. It is named from the Italian word *tener* (to hold), since this part often carried the long, sustained tones of the *cantus firmus* in Renaissance music.

Tenor banjo   A banjo with a shorter neck and fewer frets than the plectrum banjo, often used by rhythm banjo players.

Tenor clef   The C clef, when placed upon the fourth line. See page 3.

Tenor drum   A large cylindrical drum, used more frequently in marching bands and pipe bands than in the orchestra.

Tenore di grazia (It., te-NO-re di GRAH-tsee-ah)   A delicate and graceful tenor voice.

Tenore robusto (It., te-NO-re ro-BOOS-to)   A strong tenor voice

Tenor saxophone   A medium-sized member of the saxophone family, pitched in Bb and sounding a ninth lower than written. It is used extensively in jazz and wind ensembles.

Tenor trombone   See *Trombone.*

Tenth   1. A compound interval consisting of an octave and a third. 2. An organ stop tuned a tenth above the diapasons, also called decimal and double tierce.

Tenuto (It., tay-NOO-to)   1. Slightly held back in tempo, indicated typically by the abbreviation *ten.* 2. A slightly stressed attack, indicated by a dash above or below the note.

Ternary form   A three-part musical form, labeled ABA, where the B material contrasts with the A material and is usually conclusive enough to stand on its own; the traditional form of a minuet and trio or scherzo and trio.

Tertian harmony   Harmony consisting of thirds.

Terzetto (It., tair-TSE-to)   A short piece for three voices or instruments.

Tessitura (It., TE-see-TOO-rah)   The general pitch range that occurs most often in a musical part; for example, a part with mostly high pitches is said to have a "high tessitura."

Tetrachord (Gr., TET-ra-kord)   1. Notes spanning a perfect fourth. 2. A collection of any four pitches.

Texture   In music, the interaction and relative independence of musical lines, or voices. Also see *Homophony, Monophony,* and *Polyphony.*

Theme   1. A section of musical material on which part or all of a piece or movement is based. 2. The cantus firmus on which counterpoint is built. 3. The subject of a fugue. 4. A simple tune on which variations are made.

Theme and variations   A popular form in which a simple tune is stated and then repeated with various alterations, often growing more elaborate as the piece or movement progresses.

Theorbo (thee-OR-bo)   A long-necked bass lute used for basso continuo in the late 16th and early 17th centuries.

Theory   See *Music theory.*

Theremin   An electronic instrument invented by Leon Theremin in the late 1920's; it consists primarily of two antennas that control pitch and volume based on the relative proximity of the performer's hands.

Thesis (Gr., thee-sis)   Downbeat, the accented part of the bar. See *Arsis.*

Third   An interval measuring three diatonic degrees.

Third-stream   A term coined by composer and performer Gunther Schuller in 1957 to describe music that combines elements from classical and jazz styles.

Thirteenth   A compound interval consisting of an octave and a sixth.

Thirty-second note   A note whose value is a thirty-second of a whole note.

Thirty-second rest   A pause equal in duration to a thirty-second note.

Thoroughbass   See *Figured bass.*

Three-part form   See *Ternary form.*

Through-composed   See *Song.*

Thumb piano   See *Kalimba.*

Thumb-string   The melody string of the banjo.

Ti (Lat., tee)   In solfège, the seventh note of the scale; also known as *si* in many countries, where it designates the note B.

Tie   A curved line used to connect two notes of the same pitch, the second note being only a continuation of the first, without separate attack. While ties look like slurs, the function is quite different because the tie indicates the duration of one extended pitch while a slur indicates the articulation of a phrase.

Tief (Ger., teef)   Deep, low, profound.

Timbale (Fr., tam-bahl)   **Timballo** (It., tem-BAHL-lo)   A kettle drum.

Timbales   An Afro-Cuban percussion instrument usually consisting of two shallow, single-headed drums. The drums are typically mounted on a stand and played either with drumsticks or bare hands.

Timbral (TAM-brul)   Pertaining to the tone-color characteristics of an instrument, ensemble, or composition. See *Tone color.*

Timbre (Fr., TAM-bruh)   See *Tone color.*

Timbrel   An ancient Israeli percussion instrument, similar to a tambourine.

Time   Music is one of the few temporal art forms, with its various sounds and structures progressing through time. In music, the word "time" can refer to such disparate elements as the *tempo, meter, rhythm,* or simply the duration of a musical work.

Time signature   The numerical symbol at the beginning of a composition that establishes meter; the upper number shows the number of beats per measure, and the lower number shows the note value representing each beat. Additional time signatures are placed within a composition when the meter changes.

Timoroso (It., tee-mo-RO-zo)   Timorous; with hesitation.

Timpani (It. pl., TEEM-pah-nee)   A set of two, four, or five drums consisting of a cup-shaped shell of copper, over which a head is stretched; also known as the "kettle drums." It is an instrument of definite pitch, with foot pedals that tighten and loosen the head.

Tines   The prongs, or vibrating portion, of a tuning fork.

Tin Pan Alley   The nickname for the music-publishing district in Manhattan on West 28th Street, most active from the late 1880's through the early 1930's. Originally a derogatory label, referring to the simultaneous piano playing of the many song pluggers on the street, it was later used to refer to the entire popular music industry.

Tin whistle   A small, metallic end-blown flute with six holes, used in Irish folk music.

Toccata (It., to-KAH-tah)   A form of composition for keyboard instruments, most popular during the late Renaissance and Baroque periods. Getting its name from the word *toccare* (to touch), it is a technically demanding work often containing one or more fugal sections.

Toccatina (It., tok-kah-TEE-nah)   A short toccata.

Tocsin   1. An alarm bell. 2. The ringing of an alarm bell.

Todesgesang (Ger., TO-des-ge-ZAHNG) **Todeslied** (Ger., TO-des-LEET)   A dirge; a funeral song.

Totenglöckchen (Ger., TOT-n-GLÖK-sh'n)   Funeral bell.

Totenlied (Ger., TOT-n-LEET)   Funeral song, or anthem.

Totenmarsch (Ger., TOT-n-MAHRSH)   Funeral march.

Totenmusik (Ger., TOT-n-moo-zeek)   Funeral music.

Tolling   The act of ringing a church-bell in a slow, measured manner.

Tombeau (Fr., tom-bo)   Tomb; while not a musical term, this word appears in the titles of many works intended as homages.

Tom-tom   A deep cylindrical drum; drumkits are usually equipped with three or more tom-toms of varying size.

Ton (Fr., ton, Ger., ton) **Tono** (It., TO-no)   Tone, voice, key, or mode.

Tonal   Music that gravitates around a key center.

Tonal answer   In a fugue, an answer that modifies one or more notes in the process of transposing the subject to the dominant, to prolong focus on the tonic.

Tonality   See *Tonal*.

Tonart (Ger., TO-nahrt)   Mode, scale, or key.

Tone   1. A sound of consistent, definite pitch. 2. The particular quality of the sound of any voice or instrument.

Tonebars   The metal or wooden bars of varying pitch used on pitched mallet percussion instruments, including Orff instruments.

Tone cluster   See *Cluster*.

Tone color   The unique harmonic structure, envelope, and formants that make up the overall sound quality of each individual instrument or voice. Also known as timbre.

Tone poem   See *Program music*.

Tone row   In twelve-tone technique, a non-repetitive ordering of the twelve notes, or pitch classes, of the chromatic scale.

Tonette   A small, plastic end-blown flute used primarily for elementary music education before it was supplanted by the recorder.

Tone wheel   An early electronic tone generator, consisting of rotating wheels with bumps spaced to produce various pitches when rotated near an electro-magnetic coil; tone wheels were used in early Hammond organs and the Telharmonium.

Tongue   In the reed-pipe of an organ, a thin elastic slip of metal.

Tonguing   The various methods of articulating notes on wind instruments, such as staccato and legato tonguing.

Tonic   The first note of a scale; in tonal music, the fundamental "home" note to which other notes are referenced.

Tonic accent   A note which receives more emphasis, due to being higher than surrounding pitches.

Tonicization   The technique of emphasizing a note by treating it as a tonic, through the use of leading tones and cadences. Tonicization is different from modulation because of its temporary nature, often lasting only a few beats.

Tonic Sol-fa   A method of teaching vocal music, invented by Sarah Ann Glover around 1812 and afterwards refined by Rev. John Curwen, who became acquainted with the method in 1841. Its formal basis is the movable-do system, with modification for sharps and flats.

Tonleiter (Ger., TON-ligh-ter)   Scale.

Tosto (It., TOS-to)   Quick, swift, rapid.

Touch   Style of striking, or pressing the keys of an organ, pianoforte, or similar instrument; the resistance made to the fingers, by the keys of any instrument, as hard, or heavy; soft, or light touch.

Touche (Fr., toosh)   The fingerboard on a string instrument; sur la touche, bow on the fingerboard.

Touch sensitivity   The ability of a keyboard instrument to respond to varying pressure from the fingers.

Toujours (Fr., too-zhoor)   Always.

Track   In audio recording, an isolated sound channel combined with others to produce a final mix.

Trading fours/eights   A jazz technique in which several soloists alternate playing every four or eight bars.

Train wreck   The slang term for an individual or group mistake extreme enough to stop a piece during a rehearsal or performance.

Tranquillo (It., trahn-QUEE-lo)   Tranquility, calmness, quietness.

Transcription   An arrangement of a composition for an instrument not originally intended for that piece; an adaptation.

Transducer   Any device designed to convert kinetic energy into electric energy (or vice versa), such as a microphone or speaker.

Transition   Passing suddenly out of one key into another, also a passage leading from one theme to another.

Transpose, transposition   The technique of shifting musical material from one key (or pitch level) to another.

Transposed score   See *Score, transposed*.

Transposer (Fr., trans-po-zay) **Transponiren** (Ger., TRAHNS-po-NEE-ren) To transpose.

Transposing instrument Any instrument whose pitches sound differently from its written notes, often to preserve fingerings between the various members of an instrumental family. The instruments are usually named for the pitch that sounds when the instrument plays a written C; for instance, a B♭ clarinet sounds a B♭ when it plays a written C.

Transverse flute Any flute played by blowing across an opening at the head of the instrument, as opposed to an end-blown flute.

Trap set See *Drum set.*

Trascinando (It., trah-shi-NAHN-do) Dragging the tempo.

Trattenuto (It., trah-te-NOO-to) Holding back the tempo.

Traurig (Ger., TROW-rish) Heavy, sad, mournful.

Travis picking A common form of fingerpicking, usually on steel-string guitars, involving the thumb, index finger, and middle finger.

Tre (It., tre) Three.

Treble The upper part; the highest voice; the soprano.

Treble clef The G clef, placed on the second line, as illustrated on page 3.

Tre corde (It., tre KOR-de) Three strings; in piano music this means that the soft pedal is to be released.

Tremando (It., tre-MAHN-do) **Tremolando** (It., trem-o-LAHN-do) **Tremolo** (It., TRE-mo-lo) 1. A rapid repetition of a note on a bowed string or mallet percussion instrument. 2. A rapid alternation between two notes or chords on keyboard instruments or harp. 3. A roll on a percussion instrument. 4. A rapid variation in amplitude in electric guitars, basses, and organs.

Tremolant, Tremulant An organ or harmonium stop which gives to the tone a waving, trembling, or undulating effect.

Tremolo arm A lever attached to the bridge or tailpiece of an electric guitar in order to manually tighten and loosen the strings, creating tremolos and pitch bends; also known as a "whammy bar."

Très (Fr., tray) Very.

Triad Any chord consisting of three notes, each a third apart.

Triangle A piece of steel bent into triangle form, yielding a clear ringing sound of indefinite pitch when struck.

Triangle wave A non-sinusoidal waveform containing only odd harmonics; it is differentiated from the square wave by having a much faster roll-off of higher harmonics.

Trill Two adjacent notes alternating in more or less rapid succession; generally abbreviated by placing *tr* above the primary note, indicating that this note and the one immediately above are to be alternated rapidly.

Triller (Ger., TRI-ler) **Trillo** (It., TREE-lo)   See *Trill*.

Trio (It., TREE-o)   1. A composition for three voices or instruments, or the group of performers. 2. A contrasting section within multi-section movements such as a minuet or march. The Trio section is often the third segment of the movement and historically has been characterized by lighter instrumentation than the primary theme; its origin is in music of the Baroque era where the Trio section did suddenly use only three musicians.

Triole (Ger., TREE-o-le) **Triolet** (Fr., tree-o-lay)   See *Triplet*.

Trionfale (It., tree-on-FAH-le)   Triumphal.

Trio sonata   A style of multi-movement instrumental music most popular in the 17th and 18th centuries, consisting of two soloists and *Basso continuo* accompaniment. The *Sonata da camera* was in a lively, secular style, with stylized dance movements. The *Sonata da chiesa* was in a more reserved style, most often in four movements; despite its name, "church sonata," the *Sonata da chiesa* was performed in concerts as well as church services.

Triple concerto   A concerto involving three soloists.

Triple meter   A meter consisting of three beats.

Triplet   A group of three notes to be played in one beat or an otherwise-defined duration. See *Tuplet*.

Triplet feel   See *Swing time*.

Triple tonguing   A method of articulating quick triplets on woodwind and brass instruments, rapidly tonguing in a t-k-t pattern for woodwinds or t-t-k pattern for brass.

Tristezza (It., tris-TE-tsah)   Sadness, heaviness, pensiveness.

Tritone   An interval consisting of three whole steps, written as either an augmented fourth or diminished fifth; due to its dissonant nature, it was termed the "devil in music" from antiquity through the 18th century.

Trochee (Lat., tro-kay)   A dissyllabic musical foot, containing one long and one short syllable. Also see *Foot*.

Trois (Fr., trwah)   Three.

Tromba (It., TROM-bah)   1. A trumpet. 2. An 8-foot reed organ stop.

Tromba marina (It., TROM-bah mah-REE-nah)   Literally, "marine trumpet"; a bass instrument popular in the Middle Ages and Renaissance, consisting of a triangular body and a single string. The thumb was used to produce various harmonics on the string as it was bowed, producing a loud, brassy sound.

Trombone (Ger., *Posaune*, It. *Trombono*)   A brass instrument consisting of a metal tube, bent into two u-shaped sections and terminating in a flaring bell. The distinguishing feature is a double slide which can be adjusted in seven positions, each yielding a fundamental note and its harmonics. The seven positions cover a chromatic scale of two and a half octaves, as well as several strong pedal tones. Trombones are classified as soprano, alto, tenor, or bass, according to their range. The most common trombone in bands and orchestras is the tenor with a compass from the E below the bass staff to around the B♭ in the middle of the treble staff. Most professional trombones are equipped with an F attachment, which extends the lower range of the instrument and simplifies the playing of certain passages.

Trommel (Ger., TRO-mel)   Drum.

Tronco (It., TRON-ko)   An indication that sounds are to be cut short.

Trope   1. New music added to pre-existing plainchants starting in the 9th century. 2. In some atonal and serial music, an unordered pitch set, usually a hexachord.

Troppo (It., TRO-po)   Too much; non troppo, not too much.

Troubadours (Fr. pl., troo-bah-doer)   The bards and poet-musicians of Southern France around the 12th century.

Trüb (Ger., trüb)   Sad, mournful, gloomy.

Trumpet   A wind instrument consisting primarily of a bent metal tube terminating in a flared bell. It is equipped with a system of cylindrical piston valves, with each fingering yielding a different fundamental and harmonic series. The compass of the trumpet is from the G below the treble staff to the C above. The most common trumpets in the orchestra are the B♭ trumpet, C trumpet, and the B♭ or A piccolo trumpet.

Truss rod   A rod, usually made of steel, inserted into the neck of a guitar to stabilize and adjust its curvature.

Tuba   1. The bass instrument of the brass family. It consists of a conical tube bent into many coils, and is equipped with three to six piston or rotary valves. The tuba is made in different sizes and pitches, the deepest being called the *contrabass*. 2. The name of a powerful reed-stop in an organ.

Tuba mirabilis (Lat., TOO-bah mee-RAH-bee-lees)   An 8-foot reed-stop, with a high pressure of wind and powerful tone.

Tubular bells   See *Chimes*.

Tune   A melody; a succession of measured sounds, usually agreeable to the ear, and possessing a distinct and striking character.

Tuned percussion   Any percussion instrument that can play definite pitches, such as the timpani, glockenspiel, and xylophone; also known as pitched percussion.

Tuner   Any device designed to produce tuning notes and/or register the intonation of received sounds.

Tuning   The technique of adjusting to achieve uniform pitch on an instrument or within an ensemble.

Tuning fork   A small steel instrument, having two prongs, which gives a fixed tone when struck. It is used for tuning instruments, and for ascertaining or indicating the pitch of tunes.

Tuning hammer   A steel or iron implement used by piano tuners.

Tuning peg   See *Peg.*

Tuning slide   A moveable slide on brass instruments designed to adjust the pitch in small increments, for the purpose of tuning.

Tuplet   A group of notes whose duration is contracted to fit within a specified duration of time; the most common example is the triplet, in which three notes are played in the usual time of two similar ones. Tuplets are notated by a numeral below or above the affected notes, enclosed within a bracket when not already evident by a beam; more ambiguous or complicated tuplets may be expressed as a ratio, for instance 5:3 signifying five notes played in the time of three. While tuplets are by definition contracted to squeeze extra notes into a duration, some composers have also notated tuplets as expansions into a duration.

Turca   (It., TOOR-kah)   Turkish; alla Turca, in the style of Turkish music.

Turn   (It., groo-PE-to)   An ornament involving the rapid motion from a principal note to its upper neighbor and back, then to the lower neighbor and back, indicated by the symbol ∾. The turn is generally abbreviated in notation by using the turn sign placed over or after the first principal note.

Tutta   (It., TOO-tah)   **Tutto**   (It., TOO-to)   All; the whole; entirely; quite.

Tutta forza   (It., TOO-tah-FOR-tsah)   **Tutta la forza**   (It., TOO-tah lah FOR-tsah)   The whole power, as loud as possible, with the utmost force and vehemence.

Tutti   (It., TOO-tee)   All, the players or chorus; in a solo, or concerto, it means that the full orchestra is to resume playing.

Twelfth   1. A compound interval consisting of an octave and a fifth. 2. An organ stop tuned twelve notes above the diapasons.

Twelve-bar blues   The most popular style of blues music, with a twelve-measure harmonic structure traditionally involving only tonic, dominant and subdominant chords.

Twelve-string guitar   A guitar with two strings for each of its six courses.

Twelve-tone technique   A method involving the pre-compositional organization of the twelve chromatic pitches into tone rows.

Two-part form   See *Binary form.*

Two-step   1. A step found in many dances, especially in folk dances, in which the same foot advances twice in the same direction with a closing step by the other foot in between. 2. A dance in 4/4 time usually associated with Country and Western music; also known as the "Texas Two-Step."

Tympani   (It. pl., TEEM-pah-nee)   See *Timpani.*

Tyrolienne   (Fr., tee-ro-lee-en)   A song or dance peculiar to the Tyrol region between Austria and Italy.

Ud See *Oud.*

Übermässig (Ger., Ü-ber-ME-sig)   Augmented, superfluous.

Übung (Ger., Ü-boong)   An exercise; a study for the practice of some peculiar difficulty. *Übungsstück*; an exercise.

Uguale (It., oo-GWAH-le)   Equal, like, similar.

Ugualmente (It., oo-gwahl-MEN-te)   Equally, alike.

Ukulele   A small, four-stringed instrument, similar to a guitar, with origins in Hawaii.

Umfang (Ger., OOM-fahng)   Compass, extent.

Umore (It., oo-MO-ray)   Humor, playfulness.

Un (It., oon) **Una** (It., OO-nah) **Uno** (It., OO-no)   A, an, one.

Una corda (It., OO-nah KOR-dah)   One string, on one string only; in piano music it means that the soft pedal is to be used. See *Pedal.*

Unequal temperament   Any tuning system which does not calculate an equal division of the 12 pitches within an octave.

Unison   Two or more voices or instruments sounding the same note.

Unmerklich (Ger., oon-MERK-leesh)   Imperceptibly.

Un peu (Fr., uhn pu) **Un poco** (It., oon PO-ko)   A little.

Unruhig (Ger., oon-ROO-eesh)   Not peaceful, distressed.

Unter (Ger., OON-ter)   Under, below.

Unterbrechung (Ger., oon-ter-BRECH-oong)   In Schenkerian analysis, a prolongation technique where the descending line stops at scale degree 2 (over the dominant), at which point the entire structure is repeated with final closure; translated as "interruption."

Upbeat   A weak beat leading to a strong beat.

Up bow   The sign V. Used in music for bowed string instruments to signify bow motion from the tip to the frog.

Upright   1. A piano with a vertical soundboard. 2. Another name for an acoustic bass.

Up-tempo   Slang for a fast beat or pulse.

Urlinie (Ger., OOR-lin-ee)   In Schenkerian analysis, the top portion of the ursatz (fundamental structure), consisting of a line descending from scale degree 8, 5 or 3 to scale degree 1; translated as "fundamental line."

Ursatz (Ger., OOR-zahts)   In Schenkerian analysis, the two-part progression consisting of an upper portion (the Urlinie) and a lower portion (the Baßbrechung). It serves as the fundamental structure of which all tonal music is an elaboration; translated as "fundamental structure."

Urtext (Ger., OOR-text)   The edition of a musical work that adheres most closely to the composer's original intent.

COMPOSERS

Abt, Franz (1819-1885) German song composer.

Adam, Adolphe-Charles (1803-1856) French composer.

Adams, John (b. 1947) American composer.

Addinsell, Richard (1904-1977) British film composer.

Adler, Richard (b. 1921) American composer and lyricist.

Adler, Samuel (b. 1928) American composer.

Albeniz, Isaac (1861-1909) Spanish pianist and composer.

Albert, Eugène d' (1864-1932) German pianist and composer.

Alberti, Domenico (ca. 1710-1740) Italian composer. See *"Alberti bass."*

Albinoni, Tomaso (1671-1751) Venetian composer.

Albrechtsberger, Johann Georg (1736-1809) German composer.

Alkan, Charles-Valentin (1813-1888) Composer and pianist.

Anderson, Leroy (1908-1975) American composer.

Antheil, George (1900-1959) American composer.

Arcadelt, Jacob (ca. 1507-1568) Flemish composer.

Arditi, Luigi (1822-1903) Italian opera conductor and composer.

Arenski, Anton (1861-1906) Russian pianist and composer.

Argento, Dominick (b. 1927) American composer.

Arlen, Harold (1905-1986) American songwriter.

Arne, Thomas (1710-1778) British violinist and composer.

Arnold, Malcolm (1921-2006) British composer.

Auber, Daniel François Esprit (1782-1871) French opera composer.

Auric, Georges (1899-1983) French composer.

Babbitt, Milton (b. 1916) American composer.

Bach, Karl Philipp Emanuel (1714-1788) Composer and third son of J. S. Bach.

Bach, Johann Christian (1735-1782) Composer and eleventh son of J. S. Bach.

Bach, Johann Christoph Friedrich (1732-1795) Composer and ninth son of J. S. Bach.

Bach, Johann Sebastian (1685-1750) German composer.

Bach, Wilhelm Friedemann (1710-1784) Composer and second son of J. S. Bach.

Bacharach, Burt (b. 1928) American pianist and songwriter.

Bacon, Ernst (1898-1990) American pianist and songwriter.

Balakirev, Mily (1837-1910) Russian composer.

Barber, Samuel (1910-1981) American composer.

Bartók, Béla (1881-1945) Hungarian composer.

Bassett, Leslie (b. 1923) American composer.

Bax, Arnold (1883-1953) British composer.

Beach, Amy Marcy Cheney (1867-1944) American composer.

Beethoven, Ludwig van (1770-1827) German composer.

Bellini, Vincenzo (1801-1835) Italian opera composer.

Benjamin, Arthur (1893-1960) Australian composer.

Bennett, Richard Rodney (b. 1936) British composer.

Bennett, Robert Russell (1894-1981) American composer.

Berg, Alban (1885-1935) Austrian composer.

Berio, Luciano (1925-2003) Italian composer.

Berlin, Irving (1888-1989) American songwriter.

Berlioz, Hector (1803-1860) French composer and music critic.

Bernstein, Elmer (1922-2004) American film composer.

Bernstein, Leonard (1918-1990) American composer and conductor.

Billings, William (1746-1800) American composer.

Bizet, Georges (1838-1875) French opera composer.

Blackwood, Easley (b. 1933) American composer and pianist.

Bliss, Arthur (1891-1975) British composer.

Blitzstein, Marc (1905-1964) American composer.

Bloch, Ernest (1880-1959) American composer and conductor.

Blow, John (1649-1708) British composer and organist.

Boccherini, Luigi (1743-1805) Italian composer and cellist.

Boëllmann, Léon (1862-1897) French organist and composer.

Boito, Arrigo (1842-1918) Composer, librettist, and poet.

Bolcom, William (b. 1938) American composer.

Bolling, Claude (b. 1930) French jazz pianist and composer.

Bononcini, Giovanni (1670-1747) Italian opera composer.

Borodin, Alexander (1833-1887) Russian composer.

Boulanger, Lili (1893-1918) French composer.

Boulanger, Nadia (1887-1979) French composer and pedagogue.

Boulez, Pierre (b. 1925) French composer and conductor.

Boyce, William (1711-1779) British composer.

Brahms, Johannes (1833-1897) German composer.

Brant, Henry (1913-2008) Canadian-American composer.

Britten, Benjamin (1913-1976) British composer and conductor.

Brouwer, Leo (b. 1939) Cuban composer, conductor, and guitarist.

Brown, Earle (1926-2002) American composer.

Brubeck, Dave (b. 1920) American jazz pianist and composer.

Bruch, Max (1838-1920) German composer.

Bruckner, Anton (1824-1896) German symphonic composer.

Buck, Dudley (1839-1909)   American organist and composer.

Bull, John (ca. 1562-1628)   British organist and composer.

Bülow, Hans von (1830-1894)   German conductor and composer.

Burgmüller, Johann (1806-1874)   German pianist and composer.

Burleigh, Harry S. (1866-1949)   American baritone and composer.

Busoni, Feruccio (1866-1924)   Italian pianist and composer.

Buxtehude, Dietrich (ca. 1637-1707)   German organist and composer.

Byrd, William (ca. 1540-1623)   British organist and composer.

Caccini, Giulio (1551-1618)   Italian teacher and opera composer.

Cage, John (1912-1992)   American composer.

Caldara, Antonio (ca. 1670-1736)   Italian composer.

Cambini, Giuseppe Maria Gioacchino (1746-1825)   Italian composer.

Campion, Thomas (1567-1620)   British composer.

Carissimi, Giacomo (ca. 1605-1674)   Italian composer.

Carmichael, Hoagy (1899-1981)   American songwriter and pianist.

Carter, Elliott (b. 1908)   American composer.

Casadesus, Robert (1899-1972)   French pianist and composer.

Casella, Alfredo (1883-1947)   Italian composer.

Cesti, Antonio (1623-1669)   Italian composer, singer, and organist.

Chabrier, Alexis Emmanuel (1841-1894)   French composer.

Chadwick, George (1854-1931)   American composer and organist.

Chaminade, Cécile (1857-1944)   French composer and pianist.

Charpentier, Marc-Antoine (ca. 1645-1704)   French composer.

Chausson, Ernest (1855-1899)   French composer.

Chavez y Ramirez, Carlos (1899-1978)   Mexican composer.

Chen Yi (b. 1953)   Chinese-American composer.

Cherubini, Luigi (1760-1842)   Italian composer.

Chihara, Paul (b. 1938)   American composer.

Childs, Barney (1926-2000)   American composer.

Chopin, Frédéric (1810-1849)   Polish pianist and composer.

Chou, Wen-chung (b. 1923)   Chinese-American composer.

Cimarosa, Domenico (1749-1801)   Italian composer.

Clarke, Jeremiah (1673-1707)   British composer.

Clementi, Muzio (1752-1832)   Italian composer and pianist, teacher, publisher, and piano-maker.

Cohan, George M. (1878-1942)   American theater composer.

Coleman, Ornette (b. 1930)   American jazz saxophonist and composer.

Coleridge-Taylor, Samuel (1875-1912)   British composer of African descent.

Colgrass, Michael (b. 1932) American composer.

Copland, Aaron (1900-1990) American composer.

Corea, "Chick" (Armando Anthony) (b. 1941) American jazz pianist and composer.

Corelli, Arcangelo (1653-1713) Italian violinist and composer.

Corigliano, John (b. 1938) American composer.

Cornelius, Peter (1824-1874) German composer.

Couperin, François (1668-1733) French composer.

Couperin, Louis (ca. 1626-1661) French composer.

Cowell, Henry (1897-1965) American composer.

Creston, Paul (1906-1985) American composer; originally named Giuseppe Guttoveggio.

Crüger, Johann (1598-1662) German composer.

Crumb, George (b. 1929) American composer.

Cui, César Antonovitch (1835-1918) Russian composer.

Czerny, Carl (1791-1857) Austrian pianist, teacher, and composer.

Dahl, Ingolf (1912-1970) Swedish-American composer.

Dallapiccola, Luigi (1904-1975) Italian composer and teacher.

Daquin, Louis-Claude (1694-1772) French keyboardist and composer.

Dargomyzhsky, Alexander (1813-1869) Russian opera composer.

David, Ferdinand (1810-1873) German composer.

Davidovsky, Mario (b. 1934) Argentinian-American composer.

Davies, Peter Maxwell (b. 1934) British composer and conductor.

Davis, Miles (1926-1991) American jazz trumpeter and bandleader.

Debussy, Achille Claude (1862-1918) French composer.

Delibes, Léo (1836-1891) French composer.

Delius, Frederick (1863-1934) British composer.

Dello Joio, Norman (1913-2008) American composer.

Del Tredici, David (b. 1937) American composer.

Desprès, Josquin (ca. 1440-1521) Franco-Flemish composer.

Dett, Robert Nathaniel (1882-1943) African-American composer.

Diabelli, Anton (1781-1858) Austrian composer.

Diamond, David (1915-2005) American composer.

Distler, Hugo (1908-1942) German composer.

Dittersdorf, Karl Ditters von (1739-1799) Austrian composer.

Döhler, Theodor (1814-1856) Austrian pianist and composer.

Dohnanyi, Ernest von (1877-1960) Hungarian pianist and composer.

Donaldson, Walter (1893-1947) American songwriter.

Donizetti, Gaetano (1797-1848) Italian opera composer.

Dorff, Daniel (b. 1956) American composer.

Dorn, Heinrich Ludwig Egmont (1800-1892)　German composer.

Dowland, John (1563-1626)　British composer and lutenist.

Druckman, Jacob (1928-1996)　American composer.

Dubois, Théodore (1837-1924)　French organist and composer.

Dufay, Guillermus (ca. 1400-1474)　French composer.

Dukas, Paul (1865-1935)　French composer.

Dumont, Henri (1610-1684)　French keyboardist and composer.

Dunstable, John (ca. 1390-1453)　British composer.

Duparc, Henri (1848-1933)　French song composer.

Dupre, Marcel (1886-1971)　French organist, composer, and teacher.

Durante, Francesco (1684-1755)　Italian composer.

Durey, Louis (1888-1979)　French composer.

Duruflé, Maurice (1902-1986)　French composer.

Dussek, Jan Ladislav (1760-1812)　Bohemian pianist and composer.

Dvořák, Antonin (1841-1904)　Bohemian composer.

Eccles, John (ca. 1668-1735)　British composer.

Effinger, Cecil (1914-1990)　American composer and inventor.

Elgar, Sir Edward (1857-1934)　British composer.

Ellington, "Duke" (1899-1974)　American jazz composer and pianist; originally named Edward Kennedy Ellington.

Enescu, George (1881-1955)　Romanian violinist and composer.

Erb, Donald (1927-2008)　American composer.

Escobar, Luis Antonio (1925-1993)　Colombian composer.

Etler, Alvin (1913-1973)　American composer.

Evans, Gil (1912-1988)　American jazz composer and pianist.

Falla, Manuel de (1876-1946)　Spanish composer.

Farnaby, Giles (ca. 1563-1640)　British composer.

Farwell, Arthur (1872-1952)　American composer and publisher.

Fauré, Gabriel Urbain (1845-1924)　French composer.

Feldman, Morton (1926-1987)　American composer.

Field, John (1782-1837)　Irish pianist and composer.

Fillmore, J. Henry, Jr. (1881-1956)　American bandleader and composer.

Finney, Ross Lee (1906-1997)　American composer.

Fiorillo, Federigo (ca. 1753-1823)　Italian violinist and composer.

Flagello, Nicholas (1928-1994)　American composer.

Flotow, Friedrich von (1813-1883)　German opera composer.

Floyd, Carlisle (b. 1926)　American composer.

Foote, Arthur William (1853-1937)　American composer.

Foss, Lukas (1922-2009)　American pianist, conductor, and pianist.

Foster, Stephen (1826-1864)   American song composer.

Frackenpohl, Arthur (b. 1924)   American composer.

Françaix, Jean (1912-1997)   French composer.

Franchetti, Alberto (1860-1942)   Italian opera composer.

Franck, César (1822-1890)   French organist and composer.

Franz, Robert (1815-1892)   German song composer.

Frescobaldi, Giralamo (1583-1643)   Italian organist and composer.

Friml, Rudolf (1879-1972)   Bohemian-American operetta composer.

Fux, Johann Joseph (1660-1741)   Austrian composer and theorist.

Gabrieli, Andrea (ca. 1510-1586)   Italian organist and composer.

Gabrieli, Giovanni (ca. 1554-1612)   Italian organist and composer, nephew of Andrea Gabrieli.

Gabrilowitsch, Ossip (1878-1936)   Russian-American composer.

Gaburo, Kenneth (1926-1993)   American composer.

Gershwin, George (1898-1937)   American composer.

Gesualdo, Don Carlo (ca. 1560-1613)   Italian composer and lutenist.

Gevaërt, François-Auguste (1828-1908)   Belgian composer.

Giannini, Vittorio (1903-1966)   American composer.

Gibbons, Orlando (ca. 1583-1625)   British composer.

Gigout, Eugène (1844-1925)   French organist and composer.

Gilbert, Henry (1868-1928)   American composer.

Gillis, Don (1912-1978)   American composer and conductor.

Gilmore, Patrick (1829-1892)   Irish-American bandleader and composer.

Ginastera, Alberto (1916-1983)   Argentinian composer.

Giordani, Giuseppe (1743-1798)   Italian composer.

Giordano, Umberto (1867-1948)   Italian opera composer.

Glass, Philip (b. 1937) American composer.

Glazunov, Alexander (1865-1936)   Russian composer.

Gliere, Reinhold (1875-1956)   Russian composer.

Glinka, Mikhael (1804-1857)   Russian composer.

Gluck, Christoph Willibald von (1714-1787)   German composer.

Godard, Benjamin (1849-1895)   French composer.

Godowsky, Leopold (1870-1938)   Polish-American pianist and composer.

Goldmark, Karl (1830-1915)   Hungarian composer.

Goldmark, Rubin (1872-1936)   American composer.

Goldsmith, Jerry (1929-2004)   American film composer.

Goossens, Eugene (1893-1962)   British composer and conductor.

Gordon, Ricky Ian (b. 1956)   American composer.

Górecki, Henryk (b. 1933)   Polish composer.

Gossec, François-Joseph (1734-1829)   Dutch composer.

Gottschalk, Louis Moreau (1829-1869)   American pianist and composer.

Gould, Morton (1913-1996)   American conductor and composer.

Gounod, Charles (1818-1893)   French opera composer.

Grainger, Percy (1882-1961)   Australian-American composer.

Granados, Enrique y Campina (1867-1916)   Spanish composer.

Gretchaninov, Alexander (1864-1956)   Russian-American composer.

Grétry, A.E.M. (1741-1813)   French opera composer.

Grieg, Edvard Hagerup (1843-1907)   Norwegian composer.

Griffes, Charles Tomlinson (1884-1920)   American composer.

Grofé, Ferde (1892-1972)   American pianist and composer.

Guilmant, Felix Alexandre (1837-1911)   French composer.

Guthrie, Woody (1912-1967)   American folk singer and songwriter; originally named Woodrow Wilson Guthrie.

Hába, Alois (1893-1973)   Czech composer and teacher.

Hahn, Reynaldo (1874-1947)   Venezuelan-French composer.

Hailstork, Adolphus (b. 1941)   African-American composer.

Halévy, Fromental (1799-1862)   French opera composer.

Halvorsen, Johan (1864-1935)   Norwegian composer and violinist.

Hamlisch, Marvin (b. 1941)   American popular composer.

Handel, George Frideric (1685-1759)   German composer.

Handy, William Christopher (1873-1958)   African-American composer.

Hanon, Charles-Louis (1819-1900)   French pianist, composer, and pedagogue.

Hanson, Howard (1896-1981)   American composer and conductor.

Harbison, John (b. 1938)   American composer.

Harris, Roy (1898-1979)   American composer.

Harrison, Lou (1917-2003)   American composer.

Hartley, Walter Sinclair (b. 1927)   American composer.

Hasse, Johann Adolf (1699-1783)   German opera composer.

Hassler, Hans Leo (1564-1612)   German organist and composer.

Hauptmann, Moritz (1792-1868)   German composer and theorist.

Haydn, Franz Joseph (1732-1809)   Austrian composer.

Haydn, Johann Michael (1737-1806)   Austrian composer, brother of Franz Joseph Haydn.

Heller, Stephen (1813-1888)   Hungarian pianist and composer.

Henderson, Fletcher (1897-1952)   American jazz pianist, bandleader, and composer.

Hensel, Fanny (1805-1847)   German composer, sister of Felix Mendelsohn.

Henze, Hans Werner (b. 1926)   German composer.

Herbert, Victor (1859-1924)   Irish-American composer and cellist.

Herrmann, Bernard (1911-1975)   American film composer.

Hiller, Ferdinand von (1811-1885)   German conductor and composer.

Hiller, Lejaren (1924-1994)   American composer and computer-music theorist.

Hindemith, Paul (1895-1963)   German-American composer.

Hodkinson, Sydney (b. 1934)   American composer.

Holst, Gustav Theodore (1874-1934)   British composer.

Honegger, Arthur (1892-1955)   French composer.

Hopkinson, Francis (1737-1791)   American composer.

Hovhaness, Alan (1911-2000)   American composer.

Hummel, Johann Nepomuk (1778-1837)   Austrian composer.

Humperdinck, Engelbert (1854-1921)   German composer.

Husa, Karel (b. 1921)   Czech-American composer.

Ibert, Jacques (1890-1962)   French composer.

Indy, Vincent d' (1851-1931)   French composer.

Ippolitoff-Ivanoff, Michael (1859-1935) Russian composer.

Ireland, John (1879-1962)   British composer.

Isaac, Heinrich (ca. 1450-1517)   Flemish composer.

Ives, Charles Edward (1874-1954)   American composer.

Jacob, Gordon (Percival Septimus) (1895-1984)   British composer.

Janáček, Leoš (1954-1928)   Czech composer.

Janequin, Clement (ca. 1485-1558)   French composer.

Jaques-Dalcroze, Émile (1865-1950)   Swiss composer and creator of "Eurhythmics."

Jobim, Antonio Carlos (1927-1994)   Brazilian popular songwriter.

Johnston, Ben (b. 1926)   American composer.

Jommelli, Nicola (1714-1774)   Italian composer.

Joplin, Scott (1868-1917)   African-American pianist and composer.

Kabalevsky, Dmitri (1904-1987)   Russian composer.

Kagel, Mauricio (1931-2008)   Argentinian composer.

Kahn, Gus (1886-1941)   German-American songwriter and lyricist.

Kander, John (b. 1927)   American musical theater composer.

Karg-Elert, Siegfried (1877-1933)   German organist and composer.

Kay, Ulysses (1917-1995)   African-American composer.

Kennan, Kent (1913-2003)   American composer and writer on music.

Kern, Jerome (1885-1945)   American composer.

Khachaturian, Aram (1903-1978)   Russian composer.

King, Karl L. (1891-1971)   American bandleader and composer.

Kirchner, Leon (b. 1919) American composer.

Kodály, Zoltán (1882-1967) Hungarian composer and educator.

Koechlin, Charles (1867-1950) French composer and writer.

Korngold, Erich Wolfgang (1897-1957) Austrian-American composer.

Kraft, William (b. 1923) American conductor and percussionist.

Krebs, Carl August (1804-1880) German conductor and composer.

Krebs, Johann Ludwig (1713-1780) German organist and composer.

Kreisler, Fritz (1875-1962) Austrian-American violinist and composer.

Krenek, Ernst (1900-1991) Austrian-American composer.

Krieger, Johann (1651-1735) German organist and composer.

Krieger, Johann Philipp (1649-1725) German keyboardist and composer, brother of Johann Krieger.

Kubik, Gail (1914-1984) Canadian composer.

Kuhlau, Friedrich (1786-1832) German-Danish composer.

Kuhnau, Johann (1660-1722) German composer and organist.

Kurka, Robert (1921-1957) American composer.

Lachner, Franz (1803-1890) German conductor and composer.

Laderman, Ezra (b. 1924) American composer.

Lalo, Edouard (1823-1892) French-Spanish composer.

Landini, Francesco (ca. 1325-1397) Italian composer.

Langlais, Jean (1907-1991) French organist and composer.

Lasso, Orlando di (1532-1594) Franco-Flemish composer.

Lauridsen, Morten (b. 1943) American composer.

Lavignac, Albert (1846-1916) French composer and author.

Legrand, Michel (b. 1932) French composer, pianist, and conductor.

Lehar, Franz (1870-1948) Austrian-Hungarian composer.

Leoncavallo, Ruggiero (1857-1919) Italian opera composer.

Léonin (ca. 1135-ca. 1201) French composer.

Lennon, John (1940-1980) British singer and songwriter.

Leschetizky, Theodor (1830-1915) Pianist, teacher and author.

Liadov, Anatol (1855-1914) Russian composer.

Liebermann, Lowell (b. 1961) American composer and pianist.

Ligeti, Gyorgy (1923-2006) Hungarian-Austrian composer.

Liszt, Franz (1811-1886) Hungarian pianist and composer.

Lloyd Webber, Andrew (b. 1948) British musical theater composer.

Locatelli, Pietro (1695-1764) Italian composer and violinist.

Loesser, Frank (1910-1969) American musical theater composer.

Loewe, Frederich (1901-1988) Austrian-American musical theater composer.

Lotti, Antonio (ca. 1667-1740) Italian organist and composer.

Luening, Otto (1900-1996)　American composer and conductor.

Lully, Jean-Baptiste (1632-1687)　French opera composer.

Lutosławski, Witold (1913-1994)　Polish composer.

MacDowell, Edward Alexander (1860-1908)　American composer.

Machaut, Guillaume de (ca. 1300-1377)　French composer and poet.

Mahler, Gustav (1860-1911)　Austrian composer and conductor.

Mancini, Henry (1924-1994)　American composer and arranger.

Mandel, Johnny (b. 1925)　American composer and arranger.

Marchand, Louis (1669-1732)　French keyboardist and composer.

Marenzio, Luca (ca. 1553-1599)　Italian composer.

Martin, Frank (1890-1974)　Swiss composer.

Martini, Giovanni (1706-1784)　Italian composer and writer.

Martino, Donald (1931-2005)　American composer.

Martinů, Bohuslav (1890-1959)　Czech composer.

Mascagni, Pietro (1863-1945)　Italian opera composer.

Mason, Daniel Gregory (1873-1953)　American composer and teacher, grandson of Lowell Mason.

Mason, Lowell (1792-1872)　American hymn composer.

Massenet, Jules (1842-1912)　French opera composer.

Mayuzumi, Toshiro (1929-1997)　Japanese composer.

McCartney, Paul (b. 1942)　British singer and songwriter.

Méhul, Etienne-Nicolas (1763-1817)　French opera composer.

Mendelssohn (-Bartholdy), Fanny　See *Hensel, Fanny*.

Mendelssohn (-Bartholdy), Felix (1809-1847)　German composer.

Menken, Alan (b. 1949)　American theater and film composer.

Mennin, Peter (1923-1983)　American composer.

Menotti, Gian Carlo (1911-2007)　Italian-American composer.

Messiaen, Olivier (1908-1992)　French composer and theorist.

Meyerbeer, Giacomo (1791-1864)　German opera composer.

Milhaud, Darius (1892-1974)　French composer.

Mingus, Charles (1922-1979)　American jazz bassist and composer.

Monk, Thelonious (1917-1982)　American jazz pianist and composer.

Monteverdi, Claudio (1567-1643)　Italian composer.

Moore, Douglas (1893-1969)　American composer and educator.

Morley, Thomas (ca. 1557-1604)　British composer.

Morton, Ferdinand "Jelly Roll" (1890-1941)　American jazz pianist and composer.

Mouret, Jean-Joseph (1682-1738)　French composer.

Mozart, Leopold (1719-1787)　Austrian violinist, theorist, and composer, father of Wolfgang Amadeus Mozart.

Mozart, Wolfgang Amadeus (1756-1791)   Austrian composer.

Muczynski, Robert (b. 1929)   American composer.

Mulligan, Gerry (1927-1996)   American jazz saxophonist, arranger, and composer.

Mussorgsky, Modest (1839-1881)   Russian composer.

Nabokov, Nicolas (1903-1978)   Russian-American composer.

Nancarrow, Conlon (1912-1997)   American-Mexican composer.

Nelhybel, Vaclav (1919-1996)   Czech-American composer.

Nelson, Ron (b. 1929)   American composer.

Newman, Alfred (1900-1970)   American film conductor composer.

Newman, Randy (b. 1943)   American songwriter; nephew of Alfred.

Nielsen, Carl (1865-1931)   Danish composer.

Nono, Luigi (1924-1990)   Italian composer.

Obrecht, Jacob (ca. 1450-1505)   Dutch composer.

Ockeghem, Johannes (ca. 1410-1497)   Flemish composer.

Offenbach, Jacques (1819-1880)   French operetta composer.

Orff, Carl (1895-1982)   German composer and music educator.

Ornstein, Leo (1893-2002)   Russian-American composer and pianist.

Overton, Hall (1920-1972)   American composer.

Pachelbel, Johann (1653-1706)   German organist and composer.

Paderewski, Ignaz (1860-1941)   Polish pianist and composer.

Paganini, Nicolo (1782-1840)   Italian violinist and composer.

Paine, John Knowles (1839-1906)   American composer.

Paisiello, Giovanni (1740-1816)   Italian opera composer.

Palestrina, Giovanni Perluigi da (ca. 1525-1594)   Italian composer.

Parker, Horatio (1863-1919)   American organist and composer.

Parry, Charles Hubert H. (1848-1918)   British composer.

Partch, Harry (1901-1974)   American inventor and composer.

Pasatieri, Thomas (b. 1945)   American composer.

Peeters, Flor (1903-1986)   Belgian organist and composer.

Penderecki, Krzysztof (b. 1933)   Polish composer.

Pepusch, Johann Christoph (1667-1752)   German-British composer.

Pergolesi, Giovanni Battista (1710-1736)   Italian composer.

Peri, Jacopo (1561-1633)   Italian opera composer.

Perle, George (1915-2009)   American composer and music theorist.

Perotin (ca. 1155-ca. 1210)   French composer.

Persichetti, Vincent (1915-1987)   American composer.

Pezel, Johann Christoph (1639-1694)   German composer.

Phillipps, Burrill (1907-1988)   American composer.

Piccinni, Nicola (1728-1800)   Italian opera composer.

Pierné, Gabriel (1863-1937)   French organist and composer.

Pinkham, Daniel (1923-2006)   American composer.

Piston, Walter (1894-1976)   American composer and pedagogue.

Pleyel, Ignaz-Joseph (1757-1831)   Austrian-French composer.

Ponchielli, Amilcare (1834-1886)   Italian opera composer.

Popper, David (1843-1913)   Czech cellist and composer.

Porpora, Nicolo (1686-1768)   Italian composer and singing teacher.

Porter, Cole (1891-1964)   American songwriter.

Porter, Quincy (1897-1966)   American composer and violinist.

Poulenc, Francis (1889-1963)   French composer.

Powell, Mel (1923-1998)   American composer.

Praetorius, Michael (1571-1621) German composer and theorist.

Prokofiev, Sergei (1891-1953)   Russian composer.

Puccini, Giacomo (1858-1924)   Italian opera composer.

Pugnani, Gaetano (1731-1798)   Italian composer and violinist.

Purcell, Henry (1659-1695)   British composer.

Quantz, Johann Joachim (1697-1773)   German flutist, composer, and writer on music.

Quilter, Roger (1877-1953)   British composer.

Rachmaninoff, Sergei (1873-1943)   Russian pianist and composer.

Rameau, Jean-Philippe (1683-1764)   French composer and theorist.

Ran, Shulamit (b. 1949)   Israeli-American composer.

Ranjbaran, Behzad (b. 1955)   Iranian-American composer.

Ravel, Maurice (1875-1937)   French composer.

Read, Gardner (1913-2005)   American composer and author.

Reed, H. Owen (b. 1910)   American composer and conductor.

Reger, Max (1873-1916)   German composer.

Reich, Steve (b. 1936)   American composer.

Reicha, Antoine-Joseph (1770-1836)   Czech-French composer.

Reinecke, Carl (1824-1910)   German composer, pianist and teacher.

Respighi, Ottorino (1879-1936)   Italian composer.

Reynolds, Roger (b. 1934)   American composer.

Rheinberger, Joseph (1837-1901)   German organist and composer.

Riegger, Wallingford (1885-1961)   American composer and teacher.

Riley, Terry (b. 1935)   American composer.

Rimsky-Korsakov, Nikolai (1844-1908)   Russian composer.

Rochberg, George (1918-2005)   American composer.

Rodgers, Richard (1902-1979)   American songwriter.

Rodrigo, Joaquín (1901-1999)   Spanish composer.

Rogers, Bernard (1893-1968)   American composer.

Romberg, Sigmund (1887-1951)   Hungarian-American composer.

Root, George Frederick (1820-1895)   American composer.

Rorem, Ned (b. 1923)   American composer.

Rossini, Gioacchino (1792-1868)   Italian opera composer.

Rota, Nino (1911-1979)   Italian composer.

Rouse, Christopher (b. 1949)   American composer.

Roussel, Albert (1869-1937)   French composer.

Rózsa, Miklós (1907-1995)   Hungarian-American composer.

Rubinstein, Anton (1829-1894)   Russian composer and pianist.

Ruggles, Carl (1876-1971)   American composer.

Saint-Saëns, Camille (1835-1921)   French composer.

Salieri, Antonio (1750-1825)   Italian composer and teacher.

Salonen, Esa-Pekka (b. 1958)   Finnish conductor and composer.

Salzédo, (Leon) Carlos (1885-1961)   French-American harpist, composer, and pedagogue.

Salzman, Eric (b. 1933)   American composer and writer on music.

Sammartini, Giovanni (ca. 1700-1775)   Italian composer.

Sarasate, Pablo de (1844-1908)   Spanish violinist and composer.

Satie, Erik (1866-1925)   French composer.

Scarlatti, Alessandro (1660-1725)   Italian composer, father of Domenico Scarlatti.

Scarlatti, Domenico (1685-1757)   Italian composer.

Schaeffer, Pierre (1910-1995)   French composer and acoustician.

Scheidt, Samuel (1587-1654)   German organist and composer.

Schein, Johann Hermann (1586-1630)   German composer.

Schickele, Peter (b. 1935)   American composer and humorist.

Schocker, Gary (b. 1959)   American flutist and composer.

Schönberg, Arnold (1874-1951)   Austrian-American composer.

Schubert, Franz (1797-1828)   Austrian composer.

Schuller, Gunther (b. 1925)   American composer and conductor.

Schuman, William (1910-1992)   American composer.

Schumann, Clara Wieck (1819-1896)   German pianist and composer, wife of Robert Schumann.

Schumann, Robert (1810-1856)   German composer.

Schütz, Heinrich (1585-1672)   German composer.

Schwantner, Joseph (b. 1943)   American composer.

Schwartz, Arthur (1900-1984)   American composer.

Schwartz, Elliott (b. 1936)   American composer.

Scriabin, Alexander (1872-1915)   Russian pianist and composer.

Seeger, Pete (b. 1919)   American songwriter and folk singer.

Seeger, Ruth Crawford (1901-1953)   American composer, stepmother of Pete Seeger.

Serebrier, José (b. 1938)   Uruguayan-American composer and conductor.

Sessions, Roger (1896-1985)   American composer and teacher.

Shapey, Ralph (1921-2002)   American composer and conductor.

Shchedrin, Rodion (b. 1932)   Russian composer.

Shostakovitch, Dmitri (1906-1975)   Russian composer.

Sibelius, Jan (1865-1957)   Finnish composer.

Siegmeister, Elie (1909-1991)   American composer.

Smetana, Bedřich (1824-1884)   Bohemian composer.

Smith, Hale (b. 1925)   American composer.

Smyth, Ethel Mary (1858-1944)   British composer.

Soler, Antonio (1729-1783)   Catalan organist and composer.

Sondheim, Stephen (b. 1930)   American theater composer and lyricist.

Sor, Fernando (1778-1839)   Catalan guitarist and composer.

Sousa, John Philip (1856-1932)   American bandleader and composer.

Sowerby, Leo (1895-1968)   American organist and composer.

Spohr, Ludwig (1784-1859)   German composer and violinist.

Spontini, Gaspare (1774-1851)   Italian opera composer.

Stamitz, Johann Wenzel Anton (1717-1757)   Bohemian violinist and composer, father of Karl Stamitz

Stamitz, Karl Philipp (1745-1801)   Bohemian string player and composer.

Starer, Robert (1924-2001)   Austrian-American composer.

Stevens, Halsey (1908-1989)   American composer.

Still, William Grant (1895-1978)   African-American composer.

Stockhausen, Karlheinz (1928-2007)   German composer.

Stradella, Alessandro (1639-1682)   Italian composer.

Strang, Gerald (1908-1983)   American composer.

Strauss, Johann, Sr. (1804-1849)   Austrian composer.

Strauss, Johann, Jr. (1825-1899)   Austrian composer.

Strauss, Richard (1864-1949)   German composer.

Stravinsky, Igor (1882-1971)   Russian-born composer, later residing in France and America.

Strayhorn, Billy (1915-1967)   American composer and pianist.

Stucky, Steven (b. 1949)   American composer.

Subotnick, Morton (b. 1933)   American composer.

Suk, Josef (1874-1935)   Czech violinist and composer.

Sullivan, Sir Arthur (1842-1900)   British operetta composer.

Suppé, Franz von (1819-1895)   Austrian operetta composer.

Surinach, Carlos (1915-1997)   Spanish-American composer.

Süssmayr, Franz Xaver (1766-1803)   Austrian composer.

Sweelinck, Jan (1562-1621)   Dutch organist and composer.

Szymanowski, Karol (1882-1937)   Polish composer.

Tailleferre, Germaine (1892-1983)   French composer.

Takemitsu, Toru (1930-1996)   Japanese composer.

Tallis, Thomas (ca. 1505-1585)   British composer.

Taneyev, Sergei (1856-1915)   Russian composer.

Tartini, Guiseppe (1692-1770)   Italian violinist and composer.

Tchaikovsky, Piotr Ilyitch (1840-1893)   Russian composer.

Telemann, Georg Philipp (1681-1767)   German composer.

Thomas, Ambroise (1811-1896)   Franch opera composer.

Thompson, Randall (1899-1984)   American composer.

Thomson, Virgil (1896-1989)   American composer and music critic.

Tiomkin, Dimitri (1894-1979)   Ukrainian-American film composer.

Tippett, Michael (1905-1998)   British composer.

Toch, Ernst (1887-1964)   Austrian-American composer.

Tommasini, Vincenzo (1878-1950)   Italian composer.

Torelli, Giuseppe (1658-1709)   Italian composer and violinist.

Torke, Michael (b. 1961)   American composer.

Tsontakis, George (b. 1951)   American composer.

Tudor, David (1926-1996)   American composer.

Türk, Daniel Gottlob (1750-1813)   German music theorist, composer, and organist.

Uhlig, Theodor (1823-1853)   German composer.

Ussachevsky, Vladimir (1911-1990)   Russian-American composer.

Varèse, Edgard (1883-1965)   French-American composer.

Vaughan Williams, Ralph (1872-1958)   British composer.

Veracini, Francesco Maria (1690-1768)   Italian violinist and composer.

Verdi, Giuseppe (1813-1901)   Italian opera composer.

Victoria, Tomas Luis de (1548-1611)   Spanish composer.

Vieuxtemps, Henri (1820-1881)   Belgian violinist and composer.

Villa-Lobos, Heitor (1887-1959)   Brazilian composer.

Viotti, Giovanni Battista (1755-1824)   Italian violinist and composer.

Vitry, Philippe de (1291-1361)   French composer, poet, and theorist.

Vivaldi, Antonio (1678-1741)   Italian composer.

Wagner, Melinda (b. 1957)   American composer.

Wagner, Richard (1813-1883)   German opera composer.

Waller, Thomas Wright "Fats" (1904-1943) American jazz pianist, bandleader, and composer.

Walton, William (1902-1983) British composer.

Ward, Robert (b. 1917) American composer.

Ward-Steinman, David (b. 1936) American composer.

Warren, Harry (1893-1981) American popular song composer.

Weber, Carl Maria von (1786-1826) German composer.

Webern, Anton von (1883-1945) German composer.

Weelkes, Thomas (ca. 1575-1623) British composer and organist.

Weill, Kurt (1900-1950) German-American composer.

Weinberger, Jaromir (1896-1967) Czech composer.

Weisgall, Hugo (1912-1997) American composer.

Welcher, Dan (b. 1948) American composer.

Wernick, Richard (b. 1934) American composer.

Widor, Charles Marie (1845-1937) French composer and organist.

Wieniawski, Henryk (1835-1880) Polish violinist and composer.

Wilder, Alec (1907-1980) American composer.

Willaert, Adrian (ca. 1490-1562) Flemish composer.

Williams, John (b. 1932) American composer and conductor.

Willson, Meredith (1902-1984) American musical theater composer.

Wolf, Hugo (1860-1903) Austrian composer.

Wolpe, Stefan (1902-1972) German-American composer.

Wuorinen, Charles (b. 1938) American composer.

Xenakis, Yannis (1922-2001) Greek-French composer.

Yon, Pietro (1886-1943) Italian-American composer and organist.

Young, La Monte (b. 1935) American composer.

Ysaye, Eugène (1858-1931) Belgian violinist and composer.

Zador, Eugene (1894-1977) Hungarian-American composer.

Zarlino, Gioseffo (1517-1590) Italian theorist and composer.

Zelenka, Jan Dismas (1679-1745) Bohemian composer.

Zelter, Carl Friedrich (1758-1832) German composer.

Zemlinsky, Alexander (1871-1942) Austrian composer.

Zimmerman, Bernd Alois (1918-1970) German composer.

Zingarelli, Nicola Antonio (1752-1837) Italian composer.

Zwilich, Ellen Taaffe (b. 1939) American composer.

Zyman, Samuel (b. 1956) Mexican-American composer.